When r

works

Manchester University Press

The *Manchester Capitalism* book series

Manchester Capitalism is a series of short books that follow the trail of money and power across the systems of financialised capitalism. The books make powerful interventions about who gets what and why, with rigorous arguments that are accessible for the concerned citizen. They go beyond simple critiques of neoliberalism and its satellite knowledges to re-frame our problems and offer solutions about what is to be done.

Manchester was the city of both Engels and Free Trade where the twin philosophies of collectivism and free market liberalism were elaborated. It is now the home of this venture in radical thinking that primarily aims to challenge self-serving elites. We see the provincial radicalism rooted here as the ideal place from which to cast a cold light on the big issues of economic renewal, financial reform and political mobilisation.

Books in the series so far have covered diverse but related issues. How technocratic economic thinking narrows the field of the visible while popular myths about the economy spread confusion. How private finance is part of the extractive problem not the solution for development in the Global South and infrastructural needs in the UK. How politics disempowers social housing tenants and empowers reckless elites. How foundational thinking about economy and society reasserts the importance of the infrastructure of everyday life and the priority of renewal.

General editors: Julie Froud and Karel Williams

Already published:

The end of the experiment: From competition to the foundational economy

What a waste: Outsourcing and how it goes wrong

Licensed larceny: Infrastructure, financial extraction and the global South

The econocracy: The perils of leaving economics to the experts

Reckless opportunists: Elites at the end of the establishment

Foundational economy: The infrastructure of everyday life (2nd edition)

Safe as houses: Private greed, political negligence and housing policy after Grenfell

The spatial contract: A new politics of provision for an urbanized planet

The pound and the fury: Why anger and confusion reign in an economy paralysed by myth

Reclaiming economics for future generations

Bankruptcy, bubbles and bailouts: The inside history of the Treasury since 1976

Derailed: How to fix Britain's broken railways

When nothing works

From cost of living to foundational liveability

Luca Calafati, Julie Froud, Colin Haslam, Sukhdev Johal and Karel Williams

MANCHESTER UNIVERSITY PRESS

Published by Manchester University Press
Oxford Road, Manchester M13 9PL

www.manchesteruniversitypress.co.uk

British Library Cataloguing-in-Publication Data
A catalogue record for this book is available from the British Library

ISBN 978 1 5261 7370 6 hardback
ISBN 978 1 5261 7371 3 paperback

First published 2023

Typeset
by Deanta Global Publishing Services, Chennai, India
Printed in Great Britain
by Bell & Bain Ltd, Glasgow

Contents

List of exhibits   vii
Acknowledgements   xi
Abbreviations   xv

Introduction: behind the great anxiety   1

Part I: Why we need to change the lens

1   Economic policy as quagmire   27

Part II: Rethinking the economy

2   Households and foundational liveability   67
3   Inequalities between households and places   105

Part III: The mess we're in

4   Nothing works   141
5   Why the low paid need more than a pay rise   182

Contents

Part IV: What to do

6 What to do? Politics and policy   217

Notes   257
Index   288

Exhibits

The data used to create the exhibits is available at
https://foundationaleconomyresearch.com/index.php/
nothing-works-stats/

0.1	Foundational liveability	14
1.1	UK year-on-year growth rates of real GDP from 1950 to 2020	43
1.2	Percentage change in CO_2 emissions and real GDP, 1990–2020	49
1.3	Total global CO_2 emissions and real GDP, 1990–2020	50
1.4	Ecological footprint per capita of selected European countries in 2018	54
1.5	UK manufacturing real value added and employment 1970–2019	58
1.6	Contribution of the high-technology and knowledge-intensive sectors to employment, 2008 and 2021	60
1.7	State and para-state share of UK net new job creation, 2009–20	61

List of exhibits

2.1   UK households by number of persons in 1961
and 2021   74

    (a) Percentage shares of differently sized UK
households in 1961 and 2021

    (b) Absolute numbers in millions of differently
sized households

2.2   Number of economically active persons in
households ranked by gross income decile, 2020–21   78

2.3   Foundational liveability   83

2.4   Foundational balance   86

2.5   Gross, disposable and residual income for
North East England owner occupiers and
London private renters, 2020   88

2.6   Non-retired households' sources of total
income split by type in 2019–20   90

2.7   UK non-retired households' total income in
2019–20   93

3.1   How much larger UK household income
would be in 2019 if labour's share of GDP
were at the 1976 level of 57.3 per cent   112

3.2   Distribution of the 1999–2020 growth in
disposable income (after benefits and taxes)
between households according to income decile   115

3.3   GB household wealth by decile and type of
wealth, 2018–20   117

3.4   The distribution of GB household wealth by
decile, 2006–8 and 2018–20   119

3.5   Gross income for households in Newcastle-
upon-Tyne, by selected wards in 2018   122

List of exhibits

3.6	Comparison of average household purchase price in London in 1995 and 2022, by type of housing	124
3.7	Share of households claiming Universal Credit in selected wards of Newcastle-upon-Tyne, 2019 and 2022	131
3.8	UK Universal Credit recipients who are in work or have no work requirements, 2015–22	133
4.1	UK households owning at least one car or van, 1970–2018	148
4.2	Total distance travelled by cars and share of all vehicle miles travelled in Great Britain, 1949–2021	149
4.3	Annual change in jobs created and lost in the North East of England between 2010 and 2020	152
4.4	From social settlement to muddled outcomes in the UK	154
4.5	UK non-retired individuals in households receiving more in benefits than paying taxes	157
4.6	Index of the real cost of food, energy and transport, compared with wages and salaries, 2008 to 2022	160
4.7	Household weekly expenditure on four essentials, by household income decile, 2020–21	163
4.8	Households with mortgages, weekly expenditure on four essentials, by household income decile, 2020–21	166
4.9	Households with mortgages, simulated impact of higher interest rates on expenditure for four essentials, by income decile	169

List of exhibits

4.10 Average annual real growth in NHS funding
      compared with GDP, 1940–2019   175
4.11 Occupation rates of acute and general
      care overnight stay beds compared to large
      European countries, 2017   179
5.1   Increases in disposable income (after housing
      costs) resulting from moving from looking for
      work to employment for different types of
      households and tenure in postcode NE6 1AA   189
5.2   Increases in gross income and disposable
      income (after housing costs) illustration for
      four types of households with starting income
      at the bottom of the distribution (for a Byker
      household in NE6 1AA)   193
5.3   The annual cost of running a ten-year-old
      second-hand car, 2021   200
5.4   UK household car ownership by income
      decile, 2018   202
5.5   Analysis of distance travelled to work in North
      East England   203
      (a) Full-time employees travelling 5 km or
           more as a share of all full-time employees
           split by gender
      (b) Part-time employees travelling less than
           5 km as a share of all part-time employees
           split by gender

Acknowledgements

In 1936, in the middle of an earlier low, dishonest decade with a European proxy war in the background, Dylan Thomas wrote in a letter to his wife that 'our discreditable secret is that we don't know anything at all, and our horrid inner secret is that we don't care that we don't know'. In the first half of the 2020s, we can see all this performed when a Westminster minister excuses the inexcusable which government has created, and when an opposition spokesperson makes empty promises about improved economic performance and better public services. This book is written by and for those who believe it does not have to be like this, but who also realise it is difficult to know a little bit more and even harder to turn caring into doing something effective. If this book makes a contribution to that struggle, it is because it is written by a team of authors in dialogue with a network at the end of a chain.

The team consists of five academic researchers. Colin, Julie, Karel and Sukhdev have worked together as a permanent research team on funded and unfunded projects for some thirty years and, like all good teams, they include a recent recruit,

Acknowledgements

Luca, who joined some three years ago. We are in love with research and writing but disillusioned with the forms of academic knowledge production. The world has enough articles enmeshed in narrow journal debates and too many accumulated critiques and taxonomies which make very little difference. In 2019 when the team set up Foundational Economy Research Ltd (FERL), we wanted to do low cost disruptive research on various issues at different sites and also get out more to engage with practitioners, learning and writing reports as we went along. This book summarises what the team has learned.

If FERL's strategy has been fruitful so far, that is because it has been supported by a network of fellow travelling practitioners and enlightened academics who commissioned our research and, more importantly, engaged us in dialogue about what we were researching and what they were thinking and doing. The work of the team of five researchers in drafting this book was to organise concepts and results which are the joint product of the team and its support network, mostly though not entirely located in Wales. This is very directly so in the case of concepts like the three foundational aims and ways of working which were developed through dialogue when the Welsh Government commissioned the Foundational Alliance and others to come up with a template for policy review.

- Our understanding of households and places owes much to Debbie Green and Paul Relf in Morriston, Selwyn Williams and Ceri Cunnington in Blaenau Ffestiniog, and Charlotte Carpenter and the team at Karbon Homes in Newcastle-upon-Tyne.

Acknowledgements

- In Welsh Government, Deputy Minister Lee Waters has done more than anybody to embed foundational thinking and develop foundational doing. For project sponsorship, we thank officers like Ian Williams, Mark Williams, Peter Evans and John Coyne plus past and present officers in the Foundational Economy Unit of Welsh Government, headed by Aine Gawthorpe working under the Economy Minister Vaughan Gething to develop and implement foundational policy.

- We thank Joe Earle for everything he did to build and sustain the network of practitioners in Wales interested in developing the foundational economy. The strength of that network is underlined by the creation of Foundational Alliance Wales, with Jo Quinney as the organiser. The Alliance continues to depend on the initiative of creative practitioners like Keith Edwards in housing, Gary Newman of Wood Knowledge Wales and Adrian Roper, formerly CEO of Cartrefi Cymru, who are all energetic organisers and organic intellectuals.

- We also owe much to European researchers, especially from Austria, Belgium, Italy and the UK, meeting as the Foundational Economy Collective. A large collection of work on the foundational economy can be accessed at https://foundationaleconomy.com/. We have also benefitted from our dialogue with independent minded business people including Peter Folkman, Steve Jeffels and Ian McGrady.

- We are indebted to British academics including Andrew Bowman, David Edgerton, Kevin Morgan and an

Acknowledgements

anonymous reviewer who all made detailed and very helpful comments on an earlier draft of this book.

- For dissemination of our work, we have relied on downloadable reports from the FERL website at https://foundationaleconomyresearch.com/ and on books published by Manchester University Press, which has now published four team books in paperback as part of the Manchester Capitalism series. Our thanks specifically to Emma Brennan and Tom Dark at MUP for unwavering support over many years, and to Kim Walker, our editor on this book.

Finally, behind this current network is a chain of absent friends. Some like John Buchanan of the University of Sydney and John Law found time to collaborate on a couple of recent projects which influence this book. Others have been removed by retirement or death. Here we remember Mick Moran, whose untimely death in 2018 robbed us of a team member, and John (L. J.) Williams, who was a driving force in the original 1980s Aberystwyth-based team. This book is based on our research when we regrouped after Mick's death cut short a projected stream of work on citizenship. It also takes up and answers the questions raised by L. J. and others in the 1986 book *Keynes, Beveridge and Beyond* about how the decline of UK manufacturing would influence the composition of employment. You, the reader, are the next link in this chain.

Luca Calafati, Julie Froud, Colin Haslam,
Sukhdev Johal and Karel Williams
January 2023

Abbreviations

A&E	Accident and Emergency hospital facility
BMA	British Medical Association
CO_2	carbon dioxide
CPI	Consumer Prices Index
DCMS	Department for Digital, Culture, Media and Sport
EU	European Union
GB	Great Britain
GDP	gross domestic product
GVA	gross value added
IEA	Institute of Economic Affairs
IFS	Institute for Fiscal Studies
IPPR	Institute for Public Policy Research
KPI	key performance indicator
NGO	non-governmental organisation
NHS	National Health Service
OECD	Organisation for Economic Co-operation and Development
ONS	Office for National Statistics

Abbreviations

R&D	research and development
SME	small and medium-sized enterprise
SPF	Sustainable Prosperity Fund
SUV	sports utility vehicle
UC	Universal Credit
UK	United Kingdom

Introduction: behind the great anxiety

Journalists and pollsters have to try and make sense of events and reactions as they happen. In 2022 and 2023 the news pages were full of stories about the 'cost-of-living crisis', inflation and industrial disputes, especially in the public sector. The UK was living through a great anxiety about dismal events and out of control crises at home and abroad. From mid-2022, two tropes – 'nothing works' and 'everything is broken' – began to circulate in commentaries as sensemaking devices for journalists in broadsheets and tabloids of all political colours. *The Times* must win a prize as the early adopter, getting both tropes into one headline: 'Why is nothing working in broken Britain?'[1]

The Economist was a fast follower in late summer 2022 with 'Almost nothing seems to be working in Britain'.[2] Later in the year, Andrew Neil opened a thundering *Daily Mail* column with 'Nothing works in this country anymore', under the headline 'Why can't this government get ANYTHING done?'[3] And the *New Statesman* closed the year with 'Why does nothing work in the UK anymore?'[4] 'Everything is broken' has the same appeal across the political divide. *The Telegraph*'s reporter claimed that

'Britain is broken – and nobody can be bothered to do anything about it',[5] while *The Guardian*'s columnist was in no doubt 'Everything is broken because of 12 years of Tory government'.[6]

These framings were broadly in line with public opinion as measured in polls and focus groups whose results showed that a majority of the public agreed with what they were reading in their newspapers of choice. This was literally confirmed in December 2022 in a PeoplePolling survey which showed that 57 per cent of the British electorate agreed with the statement 'nothing in Britain works anymore' and only 19 per cent disagreed.[7] Although Labour voters were predictably more negative, a striking 50 per cent of Conservative voters agreed that nothing works. The head of political research at YouGov, Anthony Wells, reported 'a sense that everything is broken' amongst the electorate, and that government was being blamed because 'if anything goes wrong … people assume it's their fault'.[8]

The *New Statesman*'s blogger could assert that 'we're all agreed that everything in Britain is broken' but that agreement covered a blurred understanding of what was not working and disagreement about why everything is broken. Andrew Neill singled out dysfunctional health and transport services but also included 'eco loons' with motorway sit-down protests and small boats in the Channel. Sebastian Payne in the *Financial Times* wrote more thoughtfully about the failure of the 'palpable economy' which included the condition of high streets and job opportunities, as well as public services.[9] The centre right and centre left not surprisingly disagreed about how government was to blame. The centre right typically asked for the Conservative government to get a grip on current events and the centre left blamed Conservative government priorities over the past decade, asking for a Labour government to do better after the next election.

The argument in this book goes several steps further by presenting a new economic diagnosis and political approach to the UK's problems. The starting point is critique and an argument about economic policy as a quagmire because (regardless of who wins national elections) UK economic policy is bogged down in an unwinnable struggle and losing is unthinkable. The problem here is not just government but the UK political classes which include government and opposition, think tanks, academics and journalists. With almost no dissent, the UK political classes have committed to the objectives of faster growth and higher wages. This is not a strategy for the future but more a dream of escape from the UK's past of slow growth and stagnant wages. Our argument is that political class objectives are unattainable using any mainstream policy while they are also misconceived insofar as faster growth aggravates nature and climate emergency.

But the foundational message of hope is that the UK can do better if we rethink our problems and solutions with a direct focus on foundational liveability as what matters to households and to communities. This book proposes a three-step break with quagmire economics and ineffectual policies with the aim of changing the field of the economically visible and the politically actionable.

- The first step is to set UK problems in a new foundational liveability framework. This breaks with the individualism of gross domestic product (GDP) and gross value added (GVA) per capita measures and takes expenditure and income sharing households as the basic unit of analysis. Household liveability then depends on the alignment of three foundational pillars: disposable and residual income, essential services and social infrastructure. The income measures of disposable income after tax and benefits and residual income after paying for essentials are more relevant for liveability than gross wages. Through this new lens, the diagnosis is that all three pillars are crumbling, and a chronic UK crisis of foundational liveability has now become acute for low and medium income households.

- The second step is to add empirics so that the economic diagnosis becomes politically actionable, and we can find ways to improve foundational liveability for households. The concern here is not with synthetic reporting of liveability in terms of dashboards and indices but with heuristic empirics that help identify political points of intervention for improved liveability in specific places. Hence this book's concern with distribution to and amongst households ranked by gross, disposable and residual income because these empirics show where, how and why foundational liveability failures pinch differently placed households.

- The third step is to approach the challenge of rebuilding the three pillars of foundational liveability with a political practice of adaptive reuse, which aims at sustained meaningful improvement, not generalised claims for transformation or transition to a different state that have little connection to practice. Ambition for different priorities is necessary and commendable, but delivery is then what matters. Politics is a service activity where delivery depends on back office processes. These processes set constraints on mainstream policy delivery and open opportunities for adaptive reuse workarounds, including handing the initiative to actors who can do what the central state cannot.

The critique of the mainstream dream and the three-step foundational alternative are summarised above and developed at length in the six chapters of this book. The first chapter presents the growth and wages dream of the political classes and outlines the resulting mainstream economic policy quagmire. The last chapter presents an alternative 'what to do' analysis of politics and policies and explains the practice of adaptive reuse. The chapters in between explain the three pillar framework of foundational liveability and present economic empirics on households in all their diversity and places in their specificity.

Political economy is not an easy subject but neither is it rocket science. It should be a matter of broad political debate, reaching into communities and everyday conversations, so it is not closed off in government committees and academic seminars. As researchers and analysts who believe in participative democracy, we have a duty to make it as accessible as possible. Following this ethos, throughout the text, key empirics are presented in graphical form to make them more readable. For those who want more, every exhibit in the text is linked to source tables on the foundationaleconomyresearch.com website which will allow readers to explore data from different sources and see how it has been used. The rest of this introduction provides an overview and summary of the major arguments and empirics which define the book's approach, with key points cross-referenced to the relevant chapter sections.

Introduction

The UK is in an economic policy quagmire because the London-based political classes have committed to the objectives of faster growth and higher wages. This is not an operable strategy but a dream of escape from low growth and stagnant wages. These objectives are unattainable using any mainstream policy; they are also misconceived insofar as faster growth would only aggravate nature and climate emergency.

In a military quagmire, as classically in Vietnam for the French and the Americans, a belligerent gets bogged down in an unwinnable struggle where losing is unthinkable for political reasons. This book argues that the UK political class objectives of faster growth and higher wages have left us in an economic policy quagmire. Over time, military quagmires are self-liquidating because the struggle costs lives and money, and some defeats cannot be denied. But economic policy quagmires can be kept going for much longer by a drip feed of money and a recycling of ideas, as long as alternatives are unthinkable and undoable (Introduction to Chapter 1).

The discussion in Chapter 1 focuses on the aims of economic policy in the mainly London-based political classes. In this group we include parliamentarians in government and opposition, civil servants, academics, think tanks, and broadsheet economics and business journalists. All agree that the aim should be faster economic growth of marketable output measured by GDP and GVA. This will then allow 'higher wages', which raise living standards and allow individuals greater market choices and yield a tax dividend from growth which will finance public services like the NHS (Section 1.1).

Introduction

The political classes live politically by highlighting their differences, and intellectually by finding new distinctions. Chapter 1 highlights the shared assumptions that underpin this restless activity. It focuses on the 2019–22 period and shows how from Johnson, Truss and Sunak to Starmer, government and opposition front benches share the same dream of breaking with low growth, stagnant wages and underfunded public services. The basic line of division is then between two groups on how to get faster growth and higher wages. The techno centrists favour policies like upskilling the workforce, promoting research and development and improving transport and energy infrastructure, because increased productivity will come from combining higher quality factorial inputs. In contrast, the free market supply siders recommend tax cuts and deregulation to liberate enterprise (Section 1.1).

The UK system of economic knowledge production is centralised and hierarchical, so regional universities promote conformism and Celtic nationalists favour independence so that they can more effectively deliver the consensus aims of Westminster economic policy. If we leave aside one Green Party MP and degrowth academics and commentators, there is almost no dissent from the aims of faster growth and higher wages amongst the political classes in London, nor on the periphery in the North and West of the UK. The small Corbyn-McDonnell group which led the Labour Party from 2015–19 was old left and different insofar as it was more central statist and concerned with collective consumption, but also centre left conventional in that it backed a Green Industrial Revolution to deliver increased productivity and 'higher living standards'.[10]

Chapter 1 presents argument and evidence to show that the policy dream of faster growth is practically unrealisable. The secular rate of growth has steadily declined in recent decades and faster growth requires policies capable of reversing the trend in unfavourable national and international circumstances. The consumption-based UK economy does not have a sustainable national growth model. With wages stagnant, the UK relies on privatised Keynesianism via equity release from house price increases and cycles through boom and bust. Internationally, UK growth rates and management policies have since 2008 been upset by successive crises which are unpredictable but increasingly probable when the 2020s is a period of disorderly great power competition (Section 1.2).

The policy dream of faster national growth is more fundamentally misconceived and irresponsible at a planetary level. 'Green growth' is an illusion given existing technologies and the ineffectuality of world governments in mitigating climate change. Faster economic growth will make things worse when economic growth and increasing absolute CO_2 emissions are still in lockstep because so many national governments cannot or will not curb emissions. Here the UK is part of a larger problem when the whole Northwest European way of life is irresponsible given its ecological footprint level of resource consumption and waste generation. Becoming more responsible is peculiarly challenging for the UK in the 2020s, however. The easy bit was phasing out coal-fired power generation; the difficult bit is now curbing the emissions which the UK has outsourced through its high propensity to import (Section 1.2).

Faster growth is also associated with the blurred belief that a bigger cake of marketable output and income will allow higher wages for all (or at least for those with increasing productivity). But growth and increasing inequality are in lockstep as surely as growth and emissions. This is a matter of arithmetical ratios. As long as the upper and lower income deciles claim a commensurate share of GDP increases and the upper income deciles have a larger absolute income base, then the upper deciles will claim the lion's share of any increase in national income. From 1999 to 2020, the top three deciles of households by income obtained 48 per cent of the increase in disposable income, while the bottom three decile households collectively gained just 17 per cent (Section 3.1).

The techno centrist fixation on productivity adds crying for the moon. The techno centrists have no policies which will reliably raise productivity in the UK after a decade in the 2010s when productivity and wages stagnated. Even if productivity did increase to any significant degree, there is no basis for assuming that labour would capture the gains in higher wages. More fundamentally, higher productivity is an ill-considered objective when by any measure the current UK economy is 80 per cent services-based, and taking labour out in such activities often means worse service. The fixation with productivity is finally a distraction insofar as it diverts attention from the UK's underlying historical-political problem which is a deterioration in the composition of employment and the structural incapacity of the UK economy to generate large numbers of high wage jobs after the decline of mass manufacturing with its unionised workforce (Section 1.3).

Against this background, quagmire policy recycles tired old technocentric and free market nostrums, justified by the alibi that earlier reforms failed because they were incomplete. Thus, in the techno centrist frame, an incoming Labour government could back the Brown Commission's city region innovation clusters as the replacement for Gove/Johnson levelling up. The underlying problem here is that the political classes cannot think outside their growth, productivity and wages framework. But the good news is that there is a growing and broad-based collection of thinkers and doers, who from different perspectives are thinking beyond this framework. This is, of course, a huge task and this book can do no more than make a break and begin to think of an alternative. The first step here is the three-pillar framework of foundational liveability.

> *The first step is to set UK problems in a new foundational liveability framework. This breaks with the individualism of GDP and GVA per capita measures and takes expenditure and income sharing households as the basic unit of analysis. Household liveability then depends on the alignment of three foundational pillars: disposable and residual income, essential services and social infrastructure. Through this new lens, the diagnosis is that all three pillars are crumbling, and a chronic UK crisis of foundational liveability has now become acute for low and medium income households.*

Foundational thinking about living standards starts by breaking with meaningless averages like per capita GDP and GVA. National income accounting introduced an individualising perspective and naturalised these measures after the 1940s when it evicted earlier forms of analysis which had focused on family units and household provision. In bringing back the household as the unit of analysis, this book is not concerned with the household as the basic building block of a political social system, as with the *oikos* in the Greek city state, nor with Beveridge's patriarchal household where the wife was covered by virtue of her husband's social insurance contribution. Our aim is to understand households as a matter of fact in our everyday economic life while highlighting all their diversity in the new millennium.

Households matter because 70 per cent of the UK population lives in some 20 million multi-person households with expenditure sharing amongst members plus income sharing where there is more than one income. The variability in household composition and structure must be considered especially in a low wage society with high female participation. Thus, in UK households of couples with children, both parents work in 75 per cent of cases, typically combining the wages of one full-time and one part-time worker when couples have young children. Single parents often have no alternative to local, part-time work and are seriously disadvantaged (Section 2.1).

The next step in the argument is to put together a framework for thinking about household living standards by remixing ideas about universal basic services, universal basic income and even universal basic infrastructure which have been separately canvased in the last few years. This book brings them together because all three are foundationally necessary. All three are also disconnected from discourses about minima and essential needs which can often lead to debate about contestable standards and lists rather than how improvements can be made. The income concept can at the same time be refined by recognising that what matters is not wages but household disposable and residual income, while social infrastructure justifies its place because it is essential for the flourishing of the individuals who sustain and reproduce household resilience and capability (Section 5.3).

The key framing device is then the concept of foundational liveability which rests on the alignment of three pillars in Exhibit 0.1: disposable and residual household income; available essential foundational services like health and care; and accessible social infrastructure like public parks or libraries. All pillars are financially and/or physically interconnected.

- *All three pillars must be present and aligned for foundational liveability because citizens cannot live only by individual consumption from income.* Household members depend on collective provision of networked foundational reliance systems like health, care, education, and the pipe and cable utilities delivering water, energy and communications. They also depend on local branches of hard social infrastructure like cafes and community halls, local public parks and libraries. A UK citizen can buy over-the-counter medicines at a pharmacy or jump the NHS queue to see a consultant or GP privately. But (outside London), they cannot individually buy an ambulance service which responds rapidly to emergencies or access a local A&E facility which is open 24/7 (Section 2.1).
- *Individuals cannot live without income for on-market essentials and the income that matters is not wages or gross income but the household disposable and residual income.* In this book, household disposable income is what is left from gross wage or salary after deductions for tax and with the top-up of cash benefits. So disposable income sets the outer limit on private consumption. Residual income is then practically defined in this book as what is left of disposable income after four

essentials (housing, utilities, transport and food) – which in the UK are largely on-market – have been paid for.[11] The current 'cost-of-living crisis' is about how residual income has vanished or been eroded for many households who cannot pay for these four essentials or can only do so by sacrificing much else (Sections 2.2 and 5.1).

- *In their different ways, foundational systems and social infrastructure are just as important as income.* The importance of foundational systems (like health and care, utility supply and food distribution) is obvious because they distribute the essentials of sustenance, and if these goods and services are not accessible and affordable then life will be miserable and shortened. Social infrastructure (like cafes, clubs, community halls, parks and libraries) is important in a subtler way because it sustains all the many forms of sociability which have proven benefits for the psychological and physical health of individuals (Section 5.3).

On this basis, we can diagnose the socio-economic problem of the UK: in the middle of a cost-of-living crisis, nothing works because all three pillars of foundational liveability are crumbling. But the three-pillar diagram and diagnosis are no more than a sensemaking device, not a secret recipe. They can only help guide change when we add empirics that change what is visible to focus on issues which are not recognised and to highlight points of intervention usually not registered by the political classes. Here below are two examples of such empirics which relate to place.

- London is the high wage/high productivity exemplar and object of emulation for techno centrists. But housing costs

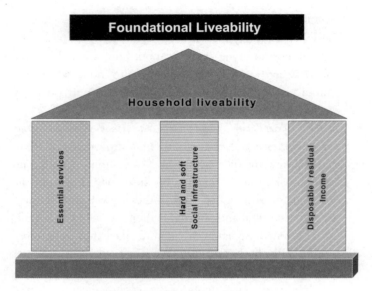

Exhibit 0.1 Foundational liveability.

in the UK have long varied dramatically by region and tenure so that the advantages of higher gross wages and disposable income are substantially eroded by high housing costs for the quarter of London households who are private renters. These households start with gross and disposable household income nearly twice as high as owner occupiers without mortgages in North East England and end with residual household income per person which is lower (Section 2.2).

- A northern city like Newcastle-upon-Tyne lags on indicators like income or GVA per capita which techno centrists vow to raise. But crediting substantially sized places like cities or regions with a unitary identity based on income or

GVA per capita averages is profoundly unhelpful. It creates an imaginary policy object when Newcastle has a mosaic character so that there is a two-to-one differential between household disposable income in a desirable middle class suburb and an inner city district like Byker. The one city offers very different foundational liveability options for households. Low income couples in a depressed district can only afford one car, leaving one of the adults – usually a woman – trapped in minimum wage employment in an overstocked local labour market (Sections 3.1 and 5.2).

The importance of these empirics is that they simultaneously shift the field of the economically visible and the politically actionable away from the political classes dreaming of higher wages and more marketable output. The variability of housing costs by region and tenure shows that foundational liveability for high and low income households depends on managing housing costs and tenures (not just wages). The importance of commuting costs means that connecting workers with jobs in a gender equitable way requires attention to childcare and bus fares. These insights are reflected in the broader foundational approach where the concern with empirics serves a useful heuristic purpose.

The second step is to add empirics so that the economic diagnosis becomes politically actionable and we can find ways to improve foundational liveability. The concern here is not with synthetic reporting of liveability in terms of dashboards and indices but with heuristic empirics that help identify political points of intervention for improved liveability – hence this book's concern with income distribution to and amongst households ranked by gross, disposable and residual income. These empirics show where, how and why the foundational liveability failures pinch differently placed households.

The starting point here is to ask why the foundational approach needs empirics and what empirics should do. The short answer is that foundational empirics should reframe problems by indicating points of political intervention. Furthermore, they should then focus effort so that policies can find leverage over outcomes and deliver meaningful improvements in foundational liveability. As in the place-based examples above, these heuristic empirics point to specific issues rather than construct synthetic indices of liveability, or dashboards with multitudes of indicators in green, amber and red.

The reference point is the three-pillar framework, but the empirical object is households in their diversity and places in their specificity. Places matter because they offer different access to jobs, essential services and social infrastructure. And places are also shaped by the characteristics of the households living there. This book presents empirics on households and places mainly based on official statistics. Over the past decade, there has been much interest in big data for its capacity to cover a wide range of topics and provide updated information. Yet official statistics are still immensely valuable, as illustrated below with some of our research findings from official data on household income and expenditure. The data is rich especially if we divide households into income or wealth deciles (on place, see Sections 3.2, 3.3 and 5.2).

In relation to households, official statistics allow us to open up the issue of distribution between labour and capital, which is invisible for the techno centrists and free marketeers although there has been a nearly ten percentage point shift in the distribution of national output from labour to capital since the 1970s. The political classes sometimes present wishful, counterfactual calculations of how British households would potentially have £10,000 more income each year if the UK had grown at the OECD average.[12] The more relevant counterfactual is that every non-retired household would actually have an extra income of more than £9,700 each year if labour's share of national output had been maintained at 1970s levels. It cannot be argued that this distributive shift against labour incomes is compensated by the diffusion of wealth because the distribution of wealth is twice as unequal as income (Section 3.1).

But this does not justify the othering of high income groups, as was classically done in the 2017 Labour manifesto *For the Many Not the Few*. Household composition is critical because having two or more wage earners in the household is a good predictor of a household being in the top half of the income distribution so that in the top three income deciles more than 70 per cent of households have two or more wage earners. The political class needs to recognise that the top income deciles are mostly not fat cat financiers and CEOs, but middle ranking members of the professional and managerial classes who benefit from assortative mating (Section 2.1).

Thus, hard empirics can focus and reorient intervention. The foundational shift is away from wishful technical attempts to grow the cake towards practical political attempts to empower labour so that workers get a larger slice of the cake

as well as better access to essential services and social infrastructure. On this basis, a more nuanced analysis can bring into
focus the ongoing problems of low income and middle income
households.

- The acute 'cost-of-living crisis' about heating and eating in
  2022–23 is one episode in a long running chronic crisis. In
  the 2010s, the cost of on-market essentials (like bus fares) was
  rising much faster than wages, so an increasing number of
  low income households had no margin of residual income.
  In the 2020s, rising interest rates for mortgage holders will
  squeeze the residual income of middle income groups who
  can expect the cost of the four essentials to increase from
  less than half to around two-thirds of disposable household
  income. Whichever party is in government can expect more
  demands for income subvention (Section 4.2).
- In a period of inflation, the immediate problem for low
  income working households is the relation between gross
  and disposable income as wages rise. Individuals on
  Universal Credit retain very little of any increase in wages
  when they face an effective marginal tax rate of around 70
  per cent. As income rises, these households immediately
  pay more tax which takes about 35 pence in the pound
  and then lose benefits at 55 pence per pound of post-tax
  income. Higher wages for the working poor are not about
  a wage/price spiral but an attempt at price/wage catch up
  which never happens (Section 5.1).
- The issues are not only about unrecognised problems with
  wages and benefits but also about the undervalued support
  of benefits in-kind. Working households in the bottom half

of the income distribution are heavily dependent on in-kind state-provided or financed services, from health and education to concessionary bus passes. For deciles 1 to 5 of non-retired households, benefits in-kind have an average market value of more than £13,000 a year for each household. Welfare state services have been underfunded since inception, partly because the political classes, like most of their electors, do not recognise the value of what households in the bottom half of the income distribution receive in-kind and could not easily pay for out of income (Sections 2.2 and 4.3).

What foundational empirics disclose is the largely unrecognised drivers of the household liveability crisis which public policy now needs to address. The crisis is an outcome of the failure of the larger post-1979 political project of market citizenship which animates the economic pursuit of marketable output and higher wages so that more can have the independent market choices of upper income deciles. This always threatened to unbalance private and collective consumption. The incoherent outcome is gross imbalance aggravated by the cost of Universal Credit wage subsidy for low income working households which is also subsidy for consumers benefiting from cheap services like parcel delivery, while employers pass their costs of employment onto taxpayers (Section 4.1).

The well-meaning intention of wage subsidy was to incentivise work and make low wages more liveable. After four decades the outcome is an incoherent, dysfunctional and unsustainable system of subsidising low income working households (with misery-level benefits for the sick, disabled and carers as an adjunct). By the 2010s, more than 40 per cent of non-retired households were receiving more in benefits than they pay in taxes. If the answer is not to be more mindless austerity cutbacks, we need a new kind of foundational politics (Section 4.1).

The third step is to approach the challenge of rebuilding the three pillars of foundational liveability with a political practice of adaptive reuse, which aims at sustained meaningful improvement. Ambition is necessary and commendable, but outcomes are what matters, and politics is a service activity where delivery depends on back office processes. These processes both set constraints on mainstream policy delivery and open opportunities for adaptive reuse workarounds, including handing the initiative to actors who can do what the central state cannot.

After making a break by providing a new economic diagnosis backed by heuristic empirics, the foundational aim of politics and policy should be to make low and middling incomes more liveable. This is not simply or mainly about redistributing income but about moving economy and society off a trajectory of deteriorating foundational liveability and securing the good life for many more through attention to all three pillars of liveability (income, essential services, social infrastructure). The benefits are less obvious for high income households in the top two or three deciles who benefit positionally from low wage, cheap private services and, if private alternatives are available, have the income to replace inadequate public provision.

Improving foundational liveability will not be easy. From financial crisis in 2008 to the Ukraine War in 2022, amidst worsening nature and climate emergency, the obstacles to reform have been such that successive crises have produced deepening mess rather than policies that deal with sector specific issues or the larger problems of financialised capitalism. Against this background, ambition is necessary, but outcomes and delivery are what matter. This book does not overpromise by targeting radical transformation or implying easy transition. Instead, it advocates purposive political gradualism and the long march around the obstacles to reform. The rationale is explained in the book's sixth and final chapter on the adaptive reuse approach to politics and policy.

The starting point is that politics (like any other service activity) has a front office that the customer sees at the point of sale and a back office of processes which determines what can be delivered – as in a restaurant with the menu on the table and, behind the pass, a kitchen and a supply chain. Our argument is that centrist politics has been too preoccupied with front office promises without attention to the back office processes which govern possibilities. These processes matter because they are both constraints on what can be delivered by mainstream pro-growth policies and opportunities for foundational pro-liveability policies. Foundational politics is the art of manoeuvring around back office constraints as much as it is about front office promises to the electorate (Section 6.1).

The central state matters because so much local delivery of foundational liveability to households is centrally funded or formatted. In the UK, the Labour Party can hope to win a general election in 2024 or 2025, with or without coalition partners. But it would then find itself in office but not in power because any incoming government will face multiple, complex constraints (Section 6.2).

Introduction

- The room for fiscal expansionism will be limited by trade deficit and the debt to GDP ratio, while an independent Bank of England with a narrow remit will control monetary policy. Even without further international crises, balancing government revenue and expenditure will be a challenge given the out-of-control wage subsidy system and increased debt servicing costs at higher rates of interest.
- Some outsourcing and privatisation could be reversed, but the state apparatus has lost the capacity to plan and organise large-scale material infrastructure projects and that capacity would have to be gradually rebuilt at all levels of government through foundational economy supply side policies.
- Regulation is much cheaper and should offer more immediate public benefits, but it has been captured by economists who prioritise competition and who have limited accounting understanding of how extractive owners behave. As we have argued, regulation needs to be more effectively refocused around physical targets supported by accounting policemen.

We would rather not start from here. The foundational response is not to despair but to propose a radical approach of adaptive reuse which eschews rebuilding to a grand design and instead works around what exists. The idea is taken from the French architects, Lacaton and Vassal, whose approach to post-war social housing developments was 'never demolish, never remove or replace, always add transfer and reuse'.[13] Their approach overlaps with the classic Lévi-Strauss concept of bricolage and the 1980s Japanese factory practice of Kaizen or continuous improvement (Section 6.2).

The radical central state has options on starter, stealth and switch policies which find and use opportunities. Starter policies play on broadly held ideas of compassion and fairness as with free school meals. Stealth policies for the public good work on technical issues like the Universal Credit taper rate which are not understood by most of the electorate. Switch policies hand the initiative to other actors who can do what the central state cannot. One big switch policy opportunity is to empower labour by repealing anti-union legislation and encouraging union organisation, rather than focusing on productivity. That would produce a change in the balance of forces between workers and employers so that workers could bargain for better wages from private and public employers (while the central state reforms the tax and benefits system to advantage lower income households) (Section 6.2).

We are not opposed to all large-scale central designs for improvement from a point in the political spectrum where Michael Oakeshott's conservatism meets James C. Scott's anarchism. But we do see how the central state has limited knowledge and capacity to initiate intelligent reform in large complex systems of multi-level government and governance. If 'public service reform' is on the political agenda, the case of top-down NHS reform since the early 1990s is a cautionary tale. Reform by a central ministry led to organisational churn that brought limited benefits and many perverse and unintended consequences; these were reinforced when operations were ineptly controlled by productivity targets (Section 6.2).

Hence the case for an open, incremental approach to social innovation, drawing on the intelligence of multiple actors who can operate with limited state support to stretch the limits of what is thinkable and doable for foundational liveability. Examples of this kind of social innovation would include local authority-sponsored reorganisation of adult home care, or Welsh Health Board 'grow your own' policies for workforce development. This recognises that the possibilities of adaptive reuse are manifold, and the relevant intelligence, knowledges and motivating values are broadly distributed amongst state, civil society and for-profit actors (Section 6.3).

The potential here is considerable but realising that potential through local experiments or regional initiatives is a work in progress. The Welsh case is instructive because it highlights the potential and the difficulties which stand in the way of achieving greater foundational liveability. There is a need for new ways of working and learning to act in alliances for change to support innovation inside and outside government (Section 6.3).

By this point, it should be clear that this book aims to change political debate on the centre and left of British politics. The premise of this book is that the foundational liveability challenges of the 2020s can only be clearly defined and addressed after we break with existing analysis of socio-economic realities that have led us into a policy quagmire. Paradigm change is beyond this team of authors, but this book does break with the policies of quagmire by presenting a new and different economic diagnosis with accompanying heuristic empirics that highlight the possibilities of political action for improved foundational liveability. This needs to be followed through with an adaptive reuse approach to politics that can go some way towards turning pro-growth constraints into pro-liveability opportunities. We do not expect readers to agree with all the positions in this book, but we hope to convince most readers that the UK political classes are caught in a policy quagmire and that all our futures depend on finding a way through to improved foundational liveability.

PART I

Why we need to change the lens

Introduction to Part I

If the economy is a machine that does not deliver for many citizens, how are we to understand its failure and begin to fix it? Our foundational starting point is that thinking and doing about the economy is misdirected towards objectives of growth, higher wages and productivity so that the political classes are stuck with unattainable objectives. Understanding the economy through this lens means that much policy effort will be wasted or misdirected.

Chapter 1 develops this critique before the rest of the book constructively proposes a different lens through which we see how the polity is failing to support households and what to do about it. Using this different lens we can then propose policies focused on foundational liveability. Our argument and examples throughout are UK based and reflect national specifics, such as the tax and benefits system. However, the UK case is not unique, and we could make similar arguments about many other West European national economies.

Chapter 1

Economic policy as quagmire

Introduction

Our argument in this chapter is that mainstream economic policy in the UK is in a quagmire. As in the case of military quagmires, it is the poor bloody infantry, not the staff officers, who pay the price for ongoing failure to achieve national objectives. The staff of policy makers and practitioners in the political classes are unable to achieve their economic objectives and unwilling to accept defeat because they cannot imagine a heterodox alternative.

Election manifestos promise to fix 'the economy' for higher living standards. Thus, in the 2019 general election, the Labour Party promised 'a fair and sustainable economy' through social intervention in the market, while the Conservative Party promised 'an even stronger and more dynamic economy' through getting Brexit done. But the economy (with a definite article) which we take for granted in all kinds of policy discourse is an invention of recent date. The *Oxford English Dictionary* records the term's first usage in its modern sense in the *Economic Journal* of 1941 and the term first appears in a party election manifesto in the *Conservative Party Manifesto* of 1950.[1]

In this new usage, the economy was defined as a distinct system that was measurable through national income accounting and amenable to policy management of aggregates like inflation. On this basis, the system would determine living standards through wages. Over time, of course, economists have had different views and management techniques have changed, as with the shift from Keynesianism to monetarism in the 1980s. At the same time, events such as the Great Financial Crisis of 2008 have raised questions about whether economic experts know what they are doing. But the principle of expert management is hard to challenge in a polity where public goals have been redefined in economic categories, as with health economics after the 1960s. Moreover, all activities are to be judged in terms of their contribution to the economy, as with the cultural and creative industries after the 1990s.

The processes that enlarged the domain of economics and buttressed its claims to expertise have worked in an imperial way to establish a kind of discursive sovereignty. Economics has evicted or subordinated other discourses so that governance through appropriate economic policy becomes the only and obvious way to actively deliver higher living standards (with or without income redistribution). From this point of view, claims and assumptions about the economy and economic policy can be usefully challenged using concepts from war studies, which tries to understand the limits on the use of military force to assert territorial claims and establish sovereignty.

The Anglo-American doyen of war studies is Lawrence Freedman. In a classic article, Freedman reflected on the term *quagmire*, used to describe military conflict where a belligerent gets bogged down in an unwinnable struggle it dares not lose.[2] Military quagmires are self-limiting and typically end in withdrawal because failure is concrete, and its direct costs are high when the belligerent 'with a high stake in the satisfactory resolution of a conflict suffers steady losses without making evident progress'.[3] The military problem is not simply unachieved objectives but the unacceptably high cost of futility in terms of money and/ or body count. Hence, the end of French and American entanglements in Vietnam or the successive Soviet and American exits from Afghanistan.

The quagmire metaphor about commitment to unattainable objectives can be transposed and applied to mainstream economic policy attempts to manage the economy. The important difference is that economic policy quagmires are often not self-limiting because failure is less evident without any equivalent of escalating costs or body bags. Quagmire without withdrawal can continue for as long as economic policy makers can claim a continuing stream of resources and political backing for new performative initiatives. In domestic economic policy areas, central government can always come up with new initiatives which incentivise lower level actors with a drip feed of project funding.

The classic example is regional policy, where successive policies have, over 50 years, conspicuously failed to reduce regional inequalities. The Cameron and May Governments had elected mayors and City Deals, the Johnson Government had 'levelling up' and the Shared Prosperity Fund, while the short-lived Truss Government had investment zones. These policies worked by encouraging competitive localism to capture resources or obtain concessions for the locality which secures local authority buy-in. Thus, when the Truss Government announced new investment zones, they were already in discussion with 38 local authorities from Blackpool to South Yorkshire and Cornwall to Essex.[4]

However, it would be wrong to suppose that if the performative game continues, economic policy will be a charade without consequences. Policies which fail to achieve their declared objectives can have secondary unintended consequences. Thus, if investment zones failed to create new economic activity, they could still divert economic activity from other places. And UK fiscal and monetary policies at the macro level are subject to the judgement of financial markets which constrain national freedom to tax and spend. From a broad perspective, the economic policy quagmire results not in dramatic defeat and withdrawal but in an ongoing multi-level mess with many more consequences for ordinary people than for policy makers.

The first section of this chapter, Section 1.1, analyses how the UK political classes understand the economy in terms of the objective of higher growth rates and higher living standards (through productivity increase) underpinned by more and better well-paid jobs. The second and third sections set out to challenge the assumptions underlying these beliefs, so that subsequent argument and evidence can put an alternative in place. Section 1.2 argues that the UK faces a decline in its growth rate which is not amenable to any orthodox economic policy fix and adds the clincher that growth in the UK and other high income countries is in any case environmentally burdensome. Section 1.3 begins to unpick the high wage/high productivity coupling by examining the relation between productivity and wages, before arguing that productivity measures and the higher productivity objective are increasingly irrelevant in the UK case.

1.1 How the political classes understand 'the economy'

Our questions in this section are: what do the UK political classes mean and intend when they talk about 'the economy'? How do they frame national economic objectives and what are their internal areas of agreement and disagreement? If we review their discourses since 2019, the short answer is that the political classes in the UK form a policy establishment which unanimously agrees on the policy objectives of economic growth and higher paid jobs but noisily differs on how to get there.

The UK political classes comprise the assortment of contesting groups who make or hope to make or influence economic policy. It includes the front benches of both major political parties regardless of the churn of personnel. Thus, Boris Johnson, Liz Truss and Rishi Sunak as successive prime ministers with their various chancellors are all included as well as their opposition shadows, Keir Starmer and Rachel Reeves. They operate with support and interventions from the Governor of the Bank of England, think tanks like the Resolution Foundation or the Institute of Economic Affairs, public-profile economists like Paul Johnson, Andy Haldane or Gerard Lyons and the broadsheet newspaper commentariat like Martin Wolf, Will Hutton or Ambrose Evans Pritchard.

This policy establishment understands the economy through the framework of national income accounting and its financial measures of output and income. This means that cyclicality and conjunctural change are of course reflected in changing tactics and commentary. By the late 2010s with a tight labour market, the capacity of the economy to create jobs and high levels of employment was generally taken for granted. In a tight labour market after the Covid-19 pandemic, policy makers first increased pressure on the jobless to take any job[5] and then worried about the half a million or so workers who had withdrawn from the labour market.[6] Recession and unemployment will change this. Then, on the ensuing upswing, the Chancellor will boast in a familiar way about the numbers of jobs created and 'the fastest growth in the G7' over the last few quarters.

But the declared long-term objectives of policy are remarkably constant and widely held, as we document below for the post-2019 period and could document for the whole period going back to the 1980s. In all kinds of policy discourses, across the political and expert spectrum, faster economic growth is the superordinate objective. For the majority, increased productivity then figures as the intermediate objective which will allow higher wages which both bring higher living standards and increase the tax revenues that fund public services.

- The superordinate objective at the national level is the growth of gross domestic product (GDP) and the measure of success is higher GDP per capita; at the regional level, the related measure is gross value added (GVA) per capita. 'Domestic product' and 'value added' are financial measures obtained by adding up marketable output (goods and services). The per capita qualifier divides the total value of output by the population. This has the effect of directing attention to productivity on the basis that increased output per unit of labour is a source of growth which can raise wages and living standards.

- This economic priority of growth goes along with a political project which we term market citizenship because the assumption is that economic growth means increasing the number of independent households reliant on private income who have market choices from wages and can do aspirational things like 'getting onto the housing ladder'. The GDP metric effectively privileges private consumption because in the UK by the 2010s, private consumption accounted for around two-thirds of nominal GDP.[7] The

> political task of government is then to solve the UK's eco-
> nomic problems by getting more citizens into jobs at higher
> wages, which will lift living standards.

- The other point of agreement is that growth will also solve
  problems about funding collective consumption because
  economic growth will generate higher tax revenues to pay
  for publicly funded services. This last proposition, about
  the tax dividend from growth, is endlessly repeated and
  universally accepted by the left and right in the UK political classes. The Brown Commission in 2022 tried to quan-
  tify it with the claim that 'every extra percentage of growth
  can increase the money available for public services by £10
  billion a year'.[8]

The Brown Commission's concern with specifics is unusual
because faster growth and higher wages are mainly about
shared assumptions and repeated assertions. But, if this is a
matter of consensus, the political classes then divert into noisy
disagreement about supply side pathways to faster growth. With
traditional state socialism marginalised, the lines of division on
pathways to faster growth are between two broad coalitions: the
dominant technocratic centrists and the insurgent free market
supply siders. Within each coalition, there is much elaboration
of small differences which are credited with intellectual and
political importance, but the basic line of division is binary.

The technocratic centrist coalition includes most economic
advisers and economically literate civil servants in the Treasury,
journalists writing in the *Financial Times*, many academics
and think tanks like the Resolution Foundation or IPPR. Its
parliamentary wing includes One Nation Conservatives,

Scottish and Welsh Nationalists and the centre left which currently dominates the Labour Party. For all these groups, raising productivity is the key to faster growth and higher wages and they believe that investment in early-stage innovation, workforce skills and physical infrastructure (especially transport infrastructure) is the key to increasing productivity. This is technocratic in that it rests on a concept of production where output is determined by the quality and quantity of inputs. Therefore, the oft-repeated policy prescriptions are for upskilling to improve the quality of labour as a productive input and for increasing the quantity of capital investment on various objects like early-stage innovation or transport infrastructure.

The free market supply sider coalition includes a minority of dissident economists like Patrick Minford and some journalists in right-wing papers like the *Daily Mail* and the *Telegraph*, with think tanks like the IEA and the Taxpayers Alliance in a vanguard role. Its parliamentary representatives are the right-wing Conservatives in and around the European Research Group. For these groups, the recipe for supply side reform is tax cuts and deregulation of everything from fracking to house building. This is explicitly a liberationist crusade because the aim is to free the market to allow individual choice and incentivise enterprise, which will deliver growth.

The Conservatives in government are divided factionally with many in the centre of the party conflicted and trying to straddle the two positions. In contrast, after electoral defeat in 2019, the Labour Party is mobilised under a technocratic centrist banner. Thus, in summer 2022, Keir Starmer as Labour leader promised that 'Labour will fight the next general election on economic growth', with 'every policy … judged by the contribution to growth and productivity'.[9] His recipe was productionist upskilling and investment in both the 'everyday economy' and the 'frontier sectors'. This pathway to green growth was termed 'modern supply side economics' by the shadow chancellor, Rachel Reeves.[10] The technocratic centre's egalitarian preference is for better wages and conditions across all regions and more policies to boost productivity. For example, the Resolution Foundation's *Stagnation Nation* report wants 'decent jobs in every place' because 'low growth and high inequality are a ... disaster for low-to-middle income Britain and the young in particular'.[11]

After their 2019 election victory, partly attributed to success in winning 'red wall' northern seats, the Johnson Government signalled interest in this agenda through its commitment to 'levelling up' laggard places and regions. Thus, Boris Johnson in his 2021 conference speech presented the standard technocratic analysis of the UK's problems as a 'low wages, low growth, low skills and low productivity' economy. In this frame, 'left-behind places' and regions are productively deficient by the measure of low GVA per capita, and the fix is raising productivity which is the governor of their underperformance. Michael Gove's 2022 White Paper, *Levelling Up the United Kingdom*, combined a social wrapper about health inequalities and community with this economic orthodoxy. For example, its remedy for internal inequalities is 'boosting productivity, pay, jobs and living standards by growing the private sector, especially in those places where they are lagging'. The mission for 'living standards' by 2030 is simply more and better jobs in the hope that 'by 2030 employment and productivity will have risen in every area of the UK'.[12]

The responses to this White Paper demonstrate the remarkable extent of policy agreement on fundamentals amongst technocratic centrists who ordinarily emphasise their differences. Centrist critics unanimously endorsed the White Paper's jobs and growth priorities but then complained that the government had no adequately resourced delivery plan. For instance, Keir Starmer observed that 'this government has no plan to get there'.[13] The broadsheet commentariat from Martin Wolf in the *Financial Times* to Will Hutton in the *Observer* responded in much the same way by arguing that commendable objectives were not being backed by adequate resources. Thus, Wolf praised 'thorough analysis, clear aims and sensible policy steps' in what was a necessary 'call to arms', but then lamented that the resources of new money were too limited to deliver the ambitious goals.[14]

The Conservative Party's misfortune is to be in government and divided between technocratic centrist and free market supply siders. All Conservatives have to rhetorically endorse the idea of a low tax state. But the leadership contest between Liz Truss and Rishi Sunak exposed differences in the timing and extent of tax cuts. The deregulationist agenda is complicated by nimbyism on the Conservative back benches, which has, for example, frustrated planning reform. There are also differences between traditionalist supply siders who favour restricting immigration and libertarian supply siders who favour large-scale immigration to deal with labour market shortages and boost growth. From this point of view, the 44-day Truss administration represented the capture of government by a group of free market insurgents at a time of energy price rise when large-scale government intervention to subvent households and businesses was politically inescapable.

The financial markets responded with panic to Chancellor Kwarteng's proposals for two years of energy price subvention and £45 billion of unfunded tax cuts without the blessing of the Office for Budgetary Responsibility. But the supply side rationale for tax cuts and deregulation was entirely orthodox. When interviewed at the beginning of her premiership Truss was clear about her priorities: 'what is important to me is we grow the British economy because that's what will ultimately deliver higher wages, more investment in towns and cities across the country, that is how we will deliver more money into people's pockets and it will also allow us to fund services like the NHS'.[15] When her Chancellor outlined his September 2022 plan for growth through tax cuts and supply side reform, he explained, 'that is how we will deliver higher wages, greater opportunities, and crucially, fund public services now and into the future'.[16]

Tony Danker of the Confederation of British Industry doubted whether Kwarteng's package would 'suddenly unlock growth' but added 'we have to grow faster, there is no alternative'.[17] When it had all gone wrong, a month later the new Chancellor Jeremy Hunt turned 'to do what is necessary for economic stability'[18] through a combination of tax rises and expenditure cuts. Even though the economy was heading into recession and at least a pause in growth, the new Chancellor endorsed 'the central insight … that economic growth is the key thing that we need'.[19] On the morning that Rishi Sunak became prime minister, an influential right-wing Conservative back bencher observed: 'what we are looking at is differences not about whether you want growth but how fast and how you look for it'.[20] For former Conservative leader Iain Duncan Smith, the task then was to balance 'getting borrowing under control' and creating a window for 'sustainable growth'.

With growth, higher wages and the tax dividend as the consensual objectives, the recurrent internal disagreements of the UK political classes are about which government policies should be adopted and whether adequate resources are being committed to delivering objectives. The quagmire outcome has been policy churn with a succession of half-implemented policies which are typically abandoned before their failure is conclusively demonstrated. Hence technocratic centrists and free market supply siders can both maintain their positions with the alibi that their reforms fail because they are incomplete. Techno centrists will complain that (adequately resourced) levelling up has not been tried, while free market supply siders will lament bad timing as they endorse Liz Truss's apology for her 'mistake', which was 'we went too far too fast'.[21]

This chapter does not take sides between the techno centrists and the free market supply siders or join the internal debates within each coalition. Instead, our argument is that faster growth and higher wages are not an operable strategy but a dream which is best understood through T. S. Eliot's contrast of 'the pain of living and the drug of dreams'. The UK in the 2010s was a country where the pain of living was negligible growth and stagnant productivity with many on low wages and more suffering from austerity cuts in public spending. The political classes' dream was then of escaping into a virtuous circle where all the negatives would be turned into positives. The political classes cannot or will not easily let go of the dream because, if achieved, it appears to offer a way to avoid all kinds of economic conflicts about distribution and difficult political choices on issues like higher taxes.

On closer examination, the dream is all very blurred, especially around 'higher wages' which are the words that politicians of left and right always use. Here they assume or assert simple relations between wages and living standards which on closer examination turn out to be wishful thinking.

- With any wage, what matters is not top-line gross wages but bottom-line disposable net income after tax and benefits. The purchasing power of net income then depends on the price of essentials like housing and energy. For example, if energy costs increase massively, they can cancel any increase in gross wages. Expenditure and income sharing in multi-person households further complicate matters. This is why think tanks like the Resolution Foundation would usually calculate household disposable income.

- There is no automaticity about the gains from increased productivity turning into wages because they can be captured by capital, not labour, and, if wages do increase, then high income households will ordinarily gain the most. As Section 1.3 notes, post-1990s experience suggests there is a partial disconnect between increased productivity and wages. As Section 3.1 demonstrates, if incomes increase, the results will usually feed inequality. The arithmetic of growth in an unequal society is such that, if upper income households start with absolutely larger incomes and claim a commensurate share of any increases, they will end up claiming the lion's share of any income increases.

In the case of successive Conservative governments, there is also a large gap between rhetoric and practice, including in relation to wages in public services. Conservative ministers say they want higher wages and a high wage economy in their speeches on the economy but they do not act on this basis when it comes to public sector pay settlements. Austerity in the 2010s meant real pay cuts for many of the 6 million or so workers in the public sector. With inflation in the 2020s, holding public sector pay increases below the Consumer Prices Index (CPI) means further real pay cuts. Matters are only confused by government requests for productivity-increasing changes in public sector working practice when, for example on the railways, such changes could not conceivably produce self-financing higher pay deals.

If political class positions on wages are confused and confusing, the next section of this chapter goes further to challenge the policy establishment's more fundamental assumptions about the attainability and desirability of sustained faster growth. Then the third and final section of this chapter looks at the UK prospects for more high paying jobs and the relevance of increased productivity to a low wage service economy.

1.2 Unattainable faster growth as false hope

This section argues that faster growth is unattainable because the UK's growth rate is declining and there is no evidence that technocratic centrist or free market supply side economic policies can shift the country onto a higher growth trajectory. Furthermore, the objective of faster growth is fundamentally misconceived and a false hope because economic growth is ecologically burdensome when it aggravates nature and climate emergency. Our argument and evidence below on these points directly challenge the shared assumptions of the UK political classes.

As we have seen, the political classes believe that output growth (with productivity increases for the centrists) solves problems by creating the possibility of higher living standards through higher gross wages and tax revenues for public services. Hence their standard exhibits are of the national GDP gap between the UK and North West European countries and the regional GVA gap between the North East or Wales and London or the South East. All these exhibits come with an explicit or implicit message about emulation and how UK government policy should and could close the national or regional gap through sustained faster economic growth.

Past experience is discouraging. Exhibit 1.1 presents year-on-year changes in UK real GDP between 1950 and 2020 and the dotted trend line shows that the secular UK rate of growth is clearly falling as our financialised national capitalism has since 2008 lurched from one unexpected international crisis to the next. And the probability is that, under Conservative or Labour governments, the UK will have slow and unsteady growth in the 2020s. The next decade is likely to be like the past decade because the UK's national growth model and the international context both militate against sustained and faster growth.

As outlined earlier in the chapter, consumption is the dominant element in the UK's GDP. With wages stagnating, the UK relies on a system of 'privatised Keynesianism'[22] based on household borrowing to boost the economy. Unregulated credit creation and debt (especially equity release through re-mortgage against rising house prices) have since the late 1980s driven domestic cycles of boom and bust. The unfavourable

international context includes three major crises in the past 15
years. The Great Financial Crisis, the Covid-19 pandemic and
the cost-of-living crisis exacerbated by the Ukraine War have all
derailed growth and complicated economic management. The
enduring legacy of the latest crisis will be the end of cheap food,
cheap energy and cheap money amidst growing geopolitical
instability. Although the form and nature of the next international crisis cannot be predicted, recurrent system-threatening
crises are structurally embedded in a globalised, financialised
economic system with political competition amidst great powers.

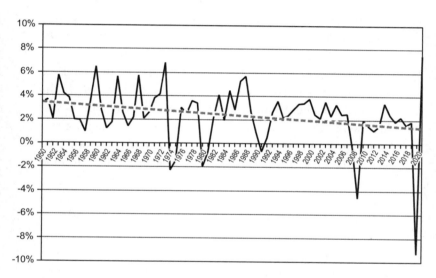

Exhibit 1.1 UK year-on-year growth rates of real GDP from 1950 to 2020.

Source: 'A millennium of macroeconomic data for the UK', Bank of England, and GDP data
tables, ONS. https://www.bankofengland.co.uk/statistics/research-datasets.

Note: The term 'real' denotes that the underlying data has removed the effects of inflation.
The data used to create the exhibits is available at https://foundationaleconomyresearch.com/
index.php/nothing-works-stats/

Against this background, the UK government could hope to avoid domestic policy mistakes in cyclical demand management that induce or aggravate recession and thereby depress growth. But the list of counter cyclical budget mistakes by 'dash for growth' Conservative chancellors is depressingly long. Reggie Maudling in 1962, Tony Barber in 1972 and Nigel Lawson in 1988 all stoked unsustainable expansion which ended in economic crisis. In 2022, Kwasi Kwarteng got to the crisis without the intervening short-lived boom. And, going forward, there are few good choices on fiscal and monetary policies for counter cyclical management in this conjuncture. Higher interest rates threaten asset prices (including housing) while weak trade performance and an 8 per cent current account deficit leave the currency exposed and increase the costs of imports.

Monetary policy will be contractionary as the Bank of England raises interest rates to curb inflation and defend the value of the pound. The scope for expansive fiscal policy is limited by the market response to Kwarteng's unfunded tax cuts which presents as something of a cautionary tale. This will constrain the ability of an incoming Labour government to fund a large-scale Green New Deal of what Roosevelt and Keynes would have called public works. Projects like large-scale home insulation and retrofit are overdue and can create short-term jobs. But the longer-term effects of accelerating green transition are uncertain. Structural change of this kind destroys as well as creates jobs in complex ways that will be difficult to predict. There is no mechanism which secures net new job creation in the UK, leave alone ensures high quality jobs in those places where jobs have been lost or are most needed.

As for all kinds of supply side policies – techno centrist and free market – these are complex long-term projects with uncertain outcomes, not a short-term fix for low growth. And in the UK, successive governments have half-heartedly tried various supply side policies – from industrial policy to investment zones – without finding any which could put the UK economy onto a different growth path, not least because of regular policy churn. Supply side policies are often taken from the technocratic centrist toolbox with prescriptions for workforce upskilling and investment in physical infrastructure and innovation, as regularly restated in a series of expert reports from the LSE Growth Commission in 2012[23] to the Economy 2030 Inquiry interim report in 2022.[24]

The Theresa May Government in 2017 favoured industrial policy for increased competitiveness in glamorous tradeable sectors, like automotive, aerospace, pharma and biotech. But supporting research and development and early-stage innovation is a long way from any kind of volume outcome. Policy makers have also recognised Mariana Mazzucato's sector-agnostic approach of 'missions' or steps towards 'grand challenges' like the ageing society.[25] This tends to encourage short-term pepper pot grants, but without the focused analysis of important foundational systems like adult care which could identify the points of intervention where significant outcomes could be levered. In 2021, the Boris Johnson Government refreshed industrial policy and embedded it in a 'plan for growth' with a focus on three issues: innovation, infrastructure and skills.[26] This signalled the arrival of just another centralised initiative, with little certainty about its life expectancy. At this point, it was also increasingly hard to tell where UK industrial policy ended and regional policy began.

Post-1970s regional policy had centred on supply side policies of making the market work better by encouraging inward investment, improving physical infrastructure and adding workforce skills. Such policies were consensually supported as ways of improving markets, but at best they are necessary but not sufficient for faster growth. Inward investment is about refilling a leaky bucket given that firms close or leave as well as enter. While state provision of training or roads at no direct cost is unfailingly popular with business organisations, the benefits in terms of jobs and growth are less clear. Higher GVA territories will, *ceteris paribus*, have a higher qualified workforce and better physical infrastructure. However, there is no evidence that, for example, adding skills will turn low GVA territories into high GVA territories.

Free market supply side deregulation offers limited gains the second time around in the 2020s when the labour market has long been deregulated and tax rates on income and profits have been competitively low since the 1980s. There is no evidence of lessons learned when the same old policies come round and round again. The short-lived investment zone proposal of September 2022 was an upscaling of the eight regional freeports announced in March 2021, which in turn were a variant of the 24 enterprise zones announced in 2011. These all variably combined regulatory concessions and financial incentives as in 1980s enterprise zones. But the 1980s zones were discontinued as failures. From the original Tym Report[27] onwards, government-commissioned and independent researchers alike have concluded that these zones created few new jobs. Up to 70 per cent of the jobs in 1980s enterprise zones were relocations from outside the zone and these relocations were usually short distances so there was negligible regional rebalancing.[28]

The revival of failed 1980s experiments in deregulation shows how supply side thinking (technocratic centrist and free market supply side) recycles the same old ideas without recognising that more of the same is unlikely to deliver faster growth and more good jobs. Worse still, faster growth is not just an unrealisable, false hope but an ecologically irresponsible and misconceived objective. Because, even if supply side policies did deliver, the UK would come up against the more fundamental problem that growth creates as many problems as it solves insofar as it aggravates the nature and climate emergency which we are politically failing to manage at international and national levels.

Under the weight of accumulating evidence and argument, the European policy consensus is slowly shifting towards recognition that 'green growth' is between improbable and impossible. In 2021 the European Environmental Agency accepted that 'it is unlikely that a long-lasting, absolute decoupling of economic growth from environmental pressures and impacts can be achieved'.[29] The UK lags behind in recognising the difficulty in decoupling growth from negative environmental impacts. The problem is not only the radical Conservative right in the Net Zero Scrutiny Group which argues that the costs of transition justify removing green taxes and increasing fossil fuel production.[30] Centrist UK politicians in government and opposition also habitually misunderstand and deny the basic relations between growth, emissions and ecological footprint. Thus, the Labour Leader of the Opposition, Keir Starmer, in a July 2022 speech claimed that 'a plan for growth needs net-zero' and 'a plan for net-zero needs growth'.[31]

As the problem is planetary, we will begin by reviewing the international evidence which confirms the position of the European Environmental Agency. We will then turn to the UK evidence which controverts the Labour leader's optimism.

On the international evidence, a landmark academic article by Hickel and Kallis in 2020 sums up the scientific evidence against green growth.[32] And that can be supplemented by *Decoupling Debunked*[33] from the European Environmental Bureau, an NGO which claims to be the 'largest network of environmental citizens' organisations in Europe'. The scientific evidence contextualises and disproves the old decoupling argument, according to which it is possible to decouple economic growth from environmental damage. The supporting empirics for this old decoupling position are summarised in data from the World Bank in Exhibit 1.2. Here GDP and global carbon emissions are related in an intensity index, that is, the amount of carbon used to generate a dollar of GDP. The graph shows that the carbon intensity of incremental growth falls from the early 1990s as nominal GDP increases faster than physical carbon emissions.

But at this point, it is necessary to distinguish between relative and absolute decoupling of growth and emissions. Exhibit 1.2 shows only that 'relative decoupling' is possible and is being achieved. This shows clearly that carbon intensity is decreasing because it is now possible to get increments of GDP growth with smaller increases in resource consumption. However, this should be distinguished from 'absolute decoupling' which would occur when the total CO_2 emissions do not increase as GDP output grows.

Economic policy as quagmire

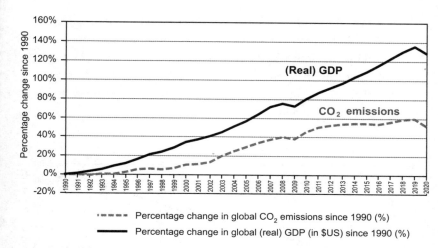

Exhibit 1.2 Percentage change in CO_2 emissions and real GDP, 1990–2020.

Source: Our World in Data (for emissions data) and World Bank national accounts data (for GDP).
https://ourworldindata.org/grapher/annual-co2-emissions-per-country?tab=table and
https://data.worldbank.org/indicator/NY.GDP.MKTP.KD.

Note: GDP at purchaser's prices is the sum of gross value added by all resident producers in the economy plus any product taxes and minus any subsidies not included in the value of the products. It is calculated without making deductions for depreciation of fabricated assets or for depletion and degradation of natural resources. Data are in constant 2015 prices, expressed in US dollars. Dollar figures for GDP are converted from domestic currencies using 2015 official exchange rates. For a few countries where the official exchange rate does not reflect the rate effectively applied to actual foreign exchange transactions, an alternative conversion factor is used. The data used to create the exhibits is available at https://foundationaleconomyresearch.com/index.php/nothing-works-stats/

At the global level, absolute decoupling has not been achieved over the past 30 years and, given available technologies and governmental behaviours, it is highly unlikely in the next decade. The historic record of absolute coupling is summarised in Exhibit 1.3 which plots global GDP in US$ trillion and the total level of global carbon emissions in billions of tonnes. Exhibit 1.3 shows that as global GDP increases so also does the absolute level of carbon emissions, with the exception of 2020 where the impacts of the Covid-19 pandemic had a striking but short-lived effect. The conclusion has to be that reducing carbon intensity per financial unit of GDP does not translate into reducing the total global carbon emissions which drive climate change.

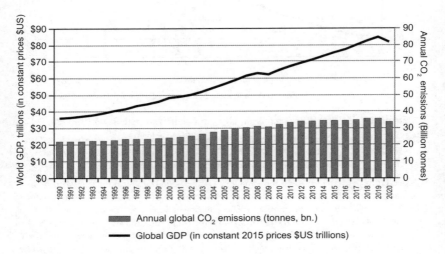

Exhibit 1.3 Total global CO_2 emissions and real GDP, 1990–2020.

Source: Our World in Data (for emissions data) and World Bank national accounts data (for GDP). https://ourworldindata.org/grapher/annual-co2-emissions-per-country?tab=table and https://data.worldbank.org/indicator/NY.GDP.MKTP.KD.

Note: GDP at purchaser's prices is the sum of gross value added by all resident producers in the economy plus any product taxes and minus any subsidies not included in the value of the products. It is calculated without making deductions for depreciation of fabricated assets or for depletion and degradation of natural resources. Data are in constant 2015 prices, expressed in US dollars. Dollar figures for GDP are converted from domestic currencies using 2015 official exchange rates. For a few countries where the official exchange rate does not reflect the rate effectively applied to actual foreign exchange transactions, an alternative conversion factor is used. The data used to create the exhibits is available at https://foundationaleconomyresearch.com/index.php/nothing-works-stats/

If we turn now to consider the UK record on growth and emissions, at first sight, there is remarkable evidence of absolute decoupling. The ONS calculates that, between 1985 and 2016, UK GDP per capita grew by 70.7 per cent while UK territorial CO_2 emissions fell by 34.2 per cent.[34] But this result is attributable to factors which make the UK territorial emissions figure misleading, and which suggest it will be difficult to maintain or improve on the historical GDP–emissions relation. The UK was from the 1980s transitioning towards a service economy so that by the late 2010s the service sector accounted for around 80 per cent of GDP and the UK had shifted mainly to importing its heavy industry and consumer goods production. This means that many of the emissions resulting from the production of goods consumed in the UK appeared in the territorial accounts of other countries. If we consider imported emissions then the absolute level of UK emissions was increasing year by year over the two decades after 1985 so that, by 2007, the UK's consumption-led CO_2 emissions (including imports) were 37 per cent higher than its territorial emissions.[35] Furthermore, 70 per cent of the reduction in emissions after 1990 comes from the energy sector and much of this can be attributed to the phasing out of coal powered electricity generation, which by the end of the 2010s accounted for no more than 2 per cent of total electricity generation.[36]

If the UK emissions/GDP growth relation is to be maintained or improved, then the UK government will have to introduce serious policies which combine 'polluter pays' carbon pricing and trading with physical restrictions on new emissions and clean-up of the provisioning systems in transport, housing and agriculture where emissions are stubbornly high. But the UK government has so far preferred to set targets for the future (like the phasing out of petrol and diesel engine new car sales by 2030) and then not engage with any of the awkward delivery issues about implementation and getting to target. As the UK Climate Change Committee observed when introducing its 2022 Progress Report, 'policies are now in place for most sectors of the economy, but a thorough review of progress finds scant evidence of delivery against these headline goals so far'.[37] Under the pressure of energy price rises, this point has perhaps now been finally taken on board by Labour which promises that, if elected, it will get serious about issues like home insulation which could deliver measurable results.

Finally, it should be remembered that the whole decoupling argument about UK emissions is narrowly focused on the impact of increments of growth for CO_2 emissions in the UK economy which is, as we have discussed earlier in this chapter, consumption based. Whatever happens to the incremental relation between growth and emissions, the high mass consumption lifestyle of the UK like other high income European countries is ecologically irresponsible. The fact that rich countries like the Nordics are large CO_2 emitters fits with the global calculation that, from 1990 to 2015, the richest 10 per cent of the world's population was responsible for 52 per cent of the cumulative carbon emissions.[38] The existing form and level of consumption in North West European countries is massively beyond planetary limits and the higher income countries are not green exemplars but the worst offenders.

This point about planetary limits emerges clearly if we shift from the narrow measure of CO_2 emissions to the broader measure of ecological footprint which is 'the impact of human activities measured in terms of the area of biologically productive land and water required to produce the goods consumed and to assimilate the wastes generated'.[39] It should be noted that even this measure underestimates environmental impact because it does not take into account negatives like ecosystem degradation, soil health and ocean acidification.

- In comparative international terms, as Exhibit 1.4 shows, the absolute size of the national footprint (in terms of resource consumption and waste generation) correlates strongly and positively with the level of GDP. European countries with high GDP like Germany and the Nordic countries are at the forefront of environmental policies. However, because of high mass consumption, these rich European countries also have a larger per capita footprint and impact on the environment than Italy, Spain or the UK.

- If then we consider individual West European countries in Exhibit 1.4, even those with lower per capita income like Spain have an absolute size footprint which is well beyond planetary limits. The sustainable footprint threshold for the 2010s and 2020s has been estimated somewhere around 1.7 hectares per capita to produce the goods consumed and assimilate the wastes generated. In the UK's case in 2018, the national footprint was 4.2 global hectares per capita. If this level of consumption and waste was applied globally, we would need two and a half planets.

These ecological footprint calculations demonstrate the unsustainability of the European way of life, and they are confirmed by other studies using completely different methodologies. For example, O'Neill *et al.* relate national capacity to meet basic human needs at a sustainable level of resource use. Here Austria, Germany and the Netherlands meet all the basic social

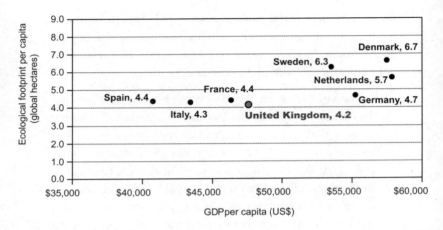

Exhibit 1.4 Ecological footprint per capita of selected European countries in 2018.

Source: OECD database (GDP per capita) and Global Footprint Network (Ecological footprint per capita). https://data.oecd.org/gdp/gross-domestic-product-gdp.htm and https://data .footprintnetwork.org/#/. The data used to create the exhibits is available at https://foundationa leconomyresearch.com/index.php/nothing-works-stats/.

needs 'but at a level of resource use that is far beyond the per capita bio-physical boundaries'.[40] From an ecological point of view, with or without more growth, all of Western Europe is unsustainable as authors like Kate Raworth and Tim Jackson have argued for some time.[41] Their arguments have been slow to breach mainstream political class thinking which dreams of growth. The more responsible policies of Labour in the UK compared with the Conservatives would produce greener growth and progress relative decoupling. But, if we review the evidence on how the planet has been and is being damaged, green economic growth is an unattainable objective with anything like current West European lifestyles. This means that the objective of growth needs to be reconsidered.

1.3 The low wages/low productivity economy

The previous section has explored the difficulty of achieving growth without further aggravating nature and climate emergencies. If this provides the high-level basis for a rethinking of the mainstream approach to the economy, we need to go further in our unravelling of the technocratic centrist agenda of creating a higher wage, higher skill, higher productivity economy. In this final section of the chapter, we begin to deconstruct this belief system by focusing on the relation between productivity and wages and questioning the relevance of the higher productivity objective.

The incontrovertible starting point for our argument is that the UK is an economy of low wages and stagnating average real wages. By the 2020s, 14 per cent of all UK jobs were classified as low paid in terms of the hourly rate, with rates at less than two-thirds of median hourly earnings, and 90 per cent of these low pay jobs were at the minimum wage. The problem of low pay is not simply the hourly rate but also the degree of under-employment. Some 28 per cent of UK jobs were classified as low paid on the basis of gross weekly earnings because they do not offer enough hours to produce an adequate wage.[42] If the UK has a bottom-heavy wage distribution, things are not getting better because real wages have been more or less flat since 2008. The ONS index of real average weekly earnings[43] was at 100 in 2004 and had risen 10 per cent higher by February 2008, just before the Great Financial Crisis downturn. Fast forward 12 years later and the real average weekly wage was just 4 per cent higher in February 2020, just before the first Covid-19 pandemic lockdown.[44]

Technocratic centrists routinely blame this stagnation on the failure of productivity growth in the 2010s. Historically the UK has year by year produced more goods and services (financially and physically) per hour worked so that labour productivity in the aggregate using financial measures has grown by about 2 per cent per annum. It is not unusual for productivity to fall in downturns like 2008–9 but in the subsequent nine years of upturn from 2010 to 2019 the ONS calculates that output per hour worked grew by just 0.4 per cent per annum. This flatlining is unprecedented in the post-1945 period[45] and in the UK and some other OECD countries it is commonly known as 'the productivity puzzle'. The standard explanation is factorial: in a survey of European economists, 40 per cent blamed low demand as the cause and 63 per cent recommended investment in skills as a policy response.[46]

This is an unhelpful cake-mix way of thinking about productivity in the 2010s as a generic recipe whose recent results disappoint. If so, the oven must be set at the wrong temperature and/or the cake mix must lack the critical self-raising ingredient. Instead, we must understand how and why the UK has become a low wage economy, and to explain that outcome, we must add a historic analysis of UK specifics over the past 50 years.

From this long-term perspective, the problem is a secular deterioration in the composition of employment, that is, a decline in the capacity of the UK economy to generate large numbers of jobs with pay levels that will support households. This reflects a sectoral shift away from male employment in the manufacturing sector after the 1970s. New knowledge-intensive and high-tech private sectors together with the expansion of state funded employment have been unable to generate enough jobs to compensate for lost manufacturing jobs. At the same time, wages in private sector employment were generally depressed by a structural shift in the distribution of national income from labour to capital. The outcome by the 2010s is a low wage, services dominated economy where, as we will argue, higher labour productivity has limited relevance as a measure or target.

The mainstream fixation on productivity combines the belief that productivity does limit wages in the long run with the hope that labour (not capital) can gain wages as output increases in the short run. But the evidence shows that pay was decoupled from productivity growth in many advanced economies in the 1990s, and that both pay and productivity have been flatlining in the UK in the 2010s. So, it is now a matter of faith to suppose that, if productivity growth resumed, labour would in fact capture the benefits of increasing UK output in the form of higher wages.[47]

In any case, if small year-by-year gains for labour were to be achieved in the 2020s, they need to be set in a 50-year perspective of long-term losses. Since the 1970s, there has been a secular decline in labour's share of output from 57.3 per cent in 1976 to 48.7 per cent in 2019 which means substantially lower incomes for the majority of households who depend on wages. Section 3.1 shows that this wage-depressing, distributive shift in GDP from labour to capital of nearly ten percentage points has depressed the average economically active household's wage income by more than £9,000 per annum since the 1970s.

From a historical perspective, this shift in distribution from labour to capital is bound up with the decline of large-scale

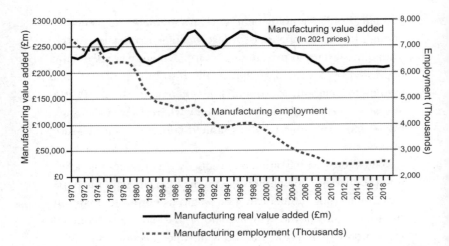

Exhibit 1.5 UK manufacturing real value added and employment 1970–2019.

Source: STAN STructural ANalysis Database, OECD. https://www.oecd.org/industry/ind/sta nstructuralanalysisdatabase.htm. The data used to create the exhibits is available at https://fou ndationaleconomyresearch.com/index.php/nothing-works-stats/.

manufacturing employment (and the associated decline in private sector trade unionism and labour bargaining power) which all has important implications for wages and productivity. Manufacturing was the key support of the male wage-earner-based economy from the 1950s to the 1970s when semi-skilled men could earn wages high enough to support a family. As we explain in Section 4.1, in 1951 5.9 million men worked in manufacturing and only 20 per cent of married women worked regularly.[48] Manufacturing was also a reliable driver of productivity increases in its heyday and through four decades of decline because, as Exhibit 1.5 shows, UK manufacturing from 1970 to 2008 produced roughly the same quantum of real net output with an ever-smaller workforce. But UK manufacturing is now too small to be a driver of better macroeconomic outcomes. By 2008 it had been reduced to a rump with fewer than 2,000 factories employing more than 200 workers,[49] food processing was the largest sector and neither output nor productivity was growing over the following decade.

The new 'frontier sectors' of knowledge-intensive services and high-tech manufacturing have not compensated for the decline of family-supporting wages in large-scale manufacturing. These sectors can create high wage jobs, but not in large numbers because the employment base in these sectors is too small. Using criteria such as tertiary educated employees, research and development (R&D) intensity and patents,[50] Eurostat counts employment in 'high tech industry and knowledge intensive services' which 'generally provide high value added and well-paid employment'.[51] As Exhibit 1.6 shows, the UK has no more than about 5 per cent of its workforce employed in the frontier sectors and this small base is not some peculiar deficiency of the British economy but a general characteristic of the larger West European economies including Germany.

Some like Moretti argue that highly educated 'idea creators' can indirectly sustain employment and prosperity in their communities through demand for local services, but it is not clear that this model of innovation-led urban development could or does work across the UK.[52]

The UK's historic problems with a deteriorating composition of employment have been buffered by the rise of dual-earner households with new opportunities for women and by the expansion of state and para-state employment for a diverse workforce. As we show in the next chapter, both parents are

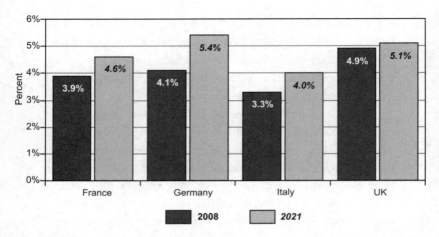

Exhibit 1.6 Contribution of the high-technology and knowledge-intensive sectors to employment, 2008 and 2021.

Source: Eurostat, 'Employment in technology and knowledge-intensive sectors at the national level, by sex (from 2008 onwards, NACE Rev. 2)', Eurostat database (accessed July 2022, online data code HTEC_EMP_NAT2). https://ec.europa.eu/eurostat/databrowser/view/htec_emp_nat2/default/table?lang=en.

Note: UK data for 2021 relates to 2019. The data used to create the exhibits is available at https://foundationaleconomyresearch.com/index.php/nothing-works-stats/.

employed in three-quarters of UK households where couples have children. But many of the second-earner jobs in dual-earner households were part-time and low paid. The contraction in state employment with post-1979 privatisation and outsourcing was balanced by the rise of para-state employment, that is, jobs in private sector firms which draw more than half of their revenue from the state. The state and the tax-funded para-state sectors did much of the heavy lifting on job creation in creating 57 per cent of all net new jobs under the New Labour governments between 1997 and 2007.[53] But, austerity budgets in the 2010s limited further state-funded job creation so that, as Exhibit 1.7 shows, state and para-state accounted for no more than 24 per cent of net new job creation in the 2010s.

The state and para-state provide essential services and, while the growth has slowed from the 1997–2007 period, these sectors still accounted for 30 per cent of net new full-time job creation in the 2010s. The central state has responded to this trend of increasing numbers by offering mean pay settlements so that (well before the current cost of living crisis), wages lagged across the public sector and many groups experienced real wage cuts. The Institute for Fiscal Studies, for example, projects a 14 per cent real terms pay cut for experienced teachers between 2010 and 2023.[54] As already noted, the hypocrisy of the central state is that it wants a higher wage economy but not in the public sector. This is a major challenge to the ideal of higher wages

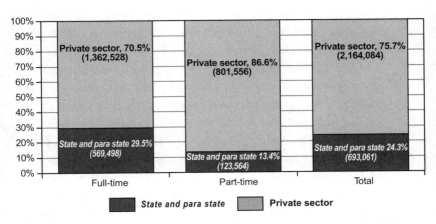

Exhibit 1.7 State and para-state share of UK net new job creation, 2009–20.

Source: Nomis database, Business Register and Employment Survey, ONS (July 2022). https://www.nomisweb.co.uk/query/select/getdatasetbytheme.asp?theme=27. The data used to create the exhibits is available at https://foundationaleconomyresearch.com/index.php/nothing-works-stats/.

fuelling prosperity given that more than one-quarter of the UK workforce is dependent on the state directly and indirectly if we include private firms like care providers in the para-state.

And this double standard on higher wages has implications for whether productivity is a useful and relevant measure in public services. Productivity in public services is measured financially as the market value of net output or value added. But in state-owned and operated services 70 per cent to 85 per cent of value added is wages paid to the workforce. In this case, because value added is a financial proxy for productivity, if the state pays the workforce more this boosts productivity. Conversely, if the state pays the workforce less that reduces productivity. So financial measures of labour productivity in the public sector reflect the capacity and willingness of the state to pay more, rather than any improvements in process efficiency. If financial measures of productivity are then discarded as meaningless in the public sector, the use of physical measures does not solve the problem but adds further complications.

In many private and public services, labour is both input and output. In such cases, taking labour out of the process generally produces a low cost service with lower quality. The results are familiar from low cost mobile, broadband and airlines, which provide limited customer service, or from budget hotels with buffet meals and no night porter. Low cost or 'budget' provision would be much the same in a school without teaching assistants, arts, sports and special needs provisions. In extreme cases, as in the UK healthcare system, a lower input of labour per unit of output results in a fragile high flow system. This point is developed in Section 4.3 which considers the case of NHS hospitals. Here, the physical productivity of staff is a matter of high throughput or flow, and more patient treatments per bed or operating theatre each year. The problem is that this high flow comes at the cost of resilience. System fragility is apparent whenever patient demand surges or delayed patient discharges block throughput, and the system struggles to cope with winter flu, even without pandemic shock.[55]

Productivity is a slippery concept in manufacturing when differences in product, process throughput and wage levels interact to influence physical productivity and cash from operations in activities like car assembly.[56] When the UK economy is dominated by services, with around 80 per cent of output or employment, productivity is a legacy concept of limited relevance to the economy as it now exists. For the reasons briefly explained above, higher financial and physical productivity is not a sensible goal or a smart way of thinking about a service-dominated economy like the UK in the 2020s.[57]

If we look at public sector service productivity, that shows no consistent upwards trend for the past 30 years, but that is an observation, not a problem justifying political preoccupation with efficiency savings or economic fixation on productivity as a lever. We need to think differently and more constructively about relevant socio-economic measures and targets in the public and the private sector which are relevant both to the quality of employment and to the outcomes of the services provided. Before we think about such targets, we will in the next chapter have to think more analytically about the benefits of high wages when most of us live in expenditure-sharing households and what matters to households is not gross household income but disposable income after tax and benefits and then residual income after essentials.

Why we need to change the lens

Overall, this chapter has shown how a high growth, high productivity, high wage economy has become the consensus objective of the main political parties and of many commentators.
But the dream of a high wage, high productivity economy is
unrealisable and misconceived at the same time as its non-reali-
sation feeds into the sense of disappointment and cynicism that
increasingly trouble our politics. The foundational argument is
then for changing the lens so that we stop trying to understand
the economy through the old lens of deficiency in input-output
terms and instead ask how we can directly improve household
liveability given the economy we have.

PART II

Rethinking the economy

Introduction to Part II

Chapter 1 outlined why the standard growth and jobs framing of 'the economy' – more and better paid jobs for individuals as the key to higher living standards – needs to be replaced. The rest of this book constructively proposes and develops a different foundational lens for rethinking the economy as a collection of households, where those in the bottom half of the income distribution have acute problems of liveability. We will show that foundational liveability has been undermined by the crumbling of each of its three supporting pillars: essential services, social infrastructure and residual income. This is the result of the failed market citizenship project which has attempted to boost individual consumption at the expense of collective provision. Rather than persisting with the failed approach of prosperity through higher productivity and incomes, the implication is that the state and other actors should come together to directly address foundational liveability.

Chapter 2

Households and foundational liveability

Introduction

This chapter takes up the challenge of thinking differently. The break is made by changing the lens through which we view the economy and defining a new object of *foundational liveability*. This involves shifting the focus from individuals to households because most of us live in multi-person households with expenditure and/or income sharing. We recognise that households depend on state and privately provided essential services from healthcare to public transport and on social infrastructure like parks and libraries. Income matters, of course, but we need to focus on disposable and residual income, which highlights the importance of housing costs and expenditures for other essentials like food and utilities.

Some have attempted to make a break by inverting the mainstream objective of growth and presenting degrowth as the new superordinate objective. This is attractive in general terms when it envisages a shift in the composition of output towards community-based ecological enterprises and more repair and reuse,[1] accompanied by income redistribution and more expenditure on public services.[2] But there are no available technical fixes for activities like flying, shipping and ruminant agriculture, and here degrowth can lurch politically towards puritan central policy prescriptions (like closing the airports[3]) which are counter-productive.

The starting point for making our break is not the growth objective but the individualism of national income accounting measures which have always been the operating metrics of growth. When national income accounting came to dominate the field from the 1940s onwards, it promoted individualised, average measures of output and income. Gross domestic product (GDP) per capita at the national level and gross value added (GVA) per capita at the regional level were accepted as standard proxy measures of living standards and economic capability. But they denied social realities about household and family which had been recognised in earlier social thinking and remain important in lived experience, as the cost-of-living crisis so clearly shows.

From the 1900s to the 1940s, the technical social science unit of analysis was not the individual but the household. In Joseph Rowntree's first York poverty survey of 1899 (and in subsequent poverty surveys), house-by-house inquiry into households was used to calculate the number of those in 'primary poverty' whose income did not cover essentials.[4] In the more vernacular thinking of social reformers like Archbishop William Temple in 1943, the family was 'the primary social unit'. Temple wrote that 'every child should find itself a member of a family housed with decency and dignity so that it may grow up … unspoilt by under feeding and overcrowding'.[5]

In lived experience, the family and its network around the household is the unit that looks after its own. Thus, Marcus Rashford the footballer and child hunger campaigner remembered his upbringing in the 2000s on a South Manchester social housing estate where 'in Wythenshawe my community was an extension of the family unit'.[6] The family struggled and Rashford says, 'I know what it feels to be hungry' because his hard-working mother was a single parent and on her low wages was never free from the 'worry about whether she would cover the next round of bills'.[7] So 'as a family we relied on breakfast clubs, free school meals' with 'Sam at the local chippy slipping him a free bag of chips when he looked hungry'.[8]

The first task is to bring households back into political economy and social thought while recovering the corollary policy concern with essentials that animated Rowntree and Temple. This needs to be done in ways that recognise present-day realities like very high rates of labour market participation, and that requires us to open up a new research agenda about the nature of the challenges to living standards and, in due course, a practical politics centred on raising foundational liveability.

The households that concern us are not standardised units, nor do we start from any normative agenda about ideal types. Our concern is not with the *oikos* as the political unit of the Greek city state nor the male breadwinner household as the economic unit of 1940s Britain, when Beveridge could suppose a wife was covered by her husband's social insurance contributions. We must now understand households in all their diversity because it is the variable composition of our households (in terms of ages, number of persons and number of economically active persons) which governs the possibilities of pooling incomes and spreading expenditure. And this variability therefore has immediate and direct implications for standards of living when so much in our society is marketised.

Consideration of standards of living then also requires some discrimination about the heterogeneity of the 'essentials' which diverse households need. Our liveability argument here is that as much as income, households need essential services like health and care, as well as social infrastructure like parks and libraries whose effective provision depends on a balance between collective and private consumption. With regard to private consumption, we can reiterate the obvious. The relevant incomes are (a) disposable household income after tax and benefits and (b) residual household income after paying for essentials like housing, utilities, food and transport.

The first section of this chapter, Section 2.1, explains how and why the diversity of the household as a social unit matters and draws out some implications for inequality.

Section 2.2 introduces our concept of *foundational liveability* which requires the alignment of three pillars providing essential services, social infrastructure and residual income. Section 2.3, the third and final section of this chapter, situates the foundational concept of liveability in relation to other concepts of liveability and in the broader context of foundational economy thinking. Thus, this second chapter starts a positive problem shift which displaces the growth and jobs, wages and productivity problematic. This opens the way for analysis of distribution to and amongst households in Chapter 3, discussion of the cost of essentials and public service provision in Chapter 4 and criticism of the tax and benefits wedge that affects low income households in Chapter 5.

2.1 Household variety and living standards

This section explains the importance of household structure and how household composition is relevant to income-based standards of living. This leads to an empirical account of how UK households and their changing structure over time fit into this framework. Here we show that multi-earner households are important because they buffer the consequences of low wages in the bottom half of the income distribution and accelerate inequality in the upper half of the income distribution. But any discussion of households must first begin by explaining the distinction between the everyday notion of family and the concept of the household as defined in official statistics.

What is the difference between a household and a family? Standard official definitions of household and family are provided by the OECD which distinguishes between one-person and multi-person households.[9] In a one-person household, a single person 'makes provision for his or her own food or other essentials' like housing. A multi-person household is 'a group of two or more persons making common provision for food or other essentials for living' under one roof and thus to some extent sharing expenditure and incomes. Members of a household may be unrelated as in a flat share. By way of contrast, a family, on the OECD definition, consists of 'those members of the household who are related ... through blood, adoption or marriage'.[10] In the UK most multi-person households are two-generation, parent/child nuclear family units though more extended family arrangements have also been common.

The distinction between single- and multi-person households is important because this has implications for income-based liveability. A multi-person household under one roof shares expenditure on some essentials and can pool incomes if there is more than one wage earner. In the multi-person household, the spreading of on-the-market costs like housing and utility bills boosts the standard of living of individuals in the household group. In an upper income multi-person household, expenditure sharing allows more spending on non-essentials and in lower income groups expenditure sharing can to some extent help buffer difficulties in paying for essentials. The boost to living standards is usually accelerated if there is more than one wage earner in the group, as in the case of couples where both partners work. But it should be remembered that when both partners work the increased income is offset by increased essential costs like childcare or transport to work.

Having explained the basic distinctions and their pertinence to living standards, how does the UK population fit into this framework? The first point has to be that only a relatively small number of UK citizens live outside ordinary households in various institutional settings. The number of those living in prisons and barracks is modest: English and Welsh jails and young offenders' institutions hold just over 81,000 prisoners[11] while just under 149,000 serve in the UK armed forces.[12] The only two substantial groups living outside households within self-contained accommodation are: first, the young and the vulnerable living in bedsits and hostels classed as 'houses in multiple occupancy' (HMO) and second, adults living in residential care homes. There are some 500,000 HMOs in England and Wales,[13] while England alone has nearly 500,000 beds in residential and care homes.[14]

These two exceptions are important, but the standard UK experience is of living in a family of relations or in a household with self-contained accommodation. In 2021, according to ONS estimates, there were 19.3 million families and 28.1 million households in the UK and, on these estimates, just under 55 million lived in families out of the total UK population of just over 67 million.[15] The issue then is about the composition of these households and how that is changing and has changed over time because over the last 50 years there have been significant changes at both ends of the size distribution.

Most attention has focused on the increase in the number of single-person households as the number of people living alone has risen. As Exhibit 2.1 shows, over a long 50-year period,

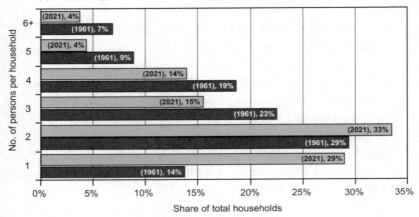

(a) *Percentage shares of differently sized UK households in 1961 and 2021*

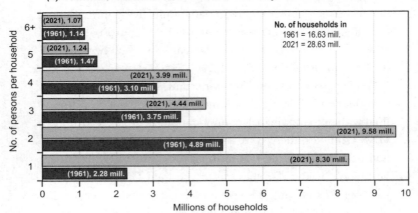

(b) *Absolute numbers in millions of differently sized households*

No. of households in
1961 = 16.63 mill.
2021 = 28.63 mill.

Exhibit 2.1 UK households by number of persons in 1961 and 2021.

Source: ONS, Families and households dataset. https://www.ons.gov.uk/peoplepopulationand community/birthsdeathsandmarriages/families/datasets/familiesandhouseholdsfamiliesan dhouseholds (accessed July 2022); ONS (2004), Household Composition by Size, Social Trends, no. 30 and no. 34. https://www.data.gov.uk/dataset/f3ba77f8-d598-4db2-a3bc-b59a1578d410 /social-trends. The data used to create the exhibits is available at https://foundationaleconomy research.com/index.php/nothing-works-stats/.

single-person households increased from 14 per cent to 29 per cent of all households. In 1961 less than 2.5 million lived alone and that number more than tripled over the next 30 years. On ONS estimates, over the past 25 years the number of people living alone rose from 6.6 million in 1996 to 8.3 million in 2021, with year-on-year increases in 22 of the past 25 years.[16] The increase in living alone is broadly spread across age groups, but the largest increase is in working age adults aged 45 to 64.[17] The rise of the single-person household is an ongoing development but maybe also the result of a once and for all shift in marriage and cohabitation arrangements.

The number of those living alone may continue to increase year on year but the percentage of those living in single-person households has barely increased from the 29 per cent level reached in 2001.

The much-discussed rise of the single-person household has stalled in percentage terms because it has been counterbalanced by barely noticed countervailing trends. At the opposite end of the distribution, there has been a decline, in percentage terms, in larger households of five or more individuals. Since 1961, the absolute number of larger households has fallen slightly from 2.6 million in 1961 to 2.3 million in 2021. However, larger households are now only half as common, falling from 15.7 per cent of the total in 1961 to 8.1 per cent by 2021. This is mainly because women are having fewer children: the standard total fertility rate measure reached a record low of 1.58 in 2020, which is not much more than half the 2.9 level of the 1960s peak.[18] Mid-sized household numbers have meanwhile been maintained and increased over the past 30 years by the gently rising number of young adults living with parents to reduce living expenses. The number of young adults aged 21 to 34 years living with parents increased from 2.3 million (19 per cent of the age cohort) in 1996 to 3.1 million (26 per cent of the age cohort) in 2021.

In a broad view of the distribution of household sizes, most UK citizens continue to live in multi-person households and there remains now, as there has been through the whole post-war period, a strong clustering in the size distribution around smaller multi-person households of two to four persons. The ONS estimates that in the UK in 2021, there were 20.3 million multi-person households as against 8.3 million single-person households, so overall 71 per cent of UK citizens lived in multi-person households. As Exhibit 2.1 shows, after more than 50 years of dramatic social change, the percentage of UK citizens living in smaller multi-person households of two to four people has fallen from 71 per cent in 1961 to 63 per cent in 2021. We can conclude that the UK is far from becoming a society of singletons.

All this matters because it has implications for living standards through the options that household structure gives or closes on expenditure sharing and income pooling. The 8.3 million single-person households have to manage without any form of expenditure sharing or income pooling. The 7.8 million couples without children often (but by no means always) have the option of pooling income from two earners and can share expenditure without the additional costs of dependent children. There are 8 million couples or single parents with dependent children including 5.2 million couples with one or two children and 1.8 million single parents with dependent children. However, these two groups are very differently placed because in the case of a single parent with dependent children, as with Marcus Rashford's mother, the needs of several individuals have to be met from one income with wage earning often also constrained by childcare responsibilities.

All of this structures the necessity and opportunity for households of different compositions and, as we will show in later chapters, does so in complex interaction with wage levels, the tax and benefits system, variable housing costs and now the cost-of-living crisis. In a country where low wages are ubiquitous, it is hardly surprising that both parents work in 75 per cent of couples with children because in 2010s Britain that was necessary for many households if they were to cover essentials and/or afford a few extras. After making this elementary point, much of the rest of this book is concerned with the complexities of the relations between income and expenditure for differently placed households. But, at this stage in the argument, we will only observe that income sharing and the general principle of 'two earners are better than one' works in a double-edged way at the household level to accelerate the inequalities of individual income.

This point about how income pooling accelerates income inequality emerges very clearly from Exhibit 2.2. Here we divide all households into ten equally sized groups or deciles, according to their gross (before tax) income from wages and benefits: the lowest income households are in decile 1 and those with the highest incomes in decile 10. The exhibit then relates household income to the number of economically active persons in each household. The 'economically active' category includes not just the employed but those who are in the workforce but currently classified as unemployed or sick. In a low unemployment year

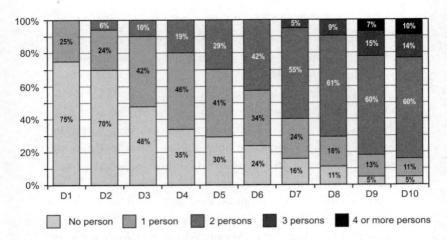

Exhibit 2.2 Number of economically active persons in households ranked by gross income decile, 2020–21.

Source: ONS, Family spending workbook 4: expenditure by household characteristic: Percentage of households by economic activity, tenure and socio-economic classification in each gross income decile group, 2020/21 (Table 50). https://www.ons.gov.uk/peoplepopulationand community/personalandhouseholdfinances/expenditure/datasets/familyspendingworkbook4 expenditurebyhouseholdcharacteristic.

Note: The underlying sorting of households is based on gross income. Base data does not always add to 100 per cent. The difference applies to four deciles and is ≤ 1 per cent plus or minus. The residual is proportionately allocated to the groups. The data used to create the exhibits is available at https://foundationaleconomyresearch.com/index.php/nothing-works-stats/.

like 2019/2020, this group can be taken as a reasonable proxy for the number of wage earners. In general terms, the number of wage earners in a household correlate positively with household position in the gross income hierarchy.

1. Having just one wage earner in the household is a good predictor of the household being in the bottom half of the income distribution. In decile 2, the second to lowest

income group, just 6 per cent of households have two wage earners, while in decile 5 only 31 per cent of households have two or more wage earners. The complication in this relation is economic inactivity, because those who are out of work and on benefits in the UK get an income which is miserably lower than almost any kind of waged employment. Economic inactivity is an even stronger driver of position in the lowest deciles with no economically active person in half to three-quarters of households in the bottom three deciles (D1, D2 and D3 in Exhibit 2.2). The bottom deciles are largely made up of economically inactive and single-earner households.

2. Having two or more wage earners in the household is a good predictor of the household being in the top half of the income distribution. In the 40 per cent of highest-income households (decile 7 and above), more than half the households have two or more wage earners; and in deciles 9 and 10 more than three-quarters of households have two or more wage earners. In the top deciles 9 and 10, less than 15 per cent of households have single earners whose income propels them into the highest income groups. This illustrates the power of assortative mating, whereby individuals tend to partner with those who are similar so that high income households disproportionally contain two managerial or professional earners on relatively high wages. According to the IPPR, there has been an increase in the proportion of people marrying within their social class, which 'exacerbates wider income inequalities by concentrating wealth and poverty in different households'.[19]

The twentieth-century welfare state was introduced to supplement the buffering capacity of the working class household which had a limited capacity to manage the insecurities of wage labour and deal with periods of interruption of weekly earnings. Even with this support, the household remained important through expenditure sharing and through income sharing of young adults living with parents. Income sharing has become increasingly important with the rise of female workforce participation to more than 70 per cent in recent years. In this context, the household by the 2010s was crucial for levelling up incomes in the bottom half of the distribution and for increasing inequality between households in the bottom and top halves. From this point of view, the cost-of-living crisis is about how households in the bottom half of the income distribution can no longer buffer the rising cost of on-market essentials.

Of course, households should not be viewed simply as atomistic units because financial and other support, most commonly care, can also be shared between households. This means that the resources available may in practice be larger or smaller as a result of income/expenditure and time/task sharing across households. For example, parents may provide support to adult children who are not living with them, just as younger workers may be supporting relatives outside their household. The representation of the household in official statistics will therefore simplify more complex relationships and affinities that can have financial as well as practical dimensions, especially in relation to the availability of time. While recognising these inter-household connections as a complexity, our analysis is in no sense invalidated. The official statistics used in this book capture the primary characteristics of households, as well as the important differences in financial and time resources between households, which will shape liveability. In turn, this will affect the ability of households to offer support to others in ways that need further investigation.

2.2 Foundational liveability defined

The previous section of this chapter explained how and why household diversity is the object of this book because household composition has important implications for income and living standards. This section adds the concept of foundational liveability which is the lens and research tool through which we understand and explore that diversity.

Household living standards are not just about numbers of earners and wages but about access to *essential services* and *social infrastructure*, as well as *residual income* after four essentials (housing, transport, utilities and food) have been paid for. The result is the three pillars concept of foundational liveability in Exhibit 2.4, which combines essential services and social infrastructure with income. This is both a concept and a research tool that is immediately used in this section to make two important points that highlight the importance of social and collective provision. First, residual income is what matters because the benefits of higher wages are eroded or even wiped out by high housing costs for some tenure groups in some regions. Second, households in the bottom half of the income distribution are heavily dependent on state benefits in cash and in-kind, the importance of which is underestimated by households and the UK political classes.

Foundational liveability as we explain it in this book develops and builds on foundational economy as we discovered it in 2013.[20] The original *Manifesto for the Foundational Economy* focused on the importance of the foundational sectors in providing essential goods and services,[21] which are the first pillar of foundational liveability. Subsequent community studies highlighted the aims and agency of ordinary people in post-industrial places. Morriston in 2019[22] highlighted the importance of social infrastructure, while Blaenau Ffestiniog in 2022[23] raised the issue of local attachment and identity in relation to place and community. Together these elements give the basis of the second pillar of foundational liveability. After questioning the relevance of productivity in the foundational economy[24] and deconstructing the meaningless figure of GVA per capita we emphasised the relevance of household residual income as the third pillar relevant to understanding living standards.[25] The concept of 'liveability', first introduced in the 2022 *Jobs and Liveability* report on the Newcastle-upon-Tyne urban area,[26] draws together several threads of this work.

The basic idea of foundational liveability is simple and can be represented graphically in the temple of liveability diagram in Exhibit 2.3. All three pillars of foundational liveability are critical for households. In a cost-of-living crisis, the income pillar claims public attention when household incomes are increasingly inadequate to pay for on-market essentials like heating and eating. But our argument in subsequent chapters will be that this crisis overlays longstanding chronic problems with all three pillars: specifically, a dysfunctional tax and benefits system which reduces disposable income for the low paid at the same time as all households suffer from a declining provision of tax-funded foundational services and social infrastructure.

Households and foundational liveability

The value of using the household as the focus is not just because of the income pooling and expenditure sharing role that the household plays, as discussed already in this chapter. The household is also a real and physical entity, located in an actual place. And place matters because the quality and availability of essential services and social infrastructure vary hugely, so that the individual household's experience of foundational liveability reflects not only its residual income but also its location.

In Exhibit 2.3, the foundational liveability of households is supported by three pillars.

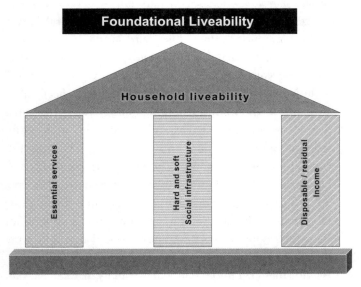

Exhibit 2.3 Foundational liveability.

1. *Essential goods and services* are those which are necessary for everyday sustenance, and which are delivered through complex reliance systems. Whether publicly provided or privately owned, these foundational goods and services are matters of collective provision, often through nationally organised networks which distribute locally. They include the welfare state services of health, education and care which are usually provided free or subsidised to some degree from tax revenue. But they also include housing, food and pipe and cable utilities – water, electricity, gas, telecommunications and broadband. These goods and services are largely or completely bought on the market and have to be paid for from household income.

2. *Social infrastructure* includes the hard infrastructure of free or affordable spaces, including parks, libraries, cultural, leisure and community centres. These are available locally and form the basis for soft infrastructure activities of all sorts, including voluntary action in civil society groups as well as individual enjoyment. This hard and soft social infrastructure is important for foundational liveability because people are creative, active and social, with a need for self-realisation, sociability and community which extends beyond the sustenance provided by essential services. The inadequacy of social infrastructure can be keenly felt. In a 2020 Survation opinion poll of 'left-behind' areas, those respondents who believed their area was not getting its fair share of resources most commonly stated that they were missing out on 'places to meet' and 'community facilities'.[27]

3. Income matters for foundational liveability in a specific way. We need to focus not on an individual's wages and gross

income but (a) disposable income after tax and benefits and then (b) residual income after paying for essentials (housing, food, transport and utilities). *Residual income* matters because so many essential foundational goods and services are on market and have to be paid for from household income. The cost-of-living crisis is about rising energy, petrol and food prices for all. Higher mortgage and rent payments mean that those in the middle as well as the bottom of the income distribution feel the pressure. The foundational issue is whether households can afford to buy on-market essentials and still have some margin of discretionary income for other purposes, or whether households cannot afford essentials and face impossible heating or eating choices.

Many now understand that the cost-of-living crisis is about negative residual income when disposable income cannot cover the cost of on-market essentials and squeezed residual income in households, up to and beyond the mid-point of the income distribution, as we explore below. This is particularly a problem where there are high housing costs (from private rents or mortgage payments) so that disposable income after taxes and benefits does not easily cover the rising cost of essentials. At the same time, alignment of these three pillars is intuitively necessary because foundational liveability fails if, for example, households have residual income but do not have accessible and affordable essential services. This can occur when good quality services like public transport or childcare are not available everywhere or are prohibitively expensive.

So, a key foundational question is about the pre-conditions for alignment of the three pillars. Our answer is that for the large majority of households, the pre-condition of alignment is a balance between collective/social provision and individual market provision, as represented in Exhibit 2.4. One argument of this book is that much of the current foundational liveability crisis for low and middle income households is the result of how the market citizenship project has naively promoted an imbalance in favour of the market, from which we are all now suffering.

There has been too much emphasis on what wage income can buy and too little recognition of the importance of the range of essential services and social infrastructure which are collectively provided. The importance of social and collective provision gets lost for two reasons which we will consider in turn. First, variation in housing costs by tenure group[28] and region means that there is not a standard household experience when it comes to the most significant expense that most

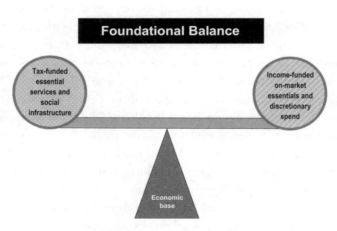

Exhibit 2.4 Foundational balance.

households face, so the implications of variable housing costs are not generally understood. Second, there is blurred public understanding and consistent underestimation of the value of in-kind public services and cash benefits in supporting households in the bottom half of the income distribution.

The first point here is that housing costs vary dramatically by region and tenure so households with higher gross and disposable incomes do not always retain a substantial advantage in terms of higher residual incomes. In extreme cases, higher gross income households may actually end up with a lower per person residual income after housing costs. This point about the erosion of high wage advantage emerges very clearly if we compare pre-crisis gross, disposable and residual income in 2020 for two substantial groups in different regions: private renters, who account for more than one-quarter of London households, and owner occupiers (with no mortgage) who account for more than one-third of households in North East England. London private renters are the urban proof that higher wages do not semi-automatically solve foundational liveability issues even in terms of household income.

As Exhibit 2.5 shows, in 2020 an average private renting London household has a gross and disposable income which is nearly twice that of the average owner occupier in North East England, but this huge advantage is substantially reduced when it comes to residual income. The household gross income of London private renters was £1,380 per week compared to £687 for the North East owner occupiers. London private renters' disposable income was £1,108 per week compared to £620 for the North East owners' group. But owner occupiers have very low housing costs because they pay neither mortgage nor

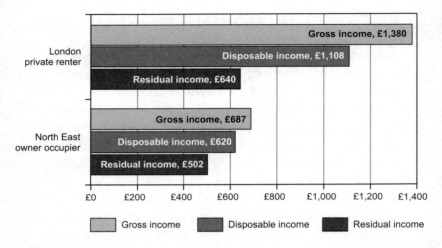

Exhibit 2.5 Gross, disposable and residual income for North East England owner occupiers and London private renters, 2020.

Source: Bespoke data from the ONS.

Note: Data is for an average household in each category. The data is for April 2019 to March 2020 fiscal year end and is therefore unaffected by the pandemic lockdowns. Gross income is the sum earned without the deduction of tax, national insurance and pensions. After the deductions, it is classified as disposable income. Residual income is derived from disposable income by deducting expenditure on rent and mortgages, food and non-alcoholic drink, utilities and transport. The data used to create the exhibits is available at https://foundationaleconomyresearch.com/index.php/nothing-works-stats/.

rent, unlike private renters in London with high housing costs which have ratcheted up with London house prices. As a result, the average private renting household in London pays 27.5 per cent of their disposable income in rent after any housing benefit obtained. The London household is then left with a residual income of £640 because the four necessities of housing, food, utilities and transport take 42 per cent of disposable income. This London household's residual income is now only 30 per cent higher than the £502 for the average North East owner occupier where their four necessities take just 19 per cent of disposable income.

London private renters are typically younger and have dependent children, so they have larger households than owner occupiers in North East England, who include many older couples who have paid off their mortgages. The residual income of £213 per person in the average London private renting household is actually below the £264 per person residual income in the average North East owner occupier household. Equally, housing benefit is critical for lower income private tenants in high rent London. The calculation above for the private renting London household is based on net rent after any housing benefit because that is what households pay directly out of their income. If we removed the housing benefit so that London private renting households had to pay gross rent, lower income renting households would all have a negative residual income problem. The foundational implication is that government needs active social policies to directly address essential services, like housing and transport whose cost and availability need to be related to household composition and the level of income support and other cash benefits.

The second important point here concerns the value of state benefits in cash and kind to all households in the bottom half of the income distribution. To examine this issue, in Exhibit 2.6 we compare the relative value of three sources of 'income': wages and salaries, cash benefits and benefits in-kind. Benefits in-kind are important to recognise because this is the value of mainly

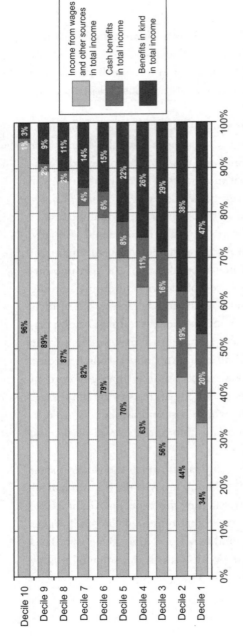

Exhibit 2.6 Non-retired households' sources of total income split by type in 2019–20 (households ranked by disposable income).

Source: ONS, Effects of taxes and benefits on UK household income: financial year ending 2020. https://www.ons.gov.uk/peoplepopulationandcommunity/persona landhouseholdfinances/incomeandwealth/bulletins/theeffectsoftaxesandbenefitsonhouseholdincome/financialyearending2020.

Notes: A retired household is one where more than 50 per cent of its income is sourced from people who (i) define themselves as retired and are aged over 50 years, or (ii) define themselves as 'Sick/Injured', not seeking work and aged at or above the State Pension Age. 'Non-retired' refers to anyone living in a household that does not meet the criteria for being a retiree. Underlying income has been equivalised using the modified-OECD scale and includes workplace pensions, individual personal pensions and annuities, Child Tax Credit and Working Tax Credit and Universal Credit and Government training scheme allowances. Council Tax and Northern Ireland rates after deducting discounts. Cash benefits are classified if they are paid directly to the recipient as a sum of money. Benefits-in-kind relate to non-cash benefits such as the National Health Service, education, free childcare and travel subsidies. The data used to create the exhibits is available at https://fou ndationaleconomyresearch.com/index.php/nothing-works-stats/ .

health and education services, plus subsidies for travel and childcare, provided by the state at no direct charge to the household. The value of benefits in-kind is imputed by the ONS on the basis of the cost of producing these services and allocated to households on the basis of their average size, which provides a rough estimate of what households would have to pay if they had to buy those services on the market. The evidence challenges the high and higher wages preoccupation and the market citizenship assumption that we can create more independent households which make market choices as they can afford to 'go private' instead of relying on state welfare provision.

Exhibit 2.6 presents data on non-retired households organised in ten income decile groups, so that decile 1 is the lowest income and decile 10 is the highest, based on household disposable income (after tax and benefits). For each income decile, we can see the relative importance of the three sources of income: wages, cash benefits and benefits in-kind. If we look at the sources of income for different deciles, then it is clear that the ideal of market citizenship through income from work is realised for the top three deciles. Cash benefits and benefits in-kind are relatively small in relation to earnings in these high income deciles, which are of course massively over-represented in the political classes who make and write about public policy.

The bottom three deciles are very differently placed because their market independence was never realised or realisable. In the top three deciles, more than 85 per cent of total household income comes from wages and other market sources of household income. Cash benefits are negligible and benefits in-kind for this group account for no more than 11 per cent of total household income. In the bottom three deciles, income from wages accounts for less than half of total income overall with cash benefits and benefits in-kind making up the balance and accounting for 45 per cent of total income in decile 3 and 65 per cent in decile 1.

In everyday UK terms, the distinction between the top three and bottom three income deciles is about a line of separation in many everyday matters. For example, this roughly corresponds to the line of division between social groups for whom access to private dentistry is unproblematic and groups for whom the unavailability of an NHS dentist is a crisis when adult treatment is required or a child needs to be added to the dentist's register. The media report that nine out of ten NHS dentist practices are not taking new adult patients and eight out of ten are not taking on children.[29] Those outside of the top three income deciles may directly feel the consequences of paying for services like dentistry, but more generally they are unlikely to realise the extent of their dependence on state benefits in-kind through services (on top of any cash benefits). While deductions from gross pay for taxation are visible in wage slips, the value of public services in-kind like education and health are poorly understood by the public, policy makers or media commentators.

Exhibit 2.7 again ranks non-retired households by decile but in this case gives the absolute value of income from work and investments, cash benefits and the ONS imputed value of benefits in-kind. Benefits in-kind are hugely important in maintaining the living standards of all households in the bottom half of the income distribution. For the lowest half of non-retired households in income deciles 1–5, benefits in-kind have an imputed value of more than £13,000, compared with wages income for these groups, which ranges from £10,000 in

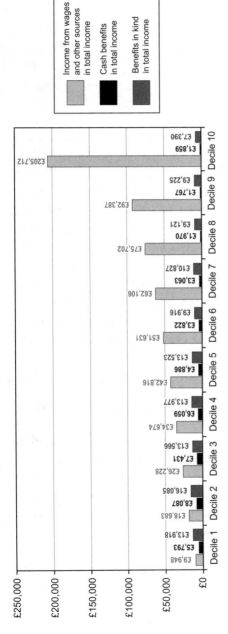

Exhibit 2.7 UK non-retired households' total income in 2019–20.

Source: ONS (May 2021), 'Effects of taxes and benefits on UK household income: financial year ending 2020'. https://www.ons.gov.uk/peoplepopulationand community/personalandhouseholdfinances/incomeandwealth/bulletins/theeffectsoftaxesandbenefitsonhouseholdincome/financialyearending2020.

Notes: A retired household is one where more than 50 per cent of its income is sourced from people who (i) define themselves as retired and are aged over 50 years, or (ii) define themselves as 'Sick/Injured', not seeking work and aged at or above the State Pension Age. 'Non-retired' refers to anyone living in a household that does not meet the criteria for being a retiree. Underlying income has been equivalised using the modified-OECD scale and includes workplace pensions, individual personal pensions and annuities, Child Tax Credit and Working Tax Credit and Universal Credit and Government training scheme allowances. Council Tax and Northern Ireland rates after deducting discounts. Cash benefits are classified if they are paid directly to the recipient as a sum of money. Benefits-in-kind relate to non-cash benefits such as the National Health Service, education, free childcare and travel subsidies. The data used to create the exhibits is available at https://foundationaleconomyresearch.com/index.php/nothing-works-stats/.

decile 1 to £43,000 in decile 5, and benefits in-kind of more than £9,000 are then a useful boost for deciles 6–9 households whose market income ranges from £52,000 to £92,000. This illustrates one aspect of the value of redistribution through the tax system.

Liveability based on using wages to buy market services is a very remote possibility for half of the non-retired households in the UK, unless we envisage a dramatic and progressive redistribution of income. In each of the bottom five deciles, as well as benefits in-kind worth more than £13,000, these households receive more than £5,500 in cash benefits. Pre-crisis, the main driver of living standard changes for households in the bottom half of the income distribution was not wages, but the quantity and quality of free or subsidised services and the generosity of cash benefits. The implication is that government should focus directly on organising support for households in all their diversity, with special attention to vulnerable households like those of single parents, rather than promoting prosperity through market citizenship.

2.3 Liveability usages and foundational context

If foundational liveability is a useful concept, we can distinguish this from place-ranking liveability, as well as situate it in the broader context of foundational thinking and doing. The word liveability (or livability in American spelling) has been in use for more than 100 years. The *Oxford English Dictionary* gives 1872 as the date of first usage of liveability in the sense of a room, house or city's 'capacity to offer comfortable living'. It then gives

1922 as the date of first usage for the more ecological concept which defines a region, environment or planet's liveability as the 'capacity to sustain life'. The foundational concept of liveability developed in this chapter effectively introduces a new working definition of the term for the 2020s which contends with other new usages including the place-ranking concept of liveability.

Consultants now produce, and place marketers consume, several index rankings of cities for liveability. Thus, we have the EIU Global Liveability Index of 172 world cities[30] or the Demos-PwC Good Growth for Cities[31] ranking of UK cities. Place rankings get attention and are good at generating media headlines about league table winners and how they change. In 2022 Vienna is globally number one for the EIU as it was in 2018 and 2019[32] while Oxford, Bournemouth, Swindon and Reading are the UK top four for Demos-PWC, which has changed method this year so comparisons cannot be made with positions in earlier years.[33] These rankings are constructed by attaching weightings to a list of measurable social and economic indicators. The EIU works with over 30 qualitative and quantitative factors across five categories: stability, healthcare, environment, education and infrastructure.[34] Demos-PwC weights twelve variables and fourteen indicators with a more social and egalitarian bias because the factors include work-life balance, affordable housing, fair distribution of income and wealth and a vibrant high street.[35]

Before turning to examine the inherent limits of the place-ranking method, it is worth recapitulating the concept of foundational liveability developed in the first two sections of this chapter and then noting how it differs quite fundamentally from place-ranking liveability. The concept of foundational liveability fuses three insights:

1. The household is the unit of analysis because most of us live in multi-person households.
2. The incomes that matter are disposable and residual income (not gross wages).
3. Foundational services and social infrastructure matter because households cannot live through private consumption.

The result is not a metric or a league table ranking device but a foundational lens which opens up the possibility of empirical research and a politics of effective policy interventions. Consequently, there are substantial differences between foundational liveability and place-ranking liveability whose working method and object are different. Foundational liveability works by tranching income and objects of expenditure for different types of households and recognising essential services and social infrastructure. Place ranking works by attaching weights to a series of economic and social indicators which define the economic and social liveability of a whole city. Foundational liveability offers a lens to examine real causal relations which can show how one place can be comfortable for some types of households and hostile for others. In contrast, place-ranking works by assigning a unitary character to a whole city or region, thus concealing as much as it reveals.

The ranking of cities by liveability index is rather like the ranking of universities by league table: positions vary according to which index you consult because the different league tables use different indicators and weightings. At the same time, the results broadly line up with the kind of status hierarchy that most people already have in their heads. When it comes to global cities, the top ten places in the EIU index are dominated by medium sized, low-density cities in Europe and Canada with Osaka and Melbourne bringing up the rear.[36] The UK's top four are all large standalone southern towns, not variegated conurbations like Greater Manchester. *Quelle surprise!*

Practically, place-ranking claims cannot be justified by any ordinary standard as the weightings of variables are arbitrary: they reflect the priorities of an imaginary subject and/or shifting public concerns. Thus, the EIU index is designed for the expat corporate manager or international agency employee contemplating a posting in a strange city or faced with a choice of postings in different cities. Hence, quality private education and healthcare are relevant. The Demos-PWC approach is altogether more serious and starts from the position that 'the focus must go beyond traditional measures of economic success such as GDP or GVA' and it now derives its weightings from a public poll of stated preferences.[37] So Demos-PWC offers a changing snapshot of what the British public say they value, which is interesting in itself but not a steady guide for politics and policy.

If we leave metrics and league tables behind, we can find an unpretentious literature which works with sensible definitions of liveability. The American Association of Retired Persons definition of a liveable community has an everyday human needs focus on affordable housing and sociability: 'a livable community is one that has affordable and appropriate housing, supportive community features and services, and adequate mobility options which together facilitate personal independence and the engagement of residents in civic and social life'.[38] Our three pillars of foundational liveability concept systematises this kind of definition and uses it to engage empirically with the varieties of households.

With these points made, we turn now to situate our concept of household liveability in the broader frame of foundational thinking and doing. This book makes a self-contained argument about how the three pillars of foundational liveability have all been undermined and provides evidence of the consequences for differently placed households. This argument and evidence focus on the household demand side of the economy, but the economy also has a supply side of firms with business models embedded in socio-technical reliance systems.[39] Available technologies and business models powerfully influence outcomes for households in terms of availability, quality and cost of essential services. Moreover, household demand and supply side provision come together in a specific historical period of possibilities and limits which in the early twenty-first century is defined by nature and climate crises.

This book's demand side analysis of liveability is thus part of a larger body of foundational economy thinking that covers firms, reliance systems and business models in an era when production and consumption overshoot planetary limits. Thus, foundational doing cannot be about just one thing; it is about holding together several related objects at the same time. This book is primarily focused on exploring the complexities of household liveability which is just one of those objects. But policy makers will usually have to relate several of these objects and consider whether success in one domain is being achieved at the expense of another, and what the trade-offs might be. This became a practical issue for the first time in 2022 when Welsh Government asked a team of foundational economy researchers and practitioners to develop a template for review of the efficacy of its foundational policies, starting with food and social care.

The Welsh team started out from the position that it was not enough to focus on what Welsh Government policies did directly for the foundational liveability of households without considering how such policies also impacted foundational goods and services providers and the extent to which they encouraged responsible suppliers with the margins to provide decent work and to reinvest. It was also absolutely essential to mitigate the burdensome ecological impact of foundational production and consumption. Hence the group proposed, and Welsh Government accepted, a template for foundational policy review which has three objectives giving a 360-degree review of foundational aims.

1. To achieve foundational liveability for households through safeguarding residual income and developing foundational services.
2. To create a financially stable and socially responsible foundational provider and supplier base, which can reinvest and pay decent wages.
3. To mitigate nature and climate emergency by making consumption and production more environmentally sustainable.

If the foundational objectives define what needs to change, the Welsh group was equally concerned with how to get change in the three dimensions. Their experience was that leading-edge thinking is easier than progressive doing. Therefore, they added the proviso that progress on the objectives depended on a political practice which combined three ways of working:

first, engage with the specifics of sector and place; second, base actions on relevant evidence; third, mobilise stakeholders in alliances for change inside and outside government. These ways of working are important because they imply that foundational politics is mutable according to time and place and that there can be no generic foundational policies because intervention should be system specific.

From this point of view, foundational politics and policy is a process of resets at micro, meso and macro levels to deal with new challenges. Thus, at micro and meso levels, in a new post-1980 era of financialised capitalism, one major challenge is dealing with extractive capitalist business models. They are fundamentally unsuited to low risk and low return utility and public service activities like water utilities or residential adult care. Business models in these activities will ordinarily produce lower quality and/or higher cost foundational services through some combination of loading operating business with debt, cash extraction and rationing of new investment by setting high hurdle rates. For example, in residential care homes in the mid-2010s, private equity's extractive business model set 12 per cent target rates of return so that this extractive model would add £100 to the weekly cost of a residential bed when compared with a 5 per cent return. When target rates of return are not achieved, debt-laden, private equity chains are fragile and prone to failure as they pass into the hands of hedge funds who have bought their debt at a discount.[40]

At macro level, there is the challenge of nature and climate emergency which cannot be blamed entirely on twenty-first-century financialised capitalism and the intrusion of its extractive business models. The problem is at least partly twentieth-century high mass consumption around forms of foundational provision which became increasingly ecologically irresponsible at scale. This is especially the case with mass auto-mobility that has brought live/work/spend disconnects, edge of town development and urban sprawl to the UK.[41] Hence in foundational economy thinking we draw the distinction between two periods: FE 1.0 from 1870 to 1950 and FE 2.0 since 2010.[42]

- Between 1870 and 1950 in FE 1.0, new reliance systems, from piped water to healthcare, made urban life safe and civilised. This was a public health triumph because, as Jane Jacobs observed, for the first time in history cities were not 'killing machines' requiring in-migration to replenish their populations. But the ecological consequences of expanded foundational provision in this form of urbanism were increasingly damaging for nature and climate. Old reliance systems are now part of the new foundational problem. A Stockholm Institute report on Wales in 2011 reported that if the whole world were to consume at the Welsh level, 2.5 planets would be required. Moreover, three foundational reliance systems of food, housing and transport accounted for 59 per cent of the Welsh ecological footprint.[43]

- By the 2020s in FE 2.0, all high income countries need reliance systems which meet urban needs within planetary limits. Practically, as we have seen in our discussion of the ecological footprint of high income countries in Chapter 1, the task is not staying within planetary limits but managing down the overshoot of planetary limits which is inherent in the North West European way of life. The challenge is considerable because it is necessary to clean up old reliance systems like energy inefficient housing and build new reliance systems like wood economy so that low carbon material can substitute for steel and cement.[44] We need to align societal and ecological objectives which were ignored in the earlier era. Thus, foundational liveability in the twenty-first century is about access to housing, transport, food and other essentials that are both affordable for households and more ecologically sustainable. The good news is that labour intensive essential services like health and care all have a low carbon footprint, as do many soft infrastructure activities. So, we can have more of what matters in services, though that does not make all our choices easy.

Thus, our book's argument about household liveability is set in a much broader ranging body of thought and practice-oriented research. Much of the learning is from Wales, a country which is, like Dylan Thomas's Swansea, an ugly, lovely place of small towns and straggling villages which have lived on after the collapse of the productive and extractive capitalism around which they were built. These Welsh learnings come from outside the centralised and hierarchical system of socio-economic knowledge production in the UK, which privileges knowledge at a distance. This centralisation often produces echo chamber framings (like the growth and wages trope), funds orthodoxy and operates without respecting either distributed social intelligence or the potential of agency in what it condescendingly describes as 'left-behind places'.

The Welsh lesson so far is that, as we will argue in Chapter 6 on politics and policy, thinking differently is always possible but doing better on any major foundational objective is difficult. When microeconomics-based regulation is ineffective and renationalisation is expensive, it is not easy to restrain and/or evict extractive business models from privatised and outsourced activities. When the local state lacks the capacity for important tasks like organising housing retrofit, it is not easy to improve the energy efficiency of housing stock. At the end of this book, readers will understand how and why we need a break and in due course a paradigm change in economic thinking, but the foundational practice of doing is necessarily gradualist and based on 'adaptive reuse' of what exists rather than transformation through building grand new designs.

Before we arrive at politics and policy, the next four chapters of this book explore the importance of foundational liveability and the specific issues that have weakened each of the three pillars over time. Chapter 3 focuses on inequalities, illustrating how the experience of households has been very different in terms of income and wealth. Chapter 5 considers the residual income problem of low income households, covering not only how the tax and benefits system creates perverse outcomes but also the specific problem of the cost of car ownership in a car-based society. Chapter 4 unpacks the notion that 'nothing works', covering not just the cost-of-living emergency as a crisis of residual income, but the longer-term chronic problems of the failure of the market citizenship project and the underfunding of essential services. The third pillar, social infrastructure, is explored in Chapter 5, underlining the importance of understanding foundational liveability as about more than income. This connects back to the importance of attachment to place, which can be the basis of economic and community revival, as we explore in Chapter 3.

Chapter 3

Inequalities between households and places

Introduction

To help understand why foundational liveability has been undermined, this chapter develops a historical and structural analysis of the contrasts between profligacy and penury which are all around us in the UK. It argues that the decline in labour's share of output since the 1970s makes households poorer and shows that high income households are well placed to claim the lion's share of any increase in the size of the wages fund. Meanwhile, meaningless averages of per capita gross value added (GVA) misrepresent the mosaic complexity of segregated places and lead to quagmire technocratic policies of 'closing the GVA gap' which do not harness the power and potential of social attachment to place.

The contrast between discretionary indulgence and pinched necessity is obvious on the high street. For example, in inner Manchester, there is a marked contrast between the retail offer on a mid-market high street like Burton Road in comfortable, middle income West Didsbury and Stockport Road in hardscrabble, multi-ethnic Longsight. These two district shopping centres are no more than three miles apart but have moved on very different trajectories over the past 30 years as West Didsbury moves up-market and Longsight moves down-market.

Burton Road retains some legacy basic retail, including an ironmonger and a chippy. But new retail, tapping discretionary spending, now dominates with café bars, tea and patisserie shops, three lifestyle homeware shops, a florist, a delicatessen, a wine shop, a craft beer shop, an osteopath and a private dentist. On or just off Stockport Road, there are two national supermarkets and one surviving bank branch. But the rest is takeaways for kebab, pizza, curry and fried chicken, plus three betting shops, three 'pound shops', several mobile phone shops, a pawnbroker and two downmarket chains (Farmfoods and Shoe Zone) selling frozen food and cheap shoes.

The same contrast separates middle and higher income households from those in the lower deciles. It is not just rich sybarites with yachts in the Med who are buying durables in ostentatious and environmentally burdensome forms. Some 40 per cent of new car sales in the UK are accounted for by SUVs, whose high rise, large frontal area can cancel out all the aerodynamic gains from lower drag coefficients in saloon design over the past century.[1] At the opposite end of the market, the problem is that consumer goods cost more and are becoming unaffordable. Used car prices have risen so a social housing tenant can no longer find a £350 banger for commuting to work.[2]

Hence there are volume sales of mid-market indulgences that nobody needs but some must have – like the Quooker, a kitchen tap that delivers not just hot and cold but boiling water with the option of chilled and sparkling as well.[3] The tap costs up to some £3,000 plus installation, and before consumables like the CO_2 cylinders which work out more expensive per litre of sparkling than bottled water from a discount store like Aldi. This is not a niche luxury but a volume product for households in the top two deciles who can afford fully fitted, open plan kitchens. Quooker has 4,500 dealers in the UK, aims to double sales volumes in the next two years and uses TV advertising to reach consumers.[4]

For many low income households, exceptional items like replacing a broken cooker or buying school uniforms require debt or several visits to the food bank. Despite a surge in Covid-19 lockdown saving, one in seven families had no savings at all in 2002–21.[5] Then, the cost-of-living crisis doubled household energy bills in one year with an average increase in costs roughly equal to one-third of what a low income couple with two children would spend on food. A September 2022 YouGov survey found that (even before winter) 24 per cent of parents with children had reduced the quantity of food they buy so as to afford other essentials and 13 per cent of these parents had eaten cold meals to save on energy bills.[6]

How are we to understand these contrasts of places and households, and how can we explain the uneven distribution of incomes which defines our present? Who or what has the agency to create a more evenly distributed future? Through the GVA lens, the problem of place is about low per capita GVA and the aim should be to close the gap with high GVA places. The low income households are a matter of regret, balanced by the hope that faster growth and productivity gains will allow higher wages for all. This chapter provides a different, more political and social, explanation.

The first section of this chapter, Section 3.1, looks backwards to the 1970s and the changing long-term distribution of output between capital and labour which determines the size of the available wage fund. We then consider the mechanics of the distribution of income between households, which determines the share that high income households can claim from an increasing fund. Section 3.1 shows that the long-term shift in the distribution of output against labour has reduced the available wage fund by a sum equal to £7,000 per household. It also demonstrates that high income households will secure most of any increase in the wage fund when their percentage increases in income operate on a larger denominator.

Our supplementary argument is that the problem and opportunity of place, regardless of high or low GVA, is always social. Section 3.2 shows how the mainstream is only reluctantly giving up its technocratic focus on GVA and related ideas about raising productivity and slowly recognising the importance of social attachment to place. Section 3.3 argues that social attachment can play a vital role as a driver and force for positive change.

3.1 Distribution to labour and amongst households

This section presents historical evidence which directly explains the contrast between household profligacy and penury as the result of long-term and embedded distribution processes. The evidence analysed below highlights two long-term developments: first, a secular decline since the 1970s in the share of national output going to labour as wages; and second, an inequitable distribution amongst households since the 1990s, with high income households gaining a disproportionate share of the income gains.

'Labour' is used as a term to mean all the workers in the UK, almost all of whom will be members of a household. The division of national output between capital and labour is relevant because labour's share of that output – as GVA or gross domestic product (GDP) – determines the size of the aggregate wage fund available to all households as incomes. If labour's share of national output in the form of wages increases over time, all households can in principle have a higher income. If the national output grows but the share going to labour as wages falls in relative terms, the outcome will be less favourable. The detailed outcomes will be determined by the second issue, which is the distribution of income between households.

In practice, not all households will benefit or lose equally from increases or decreases in the total wages fund.

Overall, the story is that looking backwards at the record of the past 20 to 50 years, the share of output going to labour has been squeezed and the mechanics of income distribution has favoured high income households. The evidence shows that the tide rises only gently because overall labour gains are damped by loss of output share and the rising tide does not lift all boats because low income households gain much less than high income households. Capital has been (and remains) positioned to capture a large share of output and the mechanics of distribution have (and will) favour high income households. By way of contrast, in mainstream thinking, distribution is a matter of hope, usually based on looking forward five to ten years when faster growth and increased productivity *might* allow higher wages, though with no basis for such optimism.

Exhibit 3.1 shows that, over the past 50 years, the division of UK output has shifted decisively against labour in the form of wages and towards capital. Labour's share of output (GDP) has declined by nearly 10 per cent from a post-war peak of 57.3 per cent of GDP in 1976 to 48.7 per cent in 2019. Why did this happen and what are the implications for households?

Some decline in labour's share of output was the inevitable economic result of the structural change in employment from manufacturing and public services to (private) services. Mass manufacturing operated with a 65 per cent plus share for labour in the 1970s and public services then or now typically run with a labour share of value added in the 65–75 per cent range. At the firm level in private services, labour typically claims no more than a 45 per cent to 50 per cent share of

the value added output. These structural effects were accelerated by a politically sponsored change in the balance of power
between increasingly organised capital and disorganised labour
from the 1980s onwards. With financialisation, capital market
discipline enforces and normalises the aggressive pursuit of
higher returns and distribution ratios by large companies and
fund investors, while the politically sponsored dismantling of
trade unionism undermined labour's bargaining power.

A simple all-household calculation can be used to illustrate
the scale of the cumulative loss for the average household
over 50 years. We can see that the decline in labour's share of
output results in a dramatic reduction in the income available
to all households. Exhibit 3.1 takes GDP as the measure of
output and calculates how much every UK household would
gain in 2019 if the share of GDP paid out in wages and salaries had been maintained at the 57.3 per cent level of 1976.
On that basis, each one of the just over 27 million UK households would have £7,083 more gross income. If we repeat the
calculation for labour in the narrow sense, there are nearly 20
million economically active households and each non-retired
household would have £9,744 more gross income as wages
in 2019.

This is only one of the many unintended and perverse consequences produced by the disempowering of organised labour
plus privatisation and outsourcing along with the deregulation
of financial markets. This Thatcherite reset of policy and politics in the 1980s (unquestioned by New Labour in the 2000s)
promised a strong national economy which had put its problems behind it. In practice, it delivered the next instalment of
UK problems. Fundamentally this was because these reforms

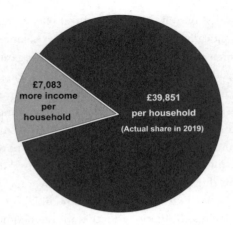

Exhibit 3.1 How much larger UK household income would be in 2019 if labour's share of GDP were at the 1976 level of 57.3 per cent.

Source: ONS (November 2019), 'Families and households in the UK: 2019'; ONS (August 2022), 'Gross Domestic Product at market prices: Current price: Seasonally adjusted £m'; and ONS (June 2022), 'Home Economy Gross Value Added (GVA) UK (S.1): Compensation of employees (D.1) Uses: Current price: £m. https://www.ons.gov.uk/peoplepopulationandcommunity/birthsdeathsand marriages/families/bulletins/familiesandhouseholds/2019; https://www.ons.gov .uk/economy/grossdomesticproductgdp/timeseries/ybha/pn2; https://www.ons .gov.uk/economy/grossvalueaddedgva/timeseries/haea/ukea.

Note: (a) In 2019 UK household's average share of GDP was £39,851; (b) counterfactually, if 2019 GDP was distributed at the 1976 level of 57.3 per cent then UK household average gross income would be £46,934, an average £7,083 higher per household. The data used to create the exhibits is available at https:// foundationaleconomyresearch.com/index.php/nothing-works-stats/.

rested on a great misrecognition of capitalism through the lens of market fundamentalist thinking.

- Unions were misrecognised as an obstacle to efficient production, when they are a necessary defence of decent settlements on wages and conditions.

- Privatisation and outsourcing were misrecognised as competition and management efficiency for consumers, when they are about sheltered positions, investors' rights and unequal contracts at the expense of public value for money and wage income for households.
- Deregulated finance was misrecognised as a machine for allocating private capital to where it was needed, when it was a rentier machine for rationing investment and extracting cash. The legacy of deregulated finance is uncontrolled debt creation in complex financial systems prone to crisis and collapse that requires state bailout, as most recently in the 2022 UK liability-driven investment crisis.[7]

Even if this great misrecognition is slowly being corrected, incremental change after a political rebalancing of power between labour and capital will only very slowly change labour's share and redress the cumulative loss of decades. And incremental change in the right direction on the division of output between capital and labour would not address a second set of issues about the uneven distribution of income gains between households. As the value of output has increased over past decades with economic growth, high income households in the top three deciles have made major income gains, while low income households have gained very little. The problem here is intractable because it is rooted in the arithmetic of ratios. If high income households and low income households get the same percentage share of any increase in national income, the absolute gains of high income households are much larger because in their case the same per cent uplift operates on a larger base.

If the decline in labour's share of national output damps aggregate household gains, the available wages fund still increases in absolute terms as national output rises over time with economic growth. What then matters to households is what comes through as disposable income after taxes and benefits. Disposable income is the relevant consideration because, as we noted in Chapter 2, in low income households, cash benefits substantially boost money income. On this basis, we can calculate the increase in disposable income for each household decile over a period of time and then consider the extent to which households have gained equally. The empirics show that over any period of a decade or more, high income households claim most of the total increase in income.

Exhibit 3.2 ranks households by income decile groups from decile 1, the lowest 10 per cent of households by income, to decile 10, the highest. It is then possible to calculate each decile's share of disposable income growth between 1999 and 2020. Over this period, the top three deciles of households receive 48 per cent of the income increase while the bottom three deciles receive 16.6 per cent. The bottom five deciles – that is, 50 per cent of all UK households – receive no more than 32.9 per cent of all the gains.

The mechanics of distribution have worked historically to accelerate income inequalities between households and this pattern is likely to continue into the future, without large changes to pay levels and to the tax and benefits system. Over the period 1999 to 2020, households in upper income deciles did not claim a much larger percentage increase in disposable income than lower income deciles. But the UK started from an initially unequal distribution of income to households, so gains

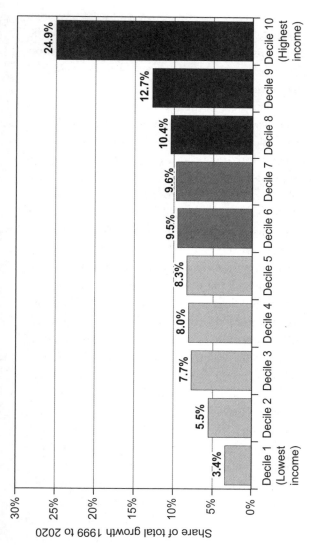

Exhibit 3.2 Distribution of the 1999–2020 growth in disposable income (after benefits and taxes) between households according to income decile.

Source: ONS (May 2021), 'Effects of taxes and benefits on UK household income: financial year ending 2020'. https://www.ons.gov.uk/peoplepopulationandcommunity/personalandhouseholdfinances/incomeandwealth/bulletins/theeffectsoftaxesandbenefitsonhouseholdincome/financialyearending2020. The data used to create the exhibits is available at https://foundationaleconomyresearch.com/index.php/nothing-works-stats/.

were unequal. Even if high income deciles enjoy a percentage increase that is no larger than lower income households, the outcome will be a consolidation of income inequality with most of the increased income accruing to those who start with the advantage of higher income.

So far, we have simply considered income because disposable and residual income are what matters for households on low or moderate incomes who overwhelmingly depend on wages and benefits. But upper income households can also benefit from their holdings of wealth which can generate capital gains as well as income. The issues here are complicated because household wealth is primarily a matter of stocks of often illiquid assets whereas income is money received in cash (or in-kind benefits) over one year. UK households hold wealth in two main forms as pension rights and house property and, as Exhibit 3.3 shows, each of these accounts for three-quarters or more of total wealth holdings in decile 5 to decile 10.[8] Pensions or owner-occupied housing do not ordinarily boost living standards by generating current income or realised capital gain until the beneficiary retires or dies, though second homes can generate rents. According to the Resolution Foundation, by 2016 some 5.5 million adults in Britain owned property in addition to their own homes, including buy-to-let properties.[9] Moreover, under current UK rules, those aged 55 and over can draw down defined contribution pensions and owner occupiers can re-mortgage, downsize or move to a cheaper area.

When these complications have been noted, the bottom line is that wealth cannot be ignored because it acts as a powerful accelerator of income inequalities. Wealth is also becoming increasingly important for high income households. In effect,

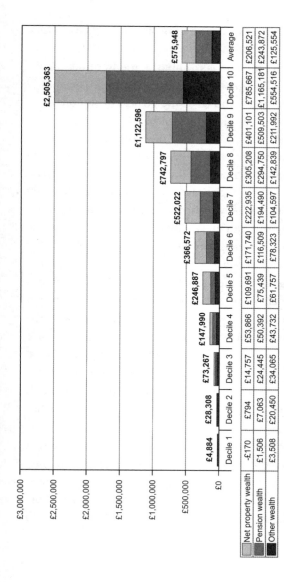

	Decile 1	Decile 2	Decile 3	Decile 4	Decile 5	Decile 6	Decile 7	Decile 8	Decile 9	Decile 10	Average
Net property wealth	-£170	£794	£14,757	£53,866	£109,691	£171,740	£222,935	£305,208	£401,101	£785,667	£206,521
Pension wealth	£1,506	£7,063	£24,445	£50,392	£75,439	£116,509	£194,490	£294,750	£509,503	£1,165,181	£243,872
Other wealth	£3,508	£20,450	£34,065	£43,732	£61,757	£78,323	£104,597	£142,839	£211,992	£554,516	£125,554

Exhibit 3.3 GB household wealth by decile and type of wealth, 2018–20.

Source: ONS (2022), 'Household total wealth in Great Britain: April 2018 to March 2020: Main results of household wealth from the seventh round of the Wealth and Assets Survey covering the period April 2018 to March 2020'. https://www.ons.gov.uk/peoplepopulationandcommunity/personalandhouseholdfinances/incomeandwealth/personalandhouseholdfinances/incomeandwealth/bulletins/totalwealthingreatbritain/april2018tomarch2020.

Note: Households are organised by total wealth holdings and then split into decile groups. The data used to create the exhibits is available at https://foundationaleconomyresearch.com/index.php/nothing-works-stats/.

the UK has increasingly shifted from an income-based to a wealth-based society, but measurement (and taxation) has not caught up. National income accounting starts from the identification of marketable output and incomes, and the issue then is about how to calculate and track the growth of national and regional output/income on an annual basis. This made sense in the world of the 1940s but since then the ratio of wealth to annual national income has unsteadily increased. The ratio of wealth to national income has doubled from three to seven times since the 1970s[10] so that understanding households only through income increasingly misses large parts of the picture.

This overhang of wealth makes household inequalities worse because holdings of wealth are hugely concentrated in the upper income deciles. Precise measurement is difficult, but the standard official source is the ONS Wealth and Assets Survey in Great Britain, which suggests the distribution of wealth between households is twice as unequal as the distribution of income.[11] If households are ranked by wealth, where decile 1 households have the least wealth and decile 10 the most, the disparities are huge because the bottom three deciles have almost no wealth, while the average top decile household has ten times the wealth of a household in the middle. And in terms of shares, there has been little change over the past 20 years. As Exhibit 3.4 shows, in 2018–20 as in 2006–8, the top decile of households held a 44 per cent share or nearly half of all household wealth. The top three deciles hold around 75 per cent or three-quarters, while the bottom three deciles have less than 2 per cent and the bottom five deciles have less than 10 per cent of all household wealth.

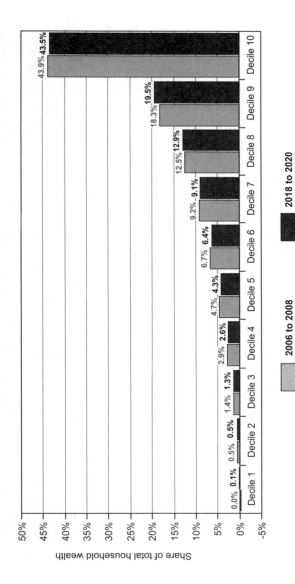

Exhibit 3.4 The distribution of GB household wealth by decile, 2006–8 and 2018–20.

Source: ONS (various years), 'Household total wealth in Great Britain'. https://www.ons.gov.uk/peoplepopulationandcommunity/personalandhouseholdfinances/incomeandwealth/bulletins/totalwealthingreatbritain/april2018tomarch2020./personalandhouseholdfinances/incomeandwealth/bulletins/totalwealthingreatbritain/april2018tomarch2020.

Note: Households are organised by total wealth holdings and then split into decile groups. The data used to create the exhibits is available at https://foundationaleconomyresearch.com/index.php/nothing-works-stats/.

This backstory about the distribution of income and wealth between capital and labour, and then amongst households, explains the painful contrast between penury and profligacy. The UK has created a dual society. The Resolution Foundation reports that disposable household incomes (equivalised for differences in household size) for those in the bottom two deciles were no higher on the eve of the pandemic in 2019–20 than in 2004–5, well before the financial crisis.[12] At the same time, in the top two deciles (generally those with two good incomes coming in) the issue is how to spend a substantial discretionary income. Much of this attracted little attention from the political classes (mainly drawn, of course, from the upper deciles) until the cost-of-living crisis dramatised the residual income pain of those in the lower deciles who cannot pay for necessities and those in the middle deciles who struggle to pay mortgages on top of higher energy and food bills.

3.2 Understanding place through the GVA lens

The political classes are currently waging a rear-guard action to defend both the GVA problem definition and its policy making assumptions while slowly recognising more social objectives and the power of attachment to place. The retreat is grudging because, as we will argue in this section, the 'both GVA and social outcomes' position on objectives is, in the terminology of Catholic theology, more attrition than contrition. That is to say, the economic concession to the importance of the social dimension involves a pragmatic recognition of the power of attachment to place. Nonetheless, per capita GVA is still a privileged indicator of a place's success or failure, and low per capita GVA is seen as a problem to be solved by increasing productivity to close the gap with high GVA places.

From a foundational liveability point of view, any understanding of place should start by recognising diversity, in particular that places of any size have a mosaic character and not a unitary identity.

1. The diversity of places by size and character is striking in England and Wales. Around 17 million people live in London and the major cities, while a further 32.9 million live in large, medium and small towns and 9.7 million in rural areas.[13] Towns can be seaside resort towns, work towns originally centred on large employers or district centres with significant retail and administrative functions. In the UK there are very many different ways of getting to be a low GVA area and it is therefore unhelpful to consider such places as a group when they are united only by a lowly place in the GVA ranking.

2. Larger settlements always have a mosaic character because of sharp two-to-one contrasts in average household income (gross or disposable) between affluent suburbs and depressed districts within one urban area. Exhibit 3.5 demonstrates the point for Newcastle-upon-Tyne, North Tyneside and the coastal town of Blyth.[14] The average gross household income is £52,500 in high income South Gosforth, compared with £24,700 in Walker South and £29,200 in the case of Byker. The Newcastle figure of average gross household income of £35,503 for the urban area as a whole smooths out these large two-to-one differences

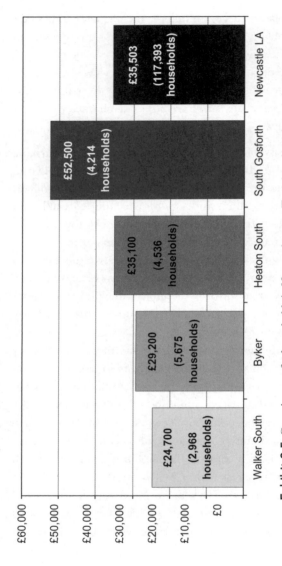

Exhibit 3.5 Gross income for households in Newcastle-upon-Tyne, by selected wards in 2018.

Source: L. Calafati, J. Froud, C. Haslam, S. Jeffels, S. Johal and K. Williams (2022), *Jobs and Liveability*, A report by Foundational Economy Research for Karbon Homes. https://foundationaleconomyresearch.com/wp-content/uploads/2022/12/FERL-Report-Jobs-Liveability-for-Karbon-Homes-Sept-2022.pdf.

Note: The gross income is the mean average per household. The data used to create the exhibits is available at https://foundationaleconomyresearch.com/index.php/nothing-works-stats/.

and unhelpfully creates an imagined object of policy, 'the Northern city'.

Matters are further complicated because within low and high average income areas there are sharp differences in income and wealth between owners and renters. Mortgage-paying households are typically higher income households and mortgage payers are acquiring an asset so that eventually they become owner occupiers. The implications of owner occupancy for the acceleration of wealth inequality are startling in London and the South East where house prices have been high and rising through most of the 2000s and the 2010s. Exhibit 3.6 shows that between 1996 and 2022 rising property prices made the average London house buyer of a modest terrace or semi-detached house nearly £25,000 a year richer through unearned and untaxed gains. The flip side of the windfall wealth gain for London home owners is the squeeze on the residual income of the one-quarter of London households who are private renters and must contribute a large fraction of disposable income in rent to pay off somebody else's mortgage. This then feeds inequality of wealth as well as income. In 2020 the average private renter in London paid 27.5 per cent of disposable income as rent.[15]

Rather than engage with this radical heterogeneity, many practitioners and academics have continued to use one GVA per capita figure to represent not just places but whole territories as large as regions or city regions, so that high per capita GVA denotes a successful place, and low per capita GVA denotes a failing place which must imitate success by raising productivity. On this basis, it is argued that the UK's place problem is the GVA deficit and inferior productivity performance of big UK

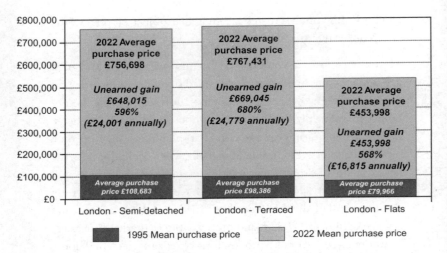

Exhibit 3.6 Comparison of average household purchase price in London in 1995 and 2022, by type of housing.

Source: Mean house prices for subnational geographies: HPSSA dataset 27, ONS (accessed 29 September 2022). https://www.ons.gov.uk/peoplepopulationandcommunity/housing/datasets/meanpricepaidforsubnationalgeographieshpssadataset27.

Note: 1995 data is for December and 2022 data is for March. The purchase prices are mean for the whole of London. The data used to create the exhibits is available at https://foundationaleconomyresearch.com/index.php/nothing-works-stats/.

cities outside London. This problem definition is legitimised by the LSE Centre for Economic Performance and academics who believe in agglomeration theory whereby the concentration of population and business in major urban settlements should produce clustering and scale effects which boost innovation and GVA productivity. The mainstream chorus is led by think tanks like the Centre for Cities which argues that 'the problem of the UK economy is that most of its big cities make very poor use of their inherent advantages'[16] because their size does not bring the higher GVA productivity bonus which agglomeration theory predicts.

From this point of view, London is the exemplary outlier with higher per capita GVA than the provincial cities and a growing share of the UK's total GVA. The core of the UK's four-nation productivity problem is then the deficit of productivity in relation to city size in major provincial cities like Birmingham, Manchester and Glasgow. This should lead to a questioning of agglomeration theory whose empirical foundations are partial.[17] But such is the power of belief in agglomeration theory that the observation of anomaly leads only to the recommendation that the problem can be fixed by scaling up and putting more capital and human resource into the lagging cities. In the Resolution Foundation's *Stagnation Nation* report, the influence of the Centre for Economic Performance as co-author is reflected in the bizarre suggestion that Manchester's productivity performance could be transformed by scaling up and adding 500,000 more people plus tens of billions in investment.[18]

This recommendation of a collective solution for Manchester goes along with some affection for the 'Dick Whittington' individual solution for those brought up in left-behind places. This solution to low GVA and productivity would be that young people with energy and ambition should take not their cats but their educational certificates and seek high wages in the big cities whose productivity would be improved by young in-migrants. The *Stagnation Nation* report does not go so far as to recommend such migration, but it does note that 'young people from most deprived areas are 2½ times less likely to leave their home area upon reaching adulthood than their peers in the least deprived places'.[19]

But any vision of how agglomeration could drive higher productivity and per capita GVA in London and major provincial
cities is the stuff of fantasy. More than 30 million live in towns
which cannot be stripped of people and resources without
political and social blowback of an unpredictable kind. And the
financial and ecological cost of expanding the infrastructure of
favoured places to accommodate in-migrants would be huge.
So the *Stagnation Nation* report declares the aim of 'delivering
on a social contract that promises you'll gain from the national
economy wherever you live'.[20] The Centre for Cities also adopts
a growth-plus-better-social-outcomes solution which combines
higher GVA and social objectives. So, levelling up 'should help
every place to reach its productivity potential' and 'levelling up
should improve standards of living across the country narrow-
ing the divergence between areas in issues such as health, education and service provision'.[21]

This is part of a larger slow defensive, centrist retreat from the
primacy of GVA which takes the form of attrition as growth/
productivity/high wages are retained as objectives while new
social outcomes are added to the list of desiderata. In 2022 this
pragmatism was politically represented in the objectives of the
UK-wide Shared Prosperity Fund (SPF) which implements the
Levelling Up White Paper. As we noted in Chapter 1, 'productivity, pay, jobs, living standards' still comes first in the White
Paper but then three of the four objectives were about the social
aspects of levelling up. This new emphasis on the social looms
even larger in the Shared Prosperity Fund introduced to replace
EU Structural Funds after Brexit. The Fund's overarching
objective is 'building pride in place and increasing life chances'
and its three investment priorities are: 'Community and Place',

'Supporting Local Business' and 'People and Skills'.[22] All relate to the *Levelling Up* White Paper Mission 9: 'By 2030, pride in place, such as people's satisfaction with their town centre and engagement in local culture and community, will have risen in every area of the UK, with the gap between top performing and other areas closing.'[23]

This downplaying of GVA and the new emphasis on the social reflects more than realism about the number of voters in 'left-behind places'. There is also a dawning recognition across the political classes that the spiralists who are prepared to move for better economic opportunities are in a minority. Accumulating evidence shows that a clear majority of people, including those living in the most deprived areas, are attached to their local area and positive about their locality as a place to live. This point emerges very clearly from the DCMS annual Community Life Survey. In the 2020–21 survey, 65 per cent of all respondents and 57 per cent of those living in the most deprived areas feel they 'very strongly' or 'fairly strongly' belong to their immediate neighbourhood. Furthermore, 79 per cent of all respondents and 62 per cent of those living in the most deprived areas are 'very or fairly satisfied with their local area as a place to live'.[24]

At the same time, the slow and half-hearted nature of the retreat from a GVA focus onto the social aspects is manifest in many ways in various documents. The recognition of the social in the Community Life Survey or by the Centre for Cities is about social attitudes and outcomes, not the political agency to change things. The official DCMS report on its Community Life Survey recognises the importance of attachment to place. However, survey findings about the absence of political agency do not find their way into that DCMS report. Responses to a question about 'whether people feel they can influence decisions affecting their local area' figure only in a separately published set of backup tables. In the 2020–21 survey, 74 per cent of respondents disagree or definitely disagree with this statement. The answers to this question have not changed very much in these surveys since 2013–14 and are much the same regardless of income.[25]

The slow retreat is continued most recently in a Demos report. This carries the concession further by legitimising the option of staying in 'left-behind' places. The report sets up an opposition between movers and stayers and argues it is wrong to focus policy on 'how towns can meet the ambitions of those that want to leave' and instead 'government should … focus on helping those that stay'.[26] This 'helping' should reflect what stayers want, which turns out to be better jobs, social facilities *and* some political agency. When Demos organised focus groups for 'stayers' they wanted orthodox economic policies of education/ training with 'better work opportunities' and 'improved opportunities for socialising' plus public engagement in participation and decision making.[27] At this point, we would suggest going all the way and rethinking place through a foundational lens where local political agency is central to improving liveability.

3.3 *Restanza* through the foundational lens

In foundational thinking about place, local political agency is the key driver of economic renewal in places wherever there are groups who want to stay and fight for a more liveable future.

Of course, in a heavily centralised political system, Westminster government and governance cannot be bypassed, given that it funds and formats so much foundational liveability. But initiative about what to do and how to do renewal has to come from dispersed places and the lower levels of national organisations. In Chapter 6 on politics and policy, we turn to consider how top-down could meet bottom-up. But, in this section, we first clear away deficiency thinking about 'left-behind places' before then thinking about the power of *restanza* and how those who choose to stay behind can be an active force for change.

Insofar as the mainstream approach has not yet relinquished the standard comparison of high and low GVA places, this sets up the problem that less successful places should close the GVA gap with more successful places. In this 'gap' way of thinking, 'left-behind places' could and should do this by rectifying their deficiencies and making themselves more worthy competitors by emulating the characteristics of more successful places. This concept of the laggard place is technically reinforced by the category of 'multiple deprived districts' which rank low, not just on income but on other criteria such as employment levels, education qualification and health outcomes.[28] Mainstream policy has been about how to remedy these deficiencies through policies like skills upgrading backed up by the discipline of Jobcentre sanctions.

From a foundational point of view, all this should be directly challenged. We need to look beyond the characteristics of places, which largely reflect residential segregation by income, and consider how the relation between the centre and periphery concentrates low incomes and expenditure in areas where there is relatively cheap private housing or social housing estates. The districts which rank low on the indices of deprivation could more reasonably be characterised as 'policy depressed' because poor wages and Universal Credit concentrate low incomes and limited purchasing power in some residential areas.

The depressive effect is localised by the mosaic character of urban districts. In the North East of England for example, if we consider districts of up to 6,000 households,[29] in Newcastle city, North Tyneside or the coastal town of Blyth some 15–30 per cent of households in a low income district will be on Universal Credit, compared with only 2–4 per cent in an affluent high GVA suburb.[30] The idea of islands of concentrated low income is clear if we look at electoral wards which typically have electorates of around 5,000 and often follow the contours of residential segregation by income. Exhibit 3.7 shows that depressed wards like Byker and Walker in Newcastle have 40 per cent of households on Universal Credit.

To understand the implications for income in depressed districts, we must consider the changing characteristics of those claiming Universal Credit, which do not at all fit media and political stereotypes.[31] Exhibit 3.8 shows the changing composition of Universal Credit recipients in Byker where the figures are broadly in line with national trends, although the percentage of claimants in work is lower in Byker. When Universal Credit was first introduced, the recipients were mainly the unemployed, but now roughly one-third of claimants are sick, disabled or carers, who will mostly have to live long-term on miserably low benefits. A further one-third of claimants are in low wage employment and caught on permanently low incomes in the poverty trap created by high marginal rates of

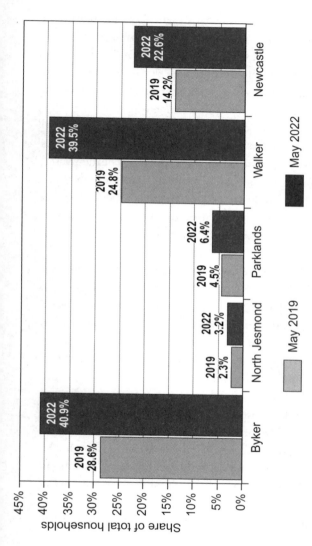

Exhibit 3.7 Share of households claiming Universal Credit in selected wards of Newcastle-upon-Tyne, 2019 and 2022.

Source: DWP, Stat-Xplore database (accessed 4 October 2022). https://stat-xplore.dwp.gov.uk/webapi/jsf/dataCatalogueExplorer.xhtml; Census 2011 – KS105EW – Household composition, Nomis and Labour Force Survey, Nomis. https://www.nomisweb.co.uk/.

Note: Number of households data is from the Census 2011. The data used to create the exhibits is available at https://foundationaleconomyresearch.com/index.php/nothing-works-stats/.

income loss in the tax and benefits system. Low incomes then produce a concentration of bottom-of-the-market purchasing power. As we shall see in the discussion of spending on essentials in Chapter 4, households in income deciles 1 and 2 spend very little on transport and are often therefore marooned on a residential island of low income and expenditure.

Furthermore, the policy-induced damage to foundational liveability goes beyond the depressing of household incomes because such damage affects all three pillars. The depressed districts which lose income as a result of benefits policy are often part of larger disadvantaged urban areas which had to cut essential services and social infrastructure disproportionately in the 2010s as a result of austerity budgets imposed by central government.[32]

Prior to 2010 low GVA urban areas like Salford and Gateshead in the North of England or Barking and Dagenham in outer London had benefited from needs-based grants designed to equalise local authority spending power. Westminster then imposed across-the-board austerity cuts in local authority budgets without regard for local need. In consequence, the Institute of Government finds, for example, that the reduction in bus services and the library closures were greatest in the most deprived areas.[33] The disparity in the scale of the cuts in the most and least deprived areas is marked. In England's ten most deprived councils, £1 in every £7 was cut from public health service expenditure. In contrast, only £1 in every £46 was cut from public health spending in the ten least deprived councils,[34] which were at the same time able to protect and in some cases increase spending on adult care, the largest item in all local

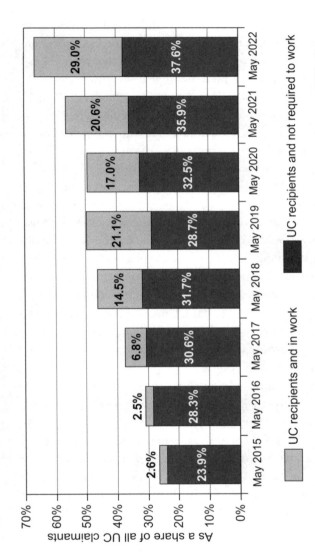

Exhibit 3.8 UK Universal Credit recipients who are in work or have no work requirements, 2015–22.

Source: DWP, Stat-Xplore database (accessed 30 September 2022), https://stat-xplore.dwp.gov.uk/webapi/jsf/dataCatalogueEx plorer.xhtml. The data used to create the exhibits is available at https://foundationaleconomyresearch.com/index.php/nothing -works-stats/.

authority budgets. In relation to foundational liveability, the weak pillar of residual income is accompanied by worsening essential services and social infrastructure so that many households in many places are hit in multiple ways.

All this becomes quagmire politics in the 2020s. After austerity budget cuts forced library closures and reduced bus services in poorer communities, local authorities were in the first half of 2022 offered the chance to compete for payments from a Shared Prosperity Fund whose objective and priorities, as we have noted, echo the *Levelling Up* White Paper mission of increasing 'people's satisfaction with their town centre and engagement in local culture and community … in every area of the UK'. While in principle this could provide some limited one-off funds to support social infrastructure in some places, the fund is very small (£2.6 billion announced in 2022[35]) in relation to the vast scale of the challenge. At the same time, the process of cuts resumed in autumn 2022 under Chancellor Jeremy Hunt, who projected public expenditure cuts in his budget partly because public services providers would not be adequately compensated for significant cost inflation.

If deficiency thinking is unhelpful and central policy is creating depressed districts, the analysis of place needs a new starting point that recognises foundational liveability. How do we find this new and different starting point? From the Community Life Survey, attachment to place is a broadly distributed asset and absence of agency over local outcomes is a pervasive liability. The foundational question is whether we can use this asset to help reduce the liability.

In foundational thinking, we do this by borrowing the concept of *restanza* from the Italian anthropologist Vito Teti[36] who lives in the Calabrian village of San Nicola da Cresa where he was born and brought up. From Teti's viewpoint, staying behind is not an easy choice but an active and difficult process in a place that must be changed:

> The adventure implicit in staying ... is no less decisive and foundational than the adventure that goes with travelling ... For many people, then, staying behind hasn't been a short cut, a symptom of laziness, a comfortable choice. On the contrary, it has been an adventure, an act of foolhardiness and, perhaps, of bravery, something presupposing both toil and pain.[37]

As Desirè Gaudioso notes, 'restanza means choosing to stay in a place in a conscious active and proactive way by actively guarding it, being aware of the past while enhancing what remains with an impulse towards the future where a new community is possible'.[38]

This practice has been borrowed from Calabria and resonates strongly in Wales. Its power has been demonstrated in the slate valleys of North Wales which have suffered 100 years of deindustrialisation with the decline of slate mining and quarrying in the Ffestiniog, Nantlle and Ogwen valleys. These places have a collective industrial past which includes the longest strike in British trade union history at Penrhyn Quarry from 1900 to 1903. They now have communities which have turned to building an economic future. In the Ffestiniog valley, Cwmni Bro federates a network of social enterprises, including not only a community pub but a hotel for the differently abled and a mountain bike trail which take revenue from tourists. The surplus is applied to community purposes including a cultural centre and high street regeneration. They have created 150 jobs in and around the town of Blaenau Ffestiniog which, with its population of just under 4,000, has more social enterprise jobs per capita than anywhere else in the UK.[39]

The community-based development in the slate valleys is not the result of importing a model or buying in consultancy but of initiative by groups of those who stayed, came back or arrived to make a difference without asking for permission or seeking publicity. Gwynedd local authority and Welsh Government are now supportive but playing catch up. Grace Blakeley's *Tribune* article in summer 2022 was the first English-language feature to cover their achievements.[40]

The distinction between stayers and movers does not fully capture the dynamic of Ffestiniog and how its future is in the balance. One key group of agents for change are the returnees who leave the valley to study or work and then actively choose to come back; another important group are the in-migrants when nearly 25 per cent of Blaenau Ffestiniog residents are not born in Wales. In our 2021 survey,[41] 50 per cent of respondents were university educated while only 20 per cent of the Blaenau Ffestiniog population as a whole have tertiary education. Respondents emphasised family and friends, language, community and natural environment as reasons for staying. They are prepared to sacrifice career prospects and higher wages if they can access essential services and housing which is affordable at local wage levels. The implication is that what Blaenau Ffestiniog needs for foundational liveability is quality essential services and affordable housing which make the jobs that are available more liveable.

The slate valleys are extraordinary because here the Welsh language sustains identity and drives action in places which have energetic and charismatic organisers who can also do management accounting. They have found not a model but a narrow pathway where continued progress requires volunteer labour and external capital funding for major new projects that are still grant dependent for start-up. Getting to the next level in Bro Ffestiniog must involve more low risk enterprises which can generate a larger surplus. For these reasons, Blaenau Ffestiniog should not be oversold as a model of the future that works. But the belief in the slate valleys is that their kind of bottom-up initiative is already relevant to the rest of Gwynedd and beyond, where community action has typically not been directed to economic renewal objectives.

Blaenau's achievements certainly justify a basic principle of foundational thinking: if civil society groups are attached to the collective life of their place, the role of public policy should be to enable them to carry on living there and empower their agency over their own future by rebuilding all three pillars of liveability. Foundational liveability for stayers, returnees and in-migrants then requires not pursuit of GVA per capita and high wage jobs but a collection of local initiatives working with public policy to support a balanced foundational liveability package of essential services and social infrastructure. This package should be related to the jobs and housing which are available and which can be made more accessible, especially for key groups like younger people. The issue then is how these basics of sustainability are to be obtained in Blaenau Ffestiniog and all the other places which have potential for economic renewal through local agency. We return to the question of what can be done to improve foundational live-ability in Chapter 6.

PART III

The mess we're in

Introduction to Part III

In Part II of this book, we looked at the diversity of household types and the inequalities of their lived experience, all set in the frame of a three-pillar foundational concept of liveability. In Part III we look at the collective mess we are in. Each one of the three pillars of foundational liveability is being undermined because the market citizenship project has failed, and the result is not high wage independence but low wage dependence. Meanwhile, residual income is being squeezed for low and middle income households, while underfunded public services like the NHS cannot deliver and there is insufficient funding for social infrastructure. Amidst all this, low income families have an income retention problem because they keep too little of their gross wages, while the costs of childcare and transport impede access to jobs.

Chapter 4

Nothing works

Introduction

This chapter presents our analysis of how and why 'nothing works'. The UK pursued a fantasy of market citizenship and independence but the outcome was uncontrolled low wage subsidy, illustrated by the way the increasing proportion of economically active households receive more in benefits than they paid in taxes. Despite this subsidy, low wage households were being squeezed by the rising cost of on-market essentials in the 2010s even before the energy price hike in 2022. At the same time, state underfunding has slowly undermined and distorted essential service provision with, for example, the acute hospital system moving from fragility before Covid-19 to breakdown.

Against this background, as our introduction noted, by mid-2022 the 'nothing works' and 'everything is broken' tropes were circulating in the media and they reflected what pollsters were finding by year end. But this was symptomatic of a great anxiety and did not indicate an agreed, precise problem definition about what was not working and why. Indeed, the tropes were the vehicle for long established tabloid definitions of UK problems and their causes. When it came to explaining why 'nothing works in this country anymore',[1] Andrew Neill in the *Daily Mail*, in classic tabloid style, named the guilty men in a list which included aimless policemen, out of touch judges, activist doctors, obstructive civil servants and incompetent ministers.

The virtue of the three pillars of foundational liveability approach outlined in Chapter 2 is that it allows us to focus on what matters for everyday lives and analyse how and why 'nothing works'. In short, the UK's 'nothing works' problem is that, even before the 54 per cent increase in typical energy bills in April 2021, all three pillars were crumbling. The foundational liveability problem is therefore not an uneven performance across the three pillars of residual income, essential services and social infrastructure, but broad front failure. This failure increasingly traps middle income as well as low income households with problems of squeezed residual income, inadequate essential services and poor quality social infrastructure.

Acute failure is clearest in the case of the NHS. Some 7 million patients were on English lists waiting for non-urgent elective treatment by 2022; the Covid backlog had lengthened waiting lists but that is no alibi for failure because waiting lists had already grown to 4 million before the pandemic. The immediate threatening problem is system failure to deal with emergencies requiring hospital treatment and the most obvious symptom here is the collapse of ambulance response times. Heart attack and stroke are in NHS terminology Category 2 life-threatening emergencies with a target ambulance response time of 18 minutes. By spring 2022, the average English Category 2 ambulance response time was nearly 40 minutes and deteriorating.[2]

Less noticed is the deterioration in social infrastructure which can be brought into focus by considering the case of the 27,000 dilapidated and neglected public parks in the UK. A 2016 survey showed 57 per cent of all adults use their park at least once a month or more often, and 90 per cent of households with children under the age of five use their park at least once a month.[3] Eighty-five per cent of our urban parks are maintained by local authorities whose park budgets were cut by £690 million between 2010 and 2021[4] as austerity cuts forced them to prioritise statutory services for adults and children over everything else. The incidence of cuts is greatest in deprived urban areas and regionally in the North East and North West of England.

In the first section of this chapter, Section 4.1, the foundational starting point is an analysis of why we are in this mess. Austerity cuts were (and are) a political choice made by chancellors in the aftermath of crisis. But we also need to understand that these choices were made in the historical context of the failure of the market citizenship project. As initiated by Thatcher and continued by New Labour, the market citizenship objective was the creation of independent high wage individuals, but the outcome was an unsustainable increase in the number of low wage, state-dependent households.

Practically, the result was a fiscally stressed state because successive governments covered up UK failure to create jobs with decent wages by deploying all kinds of wage subsidies, though this was never an officially declared policy. By the 2010s more than 40 per cent of non-retired individuals were living in households receiving more in benefits than they paid in taxes. The growth of gross domestic product (GDP) did not address this problem as the UK shifted from a high foundational liveability society in the 1950s and 1960s with three functioning pillars for a broad range of households, to a low foundational liveability society in the 2020s with three increasingly collapsed pillars for low and medium income households along with general anxiety about failing services.

The second section of this chapter, Section 4.2, shows how the demand for wage subsidies has increased dramatically in the 2020s. The cost-of-living crisis is acute for low income households partly because chronic problems about the rising cost of on-market essentials like transport and utilities had eroded their residual incomes in the 2010s. Now, general inflation, energy prices and rising interest rates are squeezing the residual income of private renting and mortgage paying households in the middle of the income distribution. This reduces the number who can buy their way out of public service and local infrastructure problems, for example, by running a second car to get around public transport deficiencies, or by joining a private gym.

The decay and collapse of underfunded public services is the most obvious symptom of a fiscally stressed state which, within the limits of the present tax system, finds it difficult to fund the capital and revenue requirements of essential services. Before the 2010s, the long-term trend rate of growth of NHS funding was more than 3 per cent per annum, but real NHS funding grew by just 1.1 per cent under the Coalition Government and then by 1.6 per cent under the Conservative Government up to 2018–19. Section 4.3 of this chapter uses the case of the NHS to explain how long-term underfunding has reformatted acute hospital services and created a fragile, high flow system whose problems are hard to fix. This adds another element of intractability to what is increasingly a wicked social crisis.

4.1 Market citizenship and the outcome of wicked crisis

This first section of this chapter tackles the origins and prehistory of the present crisis. In foundational terms, we understand the arc of UK socio-economic history since the 1970s in terms of the failure of a market citizenship project. The project's aim was to create independent individuals with market choices. But the economy could not create high wage jobs on the scale required and the outcome was a structural problem with the number of subsidy-dependent low wage households. Politics is experienced as an urgent real-time set of events and choices by actors and commentators who generally do not reflect on the arc of history. Hence the general puzzlement about how and why the UK cannot afford decent public services when GDP per capita is so much higher in the 2020s than in the 1950s.

The starting point is our account of the 1950s and 1960s as a period of high foundational liveability for households across many places and from top to bottom of society. Private consumption was sustained by a high wage male earner, typically in manufacturing employment. The corollary was low female participation with a wife or partner effectively acting as an unpaid housekeeper and child carer. Public consumption rested on generous provision of municipal public transport, social housing, schooling and healthcare, coupled with social insurance benefits that maintained the income of the unwaged when sick, unemployed or retired. Universal services, like education and healthcare, were free at the point of use and benefited all households, regardless of income. At the peak, more than 30 per cent of the population lived in social housing which was often of high quality and therefore not a form of residual provision.

Centre left Labour revisionists like Tony Crosland and the One Nation Tories like Harold Macmillan shared the idea that balance between private and public spheres was necessary, had been achieved and could be improved. The balance was demonstrated by Harold Macmillan's achievements in office. As housing minister in the early 1950s, he used 'war job' mobilisation to deliver the national target of 300,000 new houses a year[5] with council houses accounting for more than three-quarters of the new build. As Prime Minister, he won the 1959 'never had it so good' election, underpinned by a substantial increase in home ownership. Imbalance was generally seen as a defect. The best-selling success of J. K. Galbraith's *Affluent Society* in 1958 sustained a sense of the UK's moral superiority when Galbraith indicted American capitalism for its combination of private affluence and public squalor.[6]

If balance was an important achievement, we would not now want the 1950s and 1960s form of balance. It is not simply the rejection of the patriarchal household but the sense of economic progress based on mass consumption such as twin tub washing machines and second-hand cars on hire purchase for working class households. These high mass consumption solutions of the 1950s and 1960s have turned into the ecological problems of the 2010s and the 2020s. The rise of car ownership and the 'drive to society' is emblematic of the change and its consequences. As Exhibit 4.1 shows, in the early 1950s around 15 per cent of households had cars, by the 1970s half of households had cars and today we have nearly 80 per cent car ownership and multi-car households are common (Exhibit 4.1). All this decisively tilted the balance against public transport and towards journeys by private car, further encouraging out-of-town urban development, to the disadvantage of the planet and those without access to cars like female wage earners in low income households. As Exhibit 4.2 shows, by the early 1980s car use had become the default with 80 per cent of journeys made that way.

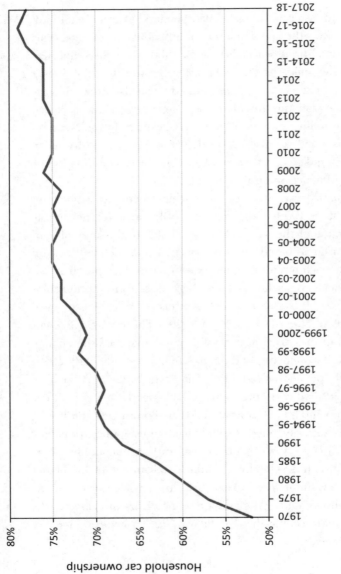

Exhibit 4.1 UK households owning at least one car or van, 1970–2018.

Source: Family Spending, 2020, Table A45, ONS. https://www.ons.gov.uk/peoplepopulationandcommunity/personalandhousehol dfinances/expenditure/datasets/percentageofhouseholdswithdurablegoodsuktablea45.

Note: Data not available in all years. The data used to create the exhibits is available at https://foundationaleconomyresearch.com/index .php/nothing-works-stats/.

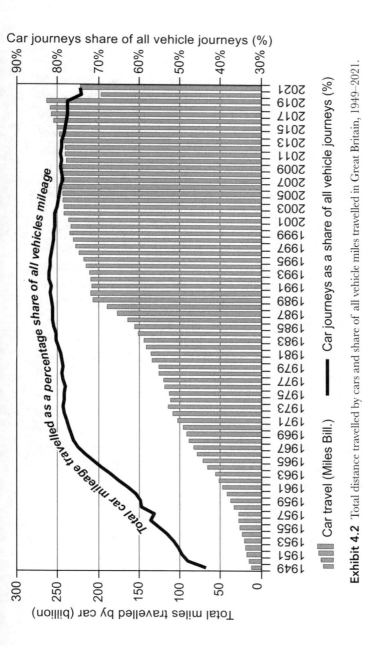

Exhibit 4.2 Total distance travelled by cars and share of all vehicle miles travelled in Great Britain, 1949–2021.

Source: National Travel Survey: 2021 data tables (Table TRA0101), Department for Transport. https://www.gov.uk/government/statistics/national-travel-survey-2021.

Note: Break in data collection methods from 1993 onwards. Total vehicle miles relate to all motor vehicles including light and heavy commercial vehicles. The data used to create the exhibits is available at https://foundationaleconomyresearch.com/index.php/nothing-works-stats/.

There was an Overton window[7] in British politics of the 1950s and 1960s which may justify Addison's description of the period as one of consensus.[8] But this was never a politically stable settlement given the disagreement about its fundamental features. Nor was it economically sustainable given the competitive weakness of British manufacturing which could not sustain the employment base and the availability of relatively well-paid employment.

- Beveridge had envisaged a 'living wage' standard for the unwaged through subsistence benefits for the old, sick and unemployed, with women to be covered by virtue of their husband's contribution. Beveridge's design was buried when the Conservative government, on the recommendations of the Phillips Committee in 1954, renounced his ambition to pay subsistence benefits.[9] The option of developing a European-style earnings-related social insurance scheme was then closed off in the 1959 General Election when the electorate rejected the Labour Party's offer of a graduated earnings-related scheme.

- The economic problem was the uncompetitiveness of UK manufacturing revealed in the 1970s, with imports rising faster than exports as Germany and Japan recovered from World War Two and sold into the UK and other contested markets.[10] Japanese exports up to the late 1980s revaluation of the Yen were then assisted by high factory productivity coupled with hourly wages which were much lower at prevailing Yen/£ exchange rates.[11] This success was the harbinger of the later irresistible rise of China and other low wage Asian producers of everything from clothing to smartphones.

As UK manufacturing went into a long decline, the Tories in the 1980s and New Labour in the 1990s were saved from having to think seriously, or do anything constructive, about continuing weak trade performance and the atrophy of the productive base. Extraction protected the Conservatives as North Sea oil fortuitously came onstream. Financialisation supported both Conservative and New Labour governments as deregulated credit boosted house prices, and re-mortgaging of homes allowed leakage into consumption. Feel-good was boosted by tapping low wage Asian factories for ever more stuff and making some of the rewards and choices of middle and upper income groups available to more households.

Most obviously, the totemic bi-partisan policies were home ownership and university education, which were both greatly expanded. Home ownership was around 35 per cent in the early 1950s, reached 50 per cent in the 1970s and then, with unregulated credit and selling off council houses, peaked at around 70 per cent in the 2000s.[12] The expansion of university education was just as spectacular. Of those born between 1965 and 1969, 16 per cent had acquired degrees by age 30. For those born a decade later, the percentage had risen to 33 per cent.[13]

Politicians boasted about the number of UK jobs created and about the UK's unemployment rates which (entirely predictably) were lower than in more regulated European national labour markets. But the UK's post-industrial service economy was not generating high wage jobs on the scale required. As Chapter 1 observed, when growth flatlined in the 2010s, the political classes increasingly recognised that the UK economy was generating too many low wage jobs with poor and regionally uneven private sector job creation. A substantial proportion

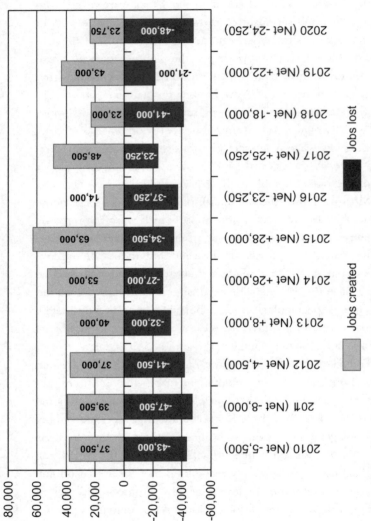

Exhibit 4.3 Annual change in jobs created and lost in the North East of England between 2010 and 2020.

Source: Business Register and Employment Survey (BRES), Nomis. https://www.nomisweb.co.uk/query/select/getdatasetbytheme.asp ?theme=27. The data used to create the exhibits is available at https://foundationaleconomyresearch.com/index.php/nothing-works-stats/.

of the extra jobs were in London, while in the North and West of the UK, there was considerable disruptive churn through hiring and firing but very limited net new job creation. For example, as Exhibit 4.3 shows, a total of just 26,250 net new jobs were created in the North East of England between 2010 and 2020 and there was positive job creation in just five of the eleven years.

The deterioration in the composition of employment meant there was a large discrepancy between the ambition and the outcomes of the market citizenship project. That gap is summarised in Exhibit 4.4. The sphere of marketised services certainly increased, most obviously with the growth of formal childcare in two-earner families. In 1980 only 22 per cent of employed mothers used some kind of formal childcare arrangement;[14] by 2018 formal childcare was being used by 62 per cent of households with children in term time. But the low income households did not have adequate wage incomes for choice or independence when around one-quarter of UK jobs are low paid on the basis of gross weekly earnings and a similar or larger percentage of working age households will be on Universal Credit by the middle of this decade. Publicly funded, high quality services were increasingly inaccessible, especially social housing as the better half of the council stock was sold off.

The outcomes of the market citizenship project did however rearrange the social limits to growth in a way that maintained and reinforced the advantage of upper income households. As Fred Hirsch[15] argued in the 1970s, many public and private goods (from tertiary education to urban car ownership) are positional in that the benefits of consumption depend on the good's availability to a select few and the exclusion of the many.

	High liveability 1950s–1970s	**Market citizenship ambition 1979–2010**	**Low liveability 2020s workfare and marketisation outcomes 2020s**
Wage income from employment	• Male wage earner in high wage, full time job with 5.9 million men in manufacturing in 1951 • Low female participation of 35% with around 20% of married women regularly working in 1951	• Assumption that post-industrial economy and flexibilised labour market could create large numbers of high wage jobs • (High wages will underpin high male and female participation, independent households and market choice)	• Dual income household with 79% male and 72% female participation • Many low pay, precarious, part time jobs in services like retail, hospitality and care (38% of women's jobs are part time) • 26% of jobs are low paid based on gross weekly earnings; 90% of low paid jobs are minimum wage
Social benefits and income support	• Insurance benefits for unwaged i.e., old, sick, cyclically unemployed • Beveridge 1942 plan for flat rate benefits covering all necessities; wives covered via husband's contribution	• Redesign benefit levels and conditionality to incentivise workforce participation • Low benefits for the employable; defined to include many on sickness benefit	• Increased dependence of low wage households on income support and housing benefit: by 2024 33% of working age households will be on UC • UC low benefits for out of work also apply to long term sick and carers; conditionality and sanctions a key feature

Exhibit 4.4 From social settlement to muddled outcomes in the UK.

Source: X09: Real Average weekly earnings using Consumer price inflation (seasonally adjusted) – Office for National Statistics; T. Cutler, J. Williams and K. Williams (1986), *Keynes, Beveridge and Beyond* (Routledge & Kegan Paul), table 3.9, p. 81; Department of Employment and Productivity (1971), *British Labour Statistics: Historical Abstract, 1886–1968*, HMSO; S. Irvine, H. Clark, M. Ward and B. Francis-Devine (March 2022), 'Women and the UK economy', Commons Library Research Briefing, House of Commons Library, https://researchbriefings. files.parliament.uk/documents/SN06838/SN06838.pdf (parliament.uk); N. Cominetti, C. McCurdy and H. Slaughter (June 2021), 'Low Pay Britain: 2021', Resolution Foundation. https://www.resolutionfoundation.org/publications/low-pay-britain-2021/ (resolution foundation.org). M. Brewer, R. Joyce, T. Waters and J. Woods (April 2019), 'Universal credit and its impact on household incomes: the long and the short of it', IFS Briefing Note BN248, The Institute for Fiscal Studies. https://ifs.org.uk/sites/default/files/output_url_files/

Provision of public goods (housing, education, healthcare)	• Extensive provision of public goods: free at point of use schooling and NHS health care • Social housing for 35% of population at peak in 1970s • Women as unpaid housekeepers and child carers	• Public goods provision less important after marketisation • More home ownership and shift to private renting as households choose how to spend incomes on the market	• Underfunded public goods: schooling, health and care services stressed • Formal childcare used by 62% of households with children 0-14 in term time • Households in social housing now falling towards 15% after right to buy with limited new build
Outcome	• A working public service state supporting/ funded by high wages via PAYE and National Insurance • Expanded state has up to 40% share of GDP • Male-centred society	• Diffused economic welfare for independent households: GDP/GVA per capita measures • High mass private consumption with less social spend, low taxes and lower state share of GDP	• Divided society (before current cost of living crisis) with many state-dependent households and squeezed residual incomes (after rent, transport and utilities) • High state share of GDP with flat and regressive tax system but the state cannot deliver public services which households need and expect

Exhibit 4.4 (Continued)

Universal_credit_and_its_impact_on_household_incomes_the_long_and_the_short_of_it_BN248.pdf (ifs.org.uk); B. Watts, S. Fitzpatrick, G. Bramley and D. Watkins (September 2014), 'Welfare Conditionality: Sanctions, Support and Behaviour Change', Joseph Rowntree Foundation. https://www.jrf.org.uk/sites/default/files/jrf/migrated/files/Welfare-conditionality-UK-Summary.pdf (jrf.org.uk); C. Belfield, J. Cribb, A. Hood and R. Joyce (July 2015), 'Living Standards, Poverty and Inequality in the UK: 2015', The Institute for Fiscal Studies. https://ifs.org.uk/sites/default/files/output_url_files/R107.pdf (ifs.org.uk); Department for Education (December 2018), 'Childcare and Early Years Survey of Parents in England, 2018', HM Government. Childcare and Early Years Survey of Parents in England 2018 (publishing.service.gov.uk); Statista (February 2022), 'Proportion of households occupied by social renters in England from 2000 to 2021' (accessed 7 October 2022), England: social rented households 2021, Statista. The data used to create the exhibits is available at https://foundationaleconomyresearch.com/index.php/nothing-works-stats/.

What Hirsch did not anticipate was that positional advantage could be maintained or increased in a society of mass consumption. High income households gained positional consumption advantage in a low wage service economy when they could afford to marketise more of what they did and save time as they benefited from the low wages paid in all kinds of personal services activities. High income households could enjoy cheap personal services in the 2010s but without the intrusion of live-in servants as in the 1910s.

The UK by the 2010s had become, rather like Brecht's Los Angeles in the 1940s, one place that could efficiently serve as heaven for the rich and hell for the poor. The added complication was that this low wage service economy outcome was fiscally stressed in ways that created a wicked problem[16] with complex, interdependent causes and no remedies within the imagination of the UK political classes. The fundamental driver of the wicked problem is that, from Margaret Thatcher onwards, successive governments have increased benefits in cash and kind for low wage households because this incentivises the workless to take up jobs and rewards those who hold down poor quality jobs.

A substantial minority of economically active households have always received more in benefits than they pay in taxes because of state aid towards the cost of bringing up children and state old age pensions for the retired. But, after the failure of market citizenship, the outcome is a society where, as Exhibit 4.5 shows, ordinarily more than 40 per cent of non-retired individuals (i.e. those of working age) live in households receiving more in benefits than they pay in taxes. Cyclical increases in unemployment are of course important drivers, and economic downturns account for the two peaks in subvention, in

1992 after the Lawson boom and in 2009–10 after the Great Financial Crisis. But from the trough in 2000, the long run trend is unsteadily upwards, and after 2009–10 the percentage receiving more in benefits did not fall back to the low of 30 per cent but stayed above 40 per cent.

Using a mainstream lens, this striking finding could be narrowly interpreted as a problem about benefits dependence. It is, of course, just as much about subsidising employers (private and public) through in-work benefits, as well as subsidising consumers of the services built on low wages. Worse still, the

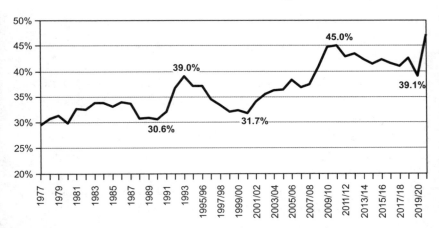

Exhibit 4.5 UK non-retired individuals in households receiving more in benefits than paying taxes.

Source: 'The Effects of Taxes and Benefits on Household Income, UK, 2020/21 – Reference Tables', ONS. https://www.ons.gov.uk/peoplepopulationandcommunity/personalandhouse holdfinances/incomeandwealth/datasets/theeffectsoftaxesandbenefitsonhouseholdincome financialyearending2014.

Note: Benefits are counted as the sum of total cash benefits and total benefits in kind. Taxes are counted as the sum of total direct taxes and total indirect taxes. Individuals in households relate to the economically active. The data used to create the exhibits is available at https://foundat ionaleconomyresearch.com/index.php/nothing-works-stats/.

low paid are trapped by a predatory tax and benefits system which we analyse in Section 5.1. In effect, after paying more tax and losing Universal Credit they retain only around 30p out of every pound of extra income. Wage subsidy, along with an ageing population and expanding service needs, explains why a fiscally stressed state was by the late 2010s struggling to fund health, care and education as well as social infrastructure as it could in the 1960s and 1970s. And that was before Covid-19 and the cost-of-living crisis, when many middle income households would need support.

4.2 The rising cost of essentials

The 'cost-of-living crisis' described in the media is about how the rising cost of essentials disproportionately hurts low income households and increasingly also hurts middle income households. It is in effect a crisis about residual income – a crisis about what, if anything, low and middle income households have left after paying for housing, food, transport, gas and electricity. The argument of this section is that low income households had worsening residual income problems by the late 2010s before the onset of an acute cost-of-living crisis in spring 2022, with a 54 per cent jump in the energy price cap in April 2022 coming on top of a 12 per cent increase in the previous October.[17] And that with a delay, through the influence of rising mortgage interest rates, middle income owner occupiers and private renters will be increasingly drawn into the crisis.

The acute crisis in 2022 did not come from a clear blue sky for low income households. More accurately, it came at the end

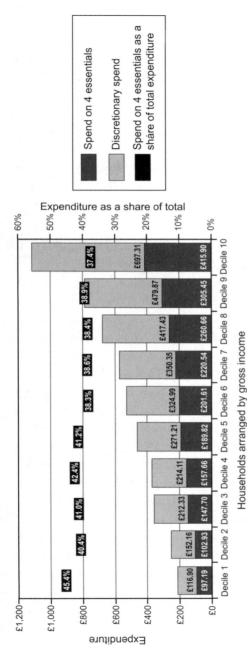

Exhibit 4.7 Household weekly expenditure on four essentials, by household income decile, 2020–21.

Source: Family Spending (Workbook 1 and 5), ONS. https://www.ons.gov.uk/peoplepopulationandcommunity/personalandhouseholdfinances/expenditure/bulletins/familyspendingintheuk/april2020tomarch2021/relateddata.

Note: Households are arranged by gross income. The four essential items are rent and mortgages, food and non-alcoholic drinks, transport and utilities. Discretionary spending is total expenditure minus the cost of the four essentials. The data used to create the exhibits is available at https://foundationaleconomyresearch.com/index.php/nothing-works-stats/.

spending on 'essentials' expands to take up available income for upper income households who can mortgage a larger house and run a second car. At the lower end of the income spectrum, lower income households need to reduce absolute expenditure and there will be less available for discretionary spending in low and middle income households.

If we look at the pattern in 2020–21 before the acute crisis, we see a double precarity of households who will struggle to cope with the rising cost of essentials and general inflation in and after 2022–23.

- Low income households were immediately vulnerable to acute crisis because they had little scope for adjustment by cutbacks in essentials because they had already restricted their spending on the two essentials of food and transport. In deciles 1 and 2, the mean weekly spend on food and transport is £36.40 and £11.10, while in decile 5 in the middle of the income distribution, the spend is £58.70 on food and £26.20 on transport. This is really striking when decile 2 includes many striving households with an average gross income which we estimate as around £25,000 and disposable income in the low twenties. Smaller household sizes and a larger number of retired people in the bottom two deciles contribute to, but do not wholly explain the difference in expenditure compared with decile 5.
- Middle income households were also exposed to acute crisis because they had a limited absolute amount of discretionary spending going into the crisis and thus no easy way of absorbing the substantial increased cost of essentials by reallocating expenditure from discretionary to essentials.

The discretionary mean weekly sum available for households coping with pinched necessity in deciles 1 and 2 was £116 and £152. But in deciles 3–5 the mean weekly discretionary sum is not hugely higher and ranges from £212 to £271. It is only in decile 6 with a discretionary margin of £361 that we reach a group which has the capacity to reallocate around £150 per week to cover the cost of rising essentials without considerable pain. This is well up the income range because we estimate the average household in decile 6 has a gross income of around £53,000 and a disposable income of around £43,000.

The argument about double precarity extending well up the income scale is confirmed by the evidence of increased food bank use. This was an indicator of stress through the decade of chronic crisis in the 2010s and it remained so in acute crisis in 2022. For example, from April to September 2022, Trussell Trust food banks distributed 1.3 million emergency food parcels, an increase of 52 per cent since 2019.[22] And there are good reasons to believe that, regardless of the trend of energy prices, the acute crisis will then develop further in 2023 and 2024 to further squeeze the discretionary spending of middle income groups of mortgage holders and private renters through their direct and indirect exposure to higher interest rates. This can be fairly easily tracked for the mortgagors whose housing costs largely consist of mortgage payments.

Approximately 30 per cent of UK households hold a mortgage and any understanding of their exposure and precarity must begin by considering how mortgage expenditures vary in relation to income across the deciles. The short answer is that

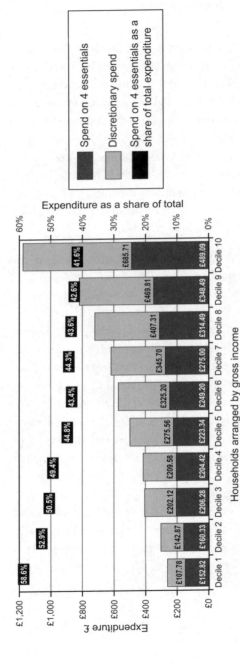

Exhibit 4.8 Households with mortgages, weekly expenditure on four essentials, by household income decile, 2020–21.

Source: Family Spending (Workbook 1 and 5), ONS. https://www.ons.gov.uk/peoplepopulationandcommunity/personalandhouseholdfinances/expenditure/bulletins/familyspendingintheuk/april2020tomarch2021/relateddata.

Note: Households are arranged by gross income. The four essential items are rent and mortgages, food and non-alcoholic drinks, transport and utilities. Discretionary spending is total expenditure minus the cost of the four essentials. The data used to create the exhibits is available at https://foundationaleconomyresearch.com/index.php/nothing-works-stats/.

the relative size of mortgage spend does not vary significantly according to income. From decile 2 to decile 10, the curve is flat for mortgage holders regardless of income, as Exhibit 4.8 shows. Housing costs account for 27 per cent of expenditure in decile 2 against 24 per cent of expenditure in decile 10, with all the deciles in between in a range from 22 to 26 per cent. House property is expensive in relation to income but it has remained attractive as an appreciating investment in many areas since the early 1990s. So, low and high income households tend to mortgage up to the limit of their income under the various lender rules about multiples of single or joint income and deposit required.

Housing costs account for around 25 per cent of total expenditure for all deciles of mortgage holders. So, it is not surprising that in 2020–21 the four essentials (housing, food, transport and energy) share of total expenditure falls in a fairly narrow range, from 53 per cent in decile 2 to 42 per cent in decile 10. Compared with all households in Exhibit 4.7, mortgage holders spend slightly more on the four essentials. Again, it is only around decile 6 (which in 2020–21 had a discretionary mean weekly margin of £325) that mortgagors have some capacity to cover the rising cost of essentials. In mortgagor deciles 3 to 5, the mean weekly discretionary sum available after the four essentials ranges from £202 to £275. If this mortgagor result for 2020–21 is similar in outline to the all households result, the sub-group of mortgage holders are then peculiarly vulnerable because they are directly exposed to higher interest rates on their mortgages.

The problem arises because the mean rate of interest on all outstanding mortgages in summer 2022 was 2.8 per cent but the Bank of England was raising interest rates as the standard monetary policy response to inflation. As rates increase, just under 20 per cent of mortgage holders will have to pay immediately because they have variable interest rate mortgages and the remaining 80 per cent have to pay as and when their fixed term mortgages expire. Most fixed term mortgages are short term so the Resolution Foundation estimates that by the end of 2024, 5.1 million of the 7.4 million mortgage holders will have been affected by rising interest rates.[23]

The exposure effects vary considerably according to assumptions about the trajectory of rate rises and the level that interest rates ultimately reach. But the effects can be explored and illustrated in the simulation exercise below which is based on the Family Spending survey. Mortgage holders are in double jeopardy in the current acute crisis because they have to cope with rising interest rates increasing their mortgage payments and with the rising prices of every other essential. This means that any realistic simulation should incorporate the effects of the increasing cost of all four essentials (Exhibit 4.9). For the average mortgage holder in each decile, the starting point is their actual pre-crisis spending on housing (at prevailing interest rates of around 2.8 per cent and at March 2021 consumer prices), and on food, energy and transport. In March 2021 the share of four essentials in total expenditure actually ranged from 48 per cent in decile 3 at the top of the low income group to 37 per cent in decile 10 at the top of the high income group.

The simulation then feeds in a counterfactual (a) using the September 2022 inflation rate of prices of the essentials and (b) 4 per cent and 6 per cent interest rates on the average mortgage

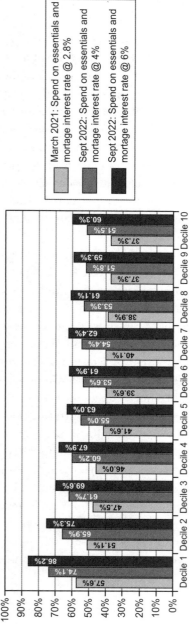

Exhibit 4.9 Households with mortgages, simulated impact of higher interest rates on expenditure for four essentials, by income decile.

Source: Simulated using data from Family Spending (Workbook 1 and 5), ONS; all data related to family spending in the UK: April 2020 to March 2021. https://www.gov.uk/peoplepopulationandcommunity/personalandhouseholdfinances/expenditure/bulletins/familyspendingintheuk/april2020to march2021/relateddata; and ONS, Consumer price inflation time series (MM23) (accessed 8 November 2022). https://www.gov.uk/economy/inflati onandpriceindices/datasets/consumerpriceindices.

Note: The data relates to households with mortgages and households are arranged by gross income. The four essential items are rent and mortgages, food and non-alcoholic drinks, transport and utilities. Discretionary spending is total expenditure minus the cost of the four essentials. The data used to create the exhibits is available at https://foundationaleconomyresearch.com/index.php/nothing-works-stats/.

in each decile which give us the very probable and possible future depending on how aggressive the Bank of England is in raising interest rates. The combined results of inflation and higher interest rates in this simulation drive up the share of expenditure allocated to essentials. In the simulation, factoring in the inflation rate in the price of essentials and 4 per cent interest rates, raises the share of four essentials in total spend by about 15 per cent across the board, ranging from 62 per cent of all spending in decile 2 to 52 per cent at decile 10. With 6 per cent interest rates, the share of the four essentials would increase by another 8–10 per cent and the range is from 70 per cent in decile 3 to 60 per cent in decile 10.

This simulation of increased expenditure shares assumes that income remains the same. The actual outcome will depend of course on the extent of compensatory wage and salary increases which households obtain. In autumn 2022, the government was trying to hold public sector gross wage increases to something like 2 per cent while few private sector employers were offering above 6–7 per cent gross subject to tax charges and benefit changes. The implication is that very few mortgagors will be able to get anything like full compensation for rising prices. A substantial section of middle income mortgage holders who have been accustomed to spending 40–45 per cent of their total expenditure on the four essentials will end up spending closer to two-thirds. Put another way, the point of comfort moves dramatically up the income scale. If we define comfort as at least £300 per week available for non-essentials, in March 2021 that point was reached by decile 6 with 40 per cent of households in the comfort zone; using September 2022 prices after 10 per cent plus inflation and with 6 per cent interest rates, the point is reached by decile 9 with only 20 per cent in the comfort zone.

And if all this is counterfactual and speculative, the incontrovertible point is that pre-crisis, the bottom half of the income distribution was never in the comfort zone and low income households are already exposed to unmanageable increases in the price of essentials. For households in the bottom three deciles, the Energy Price Guarantee did not so much solve their problems as soften the heating vs eating choices (with much then depending on accidents like winter weather and the energy efficiency of their housing). Middle income households can make some reductions in expenditure to reduce travel, food and energy costs, but these will have limits. For those who had already made economies, evidence is mounting that attempts to cover the lack of income result in increasing use of credit, especially by households in the most deprived areas,[24] as well as more borrowing from friends and family, and growing arrears, including on energy and council tax bills.[25]

4.3 Underfunded public services: the case of the NHS

The previous section has shown how residual income and the discretionary margin is an important factor that shapes foundational liveability and that individual household circumstances matter. In this section, we shift to focus on the second pillar of foundational liveability, access to essential services. Given that essential services are provided and accessed through distinctive reliance systems organised in different ways, we have to focus on a specific case. The NHS in England is an appropriate choice because the NHS is sentimentally our national treasure and in recent years has figured prominently in national discussions of failing public services. The NHS is practically a complete mess which is easy to explain but hard to sort out even with substantial increases in funding. A decade of prolonged underfunding and magical thinking about efficiency gains has distorted provision and created a fragile and dysfunctional acute hospital system, while grossly neglecting the public health issues which must be addressed if the demand for treatment is to be manageable in the long run.

The NHS is of course only one of many UK public services which do not deliver for households because of access and/or quality issues usually related to long-term underfunding and often compounded by uncontrolled privatisation or inept outsourcing. Some of the service delivery failures (like delays in 2022 in issuing passports or driving licenses) immediately inconvenience individuals and households but come with the promise that normal service will quickly be resumed. Many of the financial and physical system problems (like the cuts in per pupil school spending or the backlog in the criminal justice system) have uncertain but serious long-term consequences. The case of the NHS is particularly instructive because here we can trace the link from underfunding to a broken system whose consequences are dire and immediate.

The NHS in England and the three devolved nations provides medical services according to need that are free at the point of use for the vast majority of households in a society where only just over 10 per cent of the UK population has private health insurance.[26] At the same time an increasing number of UK citizens are paying out of pocket so that, by 2019, out of pocket expenditure by Britons on medical expenses has doubled to 1.8 per cent of GDP over the past 30 years.[27] The driver here is increasing waiting time for non-urgent hospital treatment which has been exacerbated by Covid-19. By August 2022, some 7 million, or around one in eight of the population, were on the English waiting list for non-urgent consultant-led elective treatment, and the backlog was getting longer month by month.[28]

Emergency response services are at the same time in a state of near collapse. The problems for hospital patients start when they reach hospital by ambulance or car. Accident and Emergency attendance had returned to pre-pandemic levels by Spring 2022, but the target of 95 per cent being seen within four hours has not been reached since 2013–14, and by March 2022 only 58.6 per cent of patients were being seen in four hours with a steadily downwards trend.[29] Moreover, this poor overall performance is not the result of a hospital system that works by effectively prioritising urgent cases whenever they present. The cancer target of 93 per cent of patients to be seen by a specialist consultant within two weeks of an urgent GP referral has not been met since May 2020. In August 2022 some 75.4 per cent met the first consultation target.[30]

These problems are immediately caused by the intersection of increasing demand with supply restricted by underfunding. Healthcare expenditure (including health and social care spending) has in the UK and in other high income countries more or less doubled as a percentage of GDP since the 1960s. Blame ageing populations, the availability of more sophisticated treatments and the general failure to prioritise preventive intervention in all high income countries. But the UK by the late 2010s was consistently spending a smaller fraction of GDP on health and care than other North European countries. From 2013 to 2019, the UK each year spent an average of 9.6 per cent of GDP on health and care, whereas France spent 11.4 per cent of GDP and Germany spent 11.2 per cent.[31]

The NHS has never been generously funded in relation to international comparisons but historical experience suggests it needs at least a 3 per cent real terms funding increase each year to expand services to meet demand, and probably something like a 5 per cent or more real increase every year if backlogs are to be reduced, as they were under New Labour. But in the austerity decade after 2010, real NHS funding grew by 1.1 per cent under the Coalition Government and then by just 1.6 per cent under the Conservative Government in 2018–19. The Theresa May Government reverted to mean funding increases with a more generous settlement, but a decade's damage had already been done (Exhibit 4.10).

In the austerity years there was much magical thinking about the efficiency savings which the NHS could make through meeting productivity targets, and the NHS did achieve a productivity increase of more than 2 per cent per annum between 2010–11 and 2016–17. This was illusory however because the efficiency savings were being produced by one-off measures and parsimony about wage settlements in an organisation where pay accounted for two-thirds of total costs. By 2017–18 just over 25 per cent of provider efficiency gains were delivered by one-off measures like deferring investment, freezing recruitment or making land sales, all of

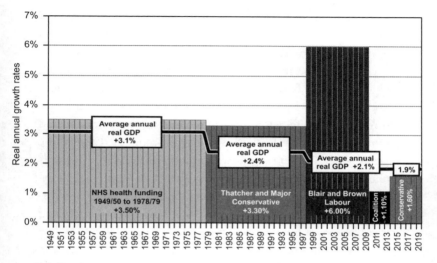

Exhibit 4.10 Average annual real growth in NHS funding compared with GDP, 1940–2019.

Source: J. Froud, C. Haslam, S. Johal, J. Law and K. Williams (June 2020), *When Systems Fail: UK Acute Hospitals and Public Health after Covid-19*, Foundational Economy Collective, pp. 42–6. https://foundationaleconomycom.files.wordpress.com/2020/08/when-systems-fail-uk-acute-hospitals-and-public-health-after-covid-19.pdf. The original NHS funding data relates to the UK NHS and is from The Health Foundation (2019), 'Labour pledges a step-change in NHS funding after almost a decade of austerity' (The Health Foundation). The data used to create the exhibits is available at https://foundationaleconomyresearch.com/index.php/nothing-works-stats/.

which did nothing for patient services.[32] According to BMA calculations from NHS data, between 2008–9 and 2021–22, there was a 35 per cent real decline in the average disposable income of hospital consultants.[33] And most grades like nurses and ambulance workers suffered deteriorating relativities and real pay cuts which have contributed to industrial action in 2022 and 2023.

Real wage cuts stored up problems of recruitment and retention from top to bottom of the system. NHS employers told the 2022 Pay Review that their lower-level employees were leaving for supermarkets, Amazon and major airports which all offer higher basic pay for entry-level roles.[34] The problems are made worse by the absence of workforce planning and by a training system which is not training enough new doctors and nurses. By late 2021, NHS employers complained that there were nearly 100,000 vacancies in the English NHS, with over one in ten posts unfilled in some regions and a national shortage of some 40,000 nurses.[35] In response, the NHS increasingly defaulted onto its long-established practice of importing 'readymade' trained nurses and doctors from countries like India and the Philippines. UK-wide, some 50,000 joined the nursing register in 2021–22 and 48 per cent of those new joiners were internationally trained.[36] It is not socially responsible for the NHS to strip trained staff from the global south when the WHO predicts a worldwide shortage of 15 million health workers by 2030, mainly in low and lower middle income countries.[37]

The story so far about service failure and the underpaid NHS workforce is a familiar one from mainstream media reports. But further analysis reveals a more fundamental problem. Funding cuts and churning reorganisation have together reconfigured key parts of the NHS so that they are unfit for health system purposes. Crucially, they lack the resilience to respond to external shocks like pandemics which are unpredictably part of mass population movements in a globalised world.

Our 2020 report[38] on the NHS response to the first wave of Covid-19 infection argued that the NHS had been structurally reconfigured so that it was inherently fragile and could not cope with a pandemic in two respects.

- First, the public health laboratory system had been reorganised around a national centre of excellence while regionally distributed laboratory capacity was effectively closed down. Consequently, mass testing had to be discontinued early in the first phase of the pandemic because the public laboratory system could not do high volume testing. A partly outsourced Covid testing system then had to be constructed at huge expense.
- Second, the acute hospital system had been reconfigured as a high flow, low stocks system which lacked the buffers to cope with a pandemic surge in demand. At the outset of the pandemic, hospital beds had to be cleared to make way for new Covid patients by discharging older patients who carried the virus into care homes. This led to more than 25,000 excess deaths in the first pandemic wave between March and September 2020.[39]

The story of laboratory organisation is a complicated one but the tale of acute hospital reconfiguration can be summarised in a few paragraphs and a couple of exhibits. In the 30 years before the pandemic, the English NHS more than halved the number of hospital beds from 299,000 in 1987–88 to 141,000 in 2019–20.[40] The hospital system was reconfigured as a low (bed) stock, high flow acute treatment system taking maximum advantage of day surgery and shorter stays in hospital.

International comparisons show this model was pushed much further in the UK than in other North West European countries; indeed, it was pushed to the point of irresponsibility in a system that was by the late 2010s running with no buffer capacity.

The UK has a smaller stock of doctors, nurses and beds in relation to population and so more citizens for every health worker and bed.[41] The UK had 352 citizens per doctor in 2018, whereas Germany had 235 and France 315 citizens per doctor. Similarly, in 2018 the UK had 128 citizens per nurse, whereas Germany had 75 citizens and France 93 citizens per nurse. Most notably, the UK in 2017 had 394 citizens per hospital bed whereas Germany had 125 citizens and France 167 citizens per hospital bed. On flow measures, like the number of patients using each bed in the course of a year, the UK leads all others in Northern and Southern Europe.[42] Using the standard OECD measure, in 2017 the UK used each bed for a new patient stay 49 times each year; in comparison, in France and Germany each bed was used 31 to 32 times, and in Italy and Spain 35 to 37 times.

The issue with this kind of high flow system is that it runs continuously at or near maximum capacity and depends on steady, constant demand because it has no safety margin of spare capacity to deal with any surge of admissions or any blockage to discharge. International comparisons in Exhibit 4.11 clearly show the UK hospital system as a high flow outlier, using scarce resources to the maximum with no capacity buffers. On the standard OECD measure, the UK bed utilisation rate rose from 87 per cent in 2010 to 94 per cent in 2017 when France, Germany, Italy and Spain all had bed utilisation rates of 60–70 per cent.[43] The fragility of the UK system is increased because many medical resources are specialised and cannot be switched to meet temporary demands for another treatment. Thus, when Covid hit in 2020, NHS England had around 100,000 acute and general beds but only 5,000 critical care beds staffed on the basis of one specialist nurse per bed.[44]

When a low stock, high flow system faces a demand backlog, as after Covid, the palliative fix is to try to increase the flow.

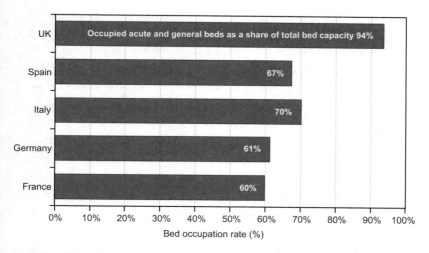

Exhibit 4.11 Occupation rates of acute and general care overnight stay beds compared to large European countries, 2017.

Source: J. Froud, C. Haslam, S. Johal, J. Law and K. Williams (June 2020), *When Systems Fail: UK Acute Hospitals and Public Health after Covid-19*, Foundational Economy Collective, pp. 42–6. https://foundationaleconomycom.files.wordpress.com/2020/08/when-systems-fail-uk-acute-hospitals-and-public-health-after-covid-19.pdf. The data used to create the exhibits is available at https://foundationaleconomyresearch.com/index.php/nothing-works-stats/.

Thus, in the NHS Covid recovery plan of 2022, the 'ambition' is to deliver up to 30 per cent more elective activity than before the pandemic.[45] But maintaining flow in the acute system will be difficult if problems in the care system block discharge of older patients when a residential home bed or home care package is not available. In the winter of 2021–22, more than one in ten general and acute NHS beds were occupied by patients who were fit to leave hospital but were not discharged.[46] The care system is in crisis because in 2022 social care funding in England is still below its real level in 2010 while the population of those over 70 with multiple long-term conditions has grown by more than 6 per cent.[47] With 165,000 care worker vacancies in autumn 2022,[48] the capacity of the care system is effectively below early 2010s levels.

It is difficult to be optimistic about the central state's ability to fix the NHS. Repair involves attending to neglected workforce basics including retention and development of existing staff, as well as recruitment to fill health and care vacancies, and gradually restoring staff salaries and relativities to levels prevailing before the real wage cuts of the 2010s. This would almost certainly require a real increase of around one-third in the wages and salary bill for health and care staff. There is also relatedly a need for extra throughput capacity and spare capacity buffers in the health and care systems, as well as capital funding to solve a maintenance backlog. At the same time, there is a need for effective preventive interventions to manage down demand increases which will otherwise overwhelm any increase in capacity. This requires very much more than reorganisation from the centre of the NHS system, not least because adult social care is commissioned by local authorities from private and other providers. Reorganisation and funding of health and care is a massive challenge for any incoming government after the general election in 2024 or 2025. Hence the need in Chapter 6 to think seriously about the politics and policy of adaptive reuse.

Chapter 5

Why the low paid need more than a pay rise

Introduction

Low income households in the UK have acute income retention problems, especially where workers have been unable to claim wage increases to compensate for price rises in a period of inflation. Each extra one pound of wages turns into about 30 pence of disposable income for those who not only pay tax on their wage increase but also lose Universal Credit. There is then a second set of problems about residual income when the costs of working for young, low income families will often include childcare and running a second-hand car. Because work is so unrewarding for those on low incomes and opens so few market choices, it is all the more important that they have access to good public services and free or cheap social infrastructure which sustain foundational liveability.

The belief and experience of middle and high income groups is that work pays and that getting a higher paid job can solve problems. This was reflected in the position of Jake Berry MP and Conservative Party Chair in autumn 2022 when wage increases were lagging behind price inflation. The 'government approach' was to rely on household solutions: 'people know they can cut their consumption or they can get a higher salary or higher wages, go out there and get that new job'.[1]

This makes sense to upper income groups in the political classes because they live in a world where they can afford to go to work and a pay rise leaves them better off. The upper income couple with children can afford childcare at the market rate and can afford to run two cars to take both wage earners in different directions in the morning. Everybody grumbles about a 40 per cent tax rate on individual gross incomes above £50,271 in 2022 and the privileged few retain advisers to deal with the annual upper limit on tax allowable pension contributions which is set at £40,000 in 2022–23.

As the first section of this chapter shows, low income households on Universal Credit live in a different world where a large pay rise turns into a small increase in disposable income. Universal Credit now incentivises work by providing income support for the low paid. Logically, benefits are withdrawn as income is increased so that those in low paid work pay more tax and lose benefits if they work longer hours or get a better paid job. In consequence, a low paid individual who gets a pay rise has a disposable income retention problem because more tax and less benefit jointly take around 70 pence from every pound of extra gross income.

The low income household also has a residual income problem which structures job choice and reduces income rewards. This is because holding down a job comes with costs if it involves a lengthy or difficult journey or formal childcare. Benefits are set very low to incentivise work but, after initially moving from benefits to work, households can be worse off in residual income terms after allowing for expenses like travel to work. And, as we show, the costs of working do structure and limit job choice, especially for female second earners in two-earner households where women are often trapped in part-time local work.

All this means that low income households need more than a pay rise. They need reform of the predatory tax and benefits system, so they retain more of their pay increases as disposable income. And they need rationalisation of the household support systems which penalise women while costing so much in terms of subsidising low wages. Households need more help with childcare and other costs of working so that they have broader job choice and a margin of residual income. And, for foundational liveability, they need more than disposable and residual income, because they also need essential services and free and accessible social infrastructure.

The importance of social infrastructure is less self-evident than in the case of health care. And so the third and final section of this chapter outlines how and why social infrastructure matters as a way of sustaining high functioning individuals and curbing the medicalisation of what community GP doctors call 'shit life syndrome'.[2] As we will see, by the late 2010s, more than 15 per cent of the English adult population was on mood changing, anti-depressant drugs.

Little of this is registered by the political classes because they remain deeply suspicious of the work ethic of low income individuals holding entry-level jobs offer-ing little job satisfaction. There is nothing new about such suspicions and stereotyping. In the 1890s the social inves-tigator Charles Booth wrote about those who never learn to do anything well and those who cannot get up in the morning. And more than 100 years later, here is George Osborne as Conservative Chancellor in 2012 anticipating real cuts in the value of benefits:

> Our conception of fairness … extends to the welfare sys-tem. We … think it's unfair that when that person leaves their home early in the morning, they pull the door behind them, they're going off to do their job, they're looking at their next-door neighbour, the blinds are down, and that family is living a life on benefits.[3]

This recurrent stereotype fixes on a few of life's casual-ties who lie abed. But what is remarkable in low income households in the 2020s is that so many men and women do go out to work, and then will work longer hours or take on more job responsibility, even though they have very lit-tle financial incentive to do so. Alan Clark[4] used the 'lions led by donkeys' trope to sum up how, in World War One, the poor bloody infantry was led by incapable and unimaginative staff officers. In the case of Universal Credit, it is mostly a case of responsible households with a work ethic disciplined by a suspicious and self-absorbed political class.

As middle income groups encounter problems about disposable and residual income, the political classes will register disposable and residual income issues, and we have an opportunity for reform. But that requires focus and prioritising the problems of low income households. Hence, the first section of this chapter, Section 5.1, deals with the rewards of work and shows how there is a large income step up when moving from benefits to work but that the disposable income gains from better jobs or more hours are limited because of the way the tax and benefits system erodes gross income. Section 5.2 illustrates the costs of work problem by looking at the expense of commuting for the motoring poor who struggle to afford a car in a car-dependent society. Section 5.3, the third and final section, develops our argument about how foundational liveability is about more than income by considering how and why social infrastructure matters.

5.1 The tax and benefits wedge from pay increases

This first section of this chapter explores the issue of whether and how work pays and shows how the tax and benefits system creates an income retention problem so that every pound of extra income turns into 30 pence of disposable income for low income households. This point is demonstrated by presenting worked examples of low paid households in and around Newcastle-upon-Tyne. The outcome for low paid households in any other region of the UK would not be very different because all operate under the same tax and benefit rules on pay increases whereby tax and pensions take 35 pence in the pound and Universal Credit is reduced by 55 pence in the pound of disposable income.

In focus groups, residents of low income districts in the Newcastle-upon-Tyne urban area told us they doubted whether work paid. One participant was clear that 'often going to work leaves you worse off' and another explained that 'by the time you pay for travel, childcare, work clothes and your lunch, you are worse off'. A third asked rhetorically, 'Can you afford to go to work?'[5] None of this fits the middle and upper income group experience where working and/or getting a better job does generally pay off financially, so that higher gross pay translates into a higher disposable income after tax. If that is not so for our focus group members, what is going on in low income households?

In considering whether and how work pays for those on low incomes, it is important to separate two distinct steps: the first step is from benefits to employment; and the second step is then to higher waged employment, whether by working longer hours in one job or getting a better paid job through internal promotion or changing employers. In the first case, 'work pays' in that moving from benefits into waged employment does raise household disposable income substantially (though costs of working may then erode residual income). Under the Universal Credit (UC) system, this differential is obtained by keeping benefits at a low level for all claimants and topping up low wages. In the second case, 'better paid work pays badly', because a higher gross wage brings limited disposable income benefit to the household when higher taxes and reduced cash benefits are taken into account.

In line with workfare thinking, the current benefits system offers a substantial financial incentive to work, with a big step up in disposable household income when individuals move from benefits to employment. For any individual claimant, the move from benefits to any kind of paid employment results in a substantial 30 per cent or more increase in gross household income as the low paid get a wage plus Universal Credit as a wage subvention. At household level, it can mean moving up from the poorest income decile, with an average annual disposable household income of £20,000 a year in 2018–19, to the second poorest decile with an average disposable household income of £33,000 a year. For example, a two adult, two child household in a socially rented property in the Newcastle districts of Byker or Percy Main with neither adult working receives a total income of £20,292 per annum in Universal Credit, Child Benefit and Council Tax Credit. If both adults move to low pay employment (typical entry-level positions) with one adult working full-time and the other part time, the disposable income (after housing costs) increases by 58 per cent to £32,078 per year, after adjustments to taxes and benefits.

As we show in Exhibit 5.1, the result is not specific to this type of household or type of tenure. The income increase on moving from benefits to employment is substantial also for households in private rented housing and for other types of households, such as single adults rather than families. For example, a single adult in private rented accommodation would see their disposable income (after taxes, benefits and housing costs) increase from £10,014 to £13,550 if they started a full-time low paid job, a gain of over one-third. Disposable income is higher for private renters compared to social renters in these illustrations because private rent is typically around 50 per cent larger and therefore benefits paid are greater for these households to help meet their higher costs.

	Single adult household		2 adults, 2 children household	
	Social renter	Private renter	Social renter	Private renter
• Disposable income after housing costs when unemployed and all adults looking for work	£8,295.56	£10,013.64	£20,292.48	£21,402.16
• Disposable income after housing costs in (low paid) work after adjustments to taxes and benefits	£11,839.36	£13,550.16	£32,078.12	£34,378.08
• **Total increase in disposable income after housing costs and after starting working**	**£3,543.80**	**£3,536.52**	**£11,785.64**	**£12,975.92**
• **% increase in disposable income after housing costs and after starting working**	**43%**	**43%**	**58%**	**61%**

Exhibit 5.1 Increases in disposable income (after housing costs) resulting from moving from looking for work to employment for different types of households and tenure in postcode NE6 1AA.

Source: Derived from data provided by Turn2Us. https://benefits-calculator. turn2us.org.uk/. This table measures disposable income after housing costs and council tax credits.

Note: NE6 1AA is in Byker, Newcastle-upon-Tyne. The data used to create the exhibits is available at https://foundationaleconomyresearch.com/index.php/ nothing-works-stats/.

Of course, these illustrative numbers do not engage with various practical and financial implications which are relevant to claimants who find a job and which affect residual income. The additional costs incurred through working, such as costs of travel and childcare, mean that Exhibit 5.1 overstates the net gains made by households moving from benefits to employment. Practically also, many of the low paid have irregular and/or temporary jobs which complicate making new Universal Credit claims and lead to delays in payments or changing amounts, which undermine household budgeting and can cause financial distress.[6]

It is also clear that the step up in disposable income from benefits to work is obtained partly by setting benefits at low levels. This has foundational liveability consequences for those on benefits including those unable to work, for example due to long-term illness or caring responsibilities, as well as for those who are involuntarily unemployed and seeking work.[7] Some Universal Credit claimants are entitled to extra payments (for severe disability or because they are approaching end of life) but this does not alter the basic point about miserably low benefits for the disabled, sick and carers. Such benefits are a major issue in low income districts where expectation of healthy life is around 52 years, and many can expect years of ill health and disability before they draw an old age pension. For that reason, Universal Credit claimants not available to work are a substantial minority of all claimants. For example, in the Newcastle-upon-Tyne local authority area in 2020, some 27 per cent of claimants who were not in work were classified as having 'no work requirements' because they have met conditions related to chronic sickness, disability or caring responsibilities.[8] In the neighbouring Northumberland and North Tyneside local authorities, the proportions are respectively 21.3 per cent and 25.3 per cent.

The step up in disposable income from benefits to work is obtained not only by low benefits but also by offering wage subvention, which is earnings related and withdrawn on a taper basis as incomes increase, like many other UK benefits. The unintended consequence is an earnings retention problem when gross pay increases in low income households. The tax and benefits systems together ensure that substantially higher individual gross pay (from more hours, pay award or a better job) translates into modest increases in disposable and residual income for a household in a poor district where typical household gross income would be between £25,000 and £35,000 (from wages and benefits). This is because under the UK tax and benefits system, taxes increase, and benefits are withdrawn as the gross income rises. Income tax, national insurance and pension take 35 pence from every extra pound of gross income; Universal Credit is then reduced by 55 pence for every one pound of disposable post-tax income above an individual claimant's 'work allowance'. This work allowance is only available for those with a health condition or responsibility for children and is currently set low at £557 per month for those not receiving any housing allowance and £335 per month for those receiving Universal Credit housing payments.

Under these current parameters, we can illustrate the impact on household disposable income of an increase in gross wage income. Take the example of a low income household with two adults and two children in a socially rented property in Newcastle with a disposable income after benefits and taxes of £32,078 a year (Exhibit 5.2). This is the Byker household that we used earlier in our example of two adults moving into work. Having secured significant financial rewards after getting two jobs, a subsequent 20 per cent increase in the main earner's gross income would translate into only a 3.6 per cent increase in household disposable income (after housing costs). This comes after the impact of a reduction of benefits including Council Tax Credit and an increase in income tax, national insurance and pension contributions.[9] A substantial 40 per cent increase in the main earner's gross income translates into a 7.2 per cent increase in household disposable income (after housing costs). Even an exceptionally large increase of 80 per cent in the income of the main earner translates only into a 14.4 per cent increase in household disposable income (after housing costs), which means just £86.60 more per week for the household of four.

As we move to other types of households and tenure, the problem of poor earnings retention remains, although with minor variations. For example, for the same proportionate increases in gross income, households that are privately renting will retain a smaller share than those that are socially renting, and the gap gets larger for relatively larger increases in gross income. Overall, relatively substantial increases in gross income for all kinds of low paid worker translate into limited increases in household disposable income: through more tax and less benefits, the low paid face an effective marginal tax rate of around 70 per cent. This greatly reduces the financial incentive to find a better job with more pay and/or more hours. If extra costs of transport or childcare are unavoidable with a new job, more gross pay may translate into less residual income.

Why the low paid need more than a pay rise

	Increase in disposable income for a single adult household in work		Increase in disposable income for 2 adults in work, 2 child household	
	Social renter (starting disposable income £11,839)	Private renter (starting disposable income £13,550)	Social renter (starting disposable income £32,078)	Private renter (starting disposable income £34,378)
20% gross income increase	2.8%	2.4%	3.6%	3.4%
40% gross income increase	8.2%	7.1%	7.2%	6.7%
60% gross income increase	14.2%	12.4%	10.8%	10.1%
80% gross income increase	17.1%	15.0%	14.4%	13.4%
100% gross income increase	25.6%	19.0%	20.2%	16.8%

Exhibit 5.2 Increases in gross income and disposable income (after housing costs) illustration for four types of households with starting income at the bottom of the distribution (for a Byker household in NE6 1AA).

Source: Derived from HMRC for tax and National Insurance thresholds and Turn2Us for Universal Credit, Child Benefit and Council Tax data (https://www.turn2us.org .uk/). Universal Credit data accessed in May 2022.

Note: Disposable income after housing costs is presented because as low income households gain more income from work, this will affect their entitlement to benefits that cover housing costs and Council Tax rebates. The data used to create the exhibits is available at https://foundationaleconomyresearch.com/index.php/ nothing-works-stats/.

These hard facts completely undermine the political classes' standard assumption that more better paid jobs will solve many of our problems. Here again we see a dual society and the limits of political class knowledge at a distance, which reflects the experience of middle and high income households who take for granted their own moderate to strong financial gains from work and often do not register that low income households live in a different world. Politicians and economists call for employability to get individuals into work and then better jobs for the low paid. But in a low wage society with extensive wage subvention, jobs and better jobs are not the only or the main levers for improved foundational liveability for many low income households. Other important considerations include more generous cash support systems for the many who cannot work; the redesign of the tax and benefits system to reduce marginal tax rates for the low paid; and ensuring access to foundational services and social infrastructure because foundational liveability does not rest solely on waged income.

It is striking that the political classes, that put so much emphasis on financial incentives to work, have constructed a system where the financial incentives to acquire a better paid job are so small for the several million employed households which were on Universal Credit in early 2020 before or after the Covid pandemic. There is no absence of work ethic or ambition amongst the vast majority of low income households. During the pandemic, many low paid key workers put themselves in harm's way in citizen-facing roles in health, care, public transport and food retailing, even without strong financial incentives to do so. Despite this revealed commitment, the same political classes were by 2022 saying it was important to resist 'irresponsible' pay claims by workers when 10 per cent plus inflation was squeezing residual income through higher energy and other essential costs. This rhetoric obscures the basic point that low income households would have to claim unfeasibly large wage increases, much higher than the rate of inflation, in order to get an increase in disposable income that compensates for rising prices. Inflation is a problem in the UK but the process is not a wage-price spiral led by wages, but a partial price-wage catch-up led by escalating prices.

5.2 The motoring poor in a car-dependent society

From the very variable financial rewards of work, we can now turn to the costs of working which have to be paid for out of household disposable income. If jobs are to be accessed and held, the costs in money and time are often considerable and can erode any residual income. Amongst these costs are the costs of commuting to work, which are often considerable and have major implications for restricting job choice in an increasingly car-dependent society where it is expensive to run a car. We focus on these issues because they have not been adequately recognised. To illustrate these points, here again we take Newcastle-upon-Tyne cases as illustrations because their story is broadly representative. Certainly, the cases illustrate the dilemmas of the two-earner low income household where running just one car is a major cost which stretches household finances.

The focus of this section is on the often neglected costs of travelling to work. But it should be remembered that this is only one of several major costs of working which eat into residual income. For those with young children, unless family can help, there will be costs of formal childcare. The high cost of formal childcare in the UK has been extensively documented in official literature, though the problems are not resolved. After taking into account state assistance with childcare costs, in 2020 the OECD calculated that childcare costs in the UK would take half of a woman's median full-time earnings for a two-earner family with two children requiring care.[10] The OECD then concluded that the costs of childcare were higher in the UK than in any other large, high income country. It is entirely understandable that low income groups in the UK make less use of formal childcare arrangements due to their unaffordability.

With travel to work costs (by car or public transport), the problem is that they cannot easily be reduced for longer distance commutes and can only be managed by restricting the choice of jobs to those closer to home. The car is key for employability in Newcastle and its edge of city employment sites. Half of the journeys to work are greater than 5 km and these longer commuting journeys typically require a car because they are irregular or orbital rather than radially in and out of the centre. If the high income household can afford a car for each working member, low income households are trapped in a dilemma. Here running even one car can become too expensive for the low income household, but not having a car can seriously limit employment opportunities because public transport is often not available or is inconvenient, slow or unreliable. Even where public transport is available then fares are often prohibitively high and have risen rapidly as we saw in the previous chapter.

Why the low paid need more than a pay rise

In current policy discussions, these themes are addressed under the label of 'transport disadvantage',[11] a broad term used to cover two sets of related issues. First, structural limitations with transportation systems and connectivity make certain journeys difficult or impossible, especially by public transport. Second, individual characteristics such as disability, work patterns, care responsibilities or income level can make public transport unusable and/or a private car unaffordable.[12] Transport disadvantage can give rise to transport poverty, as when households spend a significant amount of their income on running a car to access employment.[13] But the measurement of the extent and costs of transport disadvantage is more complicated than in the case of childcare because it involves putting together census data on the substantial distance many employees travel to work with data from other sources on the costs of car ownership and use.

London is a mega city of 10 million plus with large-scale radial commuting from suburbs to the centre using a dense public transport system. But beyond London, the country behaves quite differently, not least because public transport options are so much worse. Policy analysis has been slow to recognise the importance of post-1980 edge-of-town and city development which has created new employment sites, like business and retail parks that are designed around the car. The result is new live/work disconnects, so that almost nobody in the UK now lives in an old-fashioned work town or pit village with housing clustered around one or a few large workplaces. As with other provincial cities across the UK, Newcastle and its hinterland is a mosaic of job-rich and job-poor areas. The city centre acts as one employment pole, but since 1980 there has been substantial edge-of-town development of mono-functional industrial estates, business parks, retail parks, hospitals or universities situated on the car accessible periphery of the urban area or in 'off-roundabout' locations close to major routes.

The resulting disconnection between places of residence and the main employment sites is evidenced by the data on distance travelled to work. Data from the 2011 Census shows that just over half of the working residents (54 per cent) in the Newcastle local authority area commute more than 5 km or have no fixed workplace, and are likely to require either public transport or a car to get to work. This commute to work pattern is broadly similar in low and high income areas. The car is more convenient than public transport for reaching most employment sites from most residential areas, particularly when the whole city is accessible within a 20- to 40-minute drive (depending on traffic), regardless of where the household is located. From the Byker estate in the inner-city area to the Amazon logistics centre in the Jarrow industrial area it takes 20 minutes by car but 40 to 50 minutes by public transport, even without accounting for waiting time.[14]

The result is the primacy of the car as a means of travel to work across almost all parts of Newcastle and the surrounding urban areas, regardless of topography, transport infrastructure and household income. The car accounts for an average of 60 per cent or more of travel to work journeys across local authority areas of Newcastle, North Tyneside and Northumberland, and the story is much the same in other high and low income districts that we have studied. For half or more of urban jobs, convenient access to work locations and/or ability to work shift patterns depends on being able to drive and having car access.

This immediately excludes the one-quarter of UK adults who do not hold a full driving licence[15] from many job opportunities. For adults in this group, the cost of driving lessons and tests is a significant entry barrier to automobility. But the larger issue in low income households is whether and how to run a car, even one elderly second-hand car, as a way of accessing jobs which would otherwise be inaccessible.

For low income households in the bottom 30 per cent of the income distribution, the costs of purchase and running costs are very high in relation to their disposable income which will be in the range of £9,000 to £23,000.[16] As an illustration, consider in Exhibit 5.3 a low income household looking to buy a ten-year-old second-hand hatchback, something like a Vauxhall Astra or Ford Focus, whose annual running cost for fuel and other necessities was around £2,500 in 2021 rising to £3,000 in 2022. At the end of 2021, the cash price of a second-hand ten-year-old hatchback with three or four years of unexpired life is around £2,000. If credit is used through hire purchase[17] arranged by the dealer, the car will cost £3,000. As Exhibit 5.3 shows, the running costs of this car – tax, insurance, fuel and basic maintenance – would add £2,000 a year with petrol at £5.80 a gallon at the end of 2021. By late June 2022, petrol had risen to around £8.70 a gallon[18] and that petrol price increase had added £500 a year or £10 per week to the annual cost of running this car.

The costs of running a car mean that generally there is a positive relationship between income and car ownership. In Newcastle, we can see significant disparities in car ownership between households in relation to tenure and income level within one district. For example, taking social renting

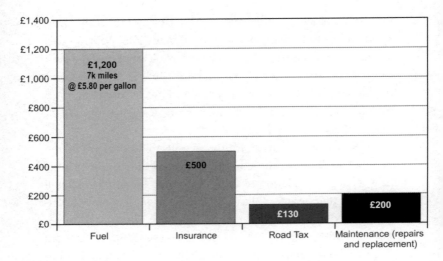

Exhibit 5.3 The annual cost of running a ten-year-old second-hand car, 2021. Total annual cost of running a car: £2,030 (£39.04 per week) (based on a second-hand, mid-range 1.4 petrol engine in Band D for road tax).

Source: RAC, 'Petrol and diesel prices in the UK: Latest fuel price data from the RAC' (accessed 29 June 2022). https://www.rac.co.uk/drive/advice/fuel-watch/. Costs are estimated for 2021. The cost of maintenance covers routine servicing but excludes large, unexpected bills. The data used to create the exhibits is available at https://foundationaleconomyresearch.com/index.php/nothing-works-stats/.

households which are generally low income, car ownership ranges from 23 per cent in North Shields to 45 per cent in Blyth Cowpen. In contrast, 95 per cent of owner occupiers with mortgages and higher incomes in these same areas have at least one car. Furthermore, two-car ownership is strikingly rare amongst low income households for obvious reasons. In Newcastle's low income districts only 3 per cent to 7 per cent of households had two or more cars or vans; by way of contrast in relatively affluent suburban districts, 25 per cent of all house-holds in Whitley Bay and 34 per cent of households in Long Horsley have two or more cars.[19]

At UK national level, with households ranged according to gross income, there is a striking pattern of variation in car own-ership according to decile position (Exhibit 5.4). In 2018 the percentage of households running a car increases with income from 35 per cent in decile 1 to 83 per cent in decile 5. In the middle of the income distribution at decile 5, only 25 per cent of households have two or more cars but in the top three deciles, 61 per cent to 74 per cent have two or more cars. Here again, the UK dualism of unthinking comfort and pinched necessity is manifest. Middle and upper income households live in a world of discretionary car ownership because they can afford one car for every working adult, with obvious consequences for the household's carbon footprint even if their cars are newer and cleaner. Many low income households live in a world of 'forced car ownership' in urban areas where studies have shown that the level of such forced ownership is related to the lack of alter-native public transport options, including for travel to work.[20]

If the annual running cost of a second-hand car was around £2,500 in late 2021 (rising to £3,000 by mid-2022) and pur-chase inevitably adds extra costs, then one car is all that two-earner, low income households can afford. And we would add that in two-earner households, forced car ownership has gen-dered consequences which disproportionately limit access to work for women. When there are two workers and only one car, typically the male takes the car to work in full-time employment and the woman walks to work or uses a short public transport journey to access the proximity labour market. This effect is so

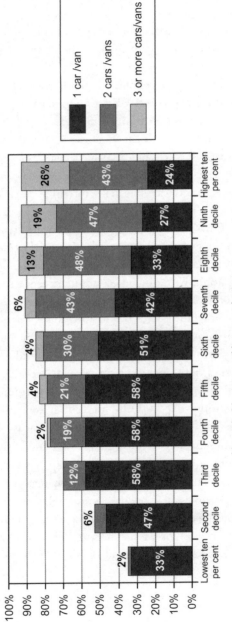

Exhibit 5.4 UK household car ownership by income decile, 2018.

Source: Office for National Statistics (January 2019), 'Percentage of households with cars by income group, tenure and household composition: Table A47'. https://www.ons.gov.uk/peoplepopulationandcommunity/personalandhouseholdfinances/expenditure/datasets/percentageofhouseholdswithc arsbyincomegrouptenureandhouseholdcompositionuktablea47.

Note: Households are organised by gross household income. The data used to create the exhibits is available at https://foundationaleconomyresearch .com/index.php/nothing-works-stats/.

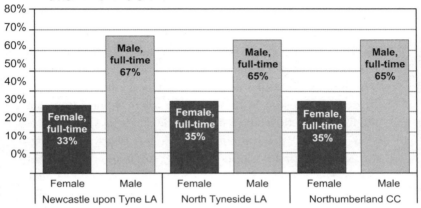

(a) Full-time employees travelling 5 km or more as a share of all full-time employees split by gender

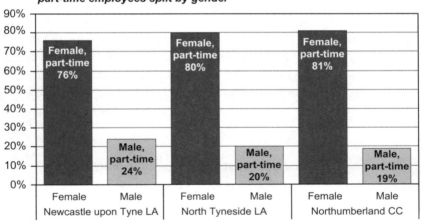

(b) Part-time employees travelling less than 5 km as a share of all part-time employees split by gender

Exhibit 5.5 Analysis of distance travelled to work in North East England.

Source: Census 2011, Nomis. https://www.nomisweb.co.uk/query/select/getdatasetbytheme.asp ?theme=75. The data used to create the exhibits is available at https://foundationaleconomy research.com/index.php/nothing-works-stats/.

strong that it is manifest not just in low income areas but right across whole local authority areas which include a mosaic of high, medium and low income areas. As Exhibit 5.5 (a and b) shows, in the Newcastle local authority area, women account for 79 per cent of part-time workers, and 76 per cent of all part-time workers travelling less than 5 km to work are women. The findings are similar in two adjacent local authority areas of North Tyneside and Northumberland where women are much less likely to be travelling longer distances to work.

If the foundational problem is transport disadvantage, and for some households transport poverty, the solution should not be to ensure more cars in lower income households. The policy response needs to address the complex causes of transport disadvantage, including the location of work and leisure activities in relation to household location, and the cost and quality of public transport. These should be priorities for households at all income levels so that there is less dependence on car-based mobility to reduce emissions and improve air quality and public health. These are not quick fixes, of course, but are consistent with strengthening the pillars of foundational liveability through improved essential services, and part of a necessary long-term shift in the focus and direction of politics and policy.

5.3 Social infrastructure: why it matters and why it is in such a mess

This section of our chapter takes up the challenge of answering some basic questions about social infrastructure which includes hard infrastructure like a library, high street or swimming pool and the soft infrastructure of group activities such as a parent and toddler group, a choir or a youth club. First, how and why does this social infrastructure matter so that it figures as the third pillar of foundational liveability alongside essential services and residual income? Second, how and why is the UK provision of accessible and affordable social infrastructure in such a mess? In the context of this chapter's argument, why does it matter that individuals in low income households have free or cheap hard and soft infrastructure so they can 'be together' in ways which allow physical exercise and cultural or creative expression?

Social infrastructure provision is currently attracting some attention on the grounds that it is necessary for a good life. Thus, we have the Bennett Institute report which defines social infrastructure as 'the amenities and spaces that bring people together to build meaningful relationships, such as cafes, libraries and lidos'.[21] Similarly, Eric Klinenberg's book relates social infrastructure to social science understandings by defining it as 'the physical conditions that determine whether social capital develops'.[22] But it is easier for policy makers to see how and why households need and must have a margin of income after paying for housing, transport, food and utilities, or how and why accessible and affordable health or transport services matter.[23] These first two pillars of foundational liveability are about provision and systems that are manifestly necessary for human survival in a modicum of comfort and dignity. Social infrastructure, as the third pillar of foundational liveability, is about systems which are relevant for human flourishing through thriving social relations and positive emotional states.

How then do we think about the foundational liveability value of social infrastructure? Here it is useful to start from

Amartya Sen's argument that development is not about more resources with market value and a greater choice of goods and services. What matters for Sen is the citizens' freedom to 'live a life they have reason to value', which of course presupposes that individuals have agency so that 'a person has the ability to do or be certain things that she has reason to value'.[24] In these terms, the realisation of freedom is then a matter of capabilities and functioning.

Building on Iris Marion Young,[25] foundational thinking goes beyond classic liberal thinking, which focuses mainly on rights and abstracts from business models and power structures. The foundational emphasis is that any discussion of individual and collective capability must be connected to the material and institutional systems that underpin human agency. From this perspective, freedom depends on reliance systems delivering essential services and social infrastructure which can then sustain all the various forms of individual expression and sociability.

That raises a further question of how and why we should value the infrastructure systems that sustain individual expression and sociability. The current academic literature on social infrastructure emphasises socio-economic outcomes and argues that social infrastructure matters because it makes economy and society work in ways that sustain the polity, economy and society. The second edition of Klinenberg's book is subtitled *How to Build a More Equal and United Society* because 'robust social infrastructure, does not just protect our democracy, it contributes to economic growth'.[26] The Bennett Institute report recognises 'economic value' through town centre regeneration, boosting skills and employment, 'social value' through community resilience and integration and 'civic value' through identity and political participation.

The foundational approach to the value of individual and collective expression and sociability is broader because our argument is that this is an end in itself as a fundamental component of what makes life fulfilling and healthy. The background here is that a large part of the population is not in a good mental or physical state with repercussions on how they are able to contribute to household, community and social life. In 2017–18, 7.3 million adults or 17 per cent of the English adult population were on mood changing anti-depressant medication.[27] Obesity has more or less doubled in the adult population since the early 1990s, so that by 2018 some 28 per cent of the English adult population were obese with prospects of morbidity and quality of life problems in their later years.[28] This is not about rights but about how a substantial minority of citizens find everyday life oppressive and/or engage in behaviours which are self-harming.

Considering the mess we are in, as explored in this book, it is hardly surprising that the UK has so many depressed or self-harming citizens. Against this background, social infrastructure is important because it sustains socialisation, physical activity and creative expression, which can all have direct and measurable effects on the mental and physical health of individuals.

- Socialisation: In general, isolated individuals have worse mental and physical health conditions than people who socialise and are part of positive social networks.[29] The evidence on this topic is mounting with recent epidemiological evidence showing that 'an active social life is one of the strongest predictors of longevity and good health',[30] 'with women's lives prolonged by five years and men's by six years'.[31]

- Physical activity: Physical exercise is linked to positive health outcomes, and nearly 40 per cent of the adult population is not 'physically active' on the official UK definition. Exercise is not simply about cardiovascular fitness. Physical activity can reduce the incidence of certain types of cancer (breast cancer, colorectal cancer, prostate cancer) potentially by up to 40 per cent while also being crucial to surviving cancer after treatment where prospective studies show it leads to increases in survivorship by 50 to 60 per cent.[32] There are many other areas where physical exercise has profound effects on our health: exercise can prevent falls,[33] which are a leading cause of injury-related mortality and morbidity in older people. Exercise can also prevent and treat depression, which is a leading cause of workdays lost with skyrocketing collective costs.[34]

- Creative expression: It has been long established in psychology and pedagogy that creative expression – including in play, arts, crafts and science – has positive effects on mental health and human development.[35] This point is widely accepted in the case of children, but in adults the importance of creative activities is less recognised. Yet, recent studies[36] confirm its importance and its indirect implications for physical health. The growing field of psychoneuroimmunology[37] is uncovering a strong connection between emotional states and diseases, hence creative activities influencing mental states can also have positive effects on our physical states.

In all these ways, social infrastructure is a key support of individuals' health and fulfilment, creating the necessary preconditions for positive contribution in the household and, more broadly, in social and political life. On this basis, access to good quality infrastructure is directly critical for foundational liveability, alongside essential services and residual income whose direct effects are more obvious.

It is therefore important to consider how we might have more of this good thing. Klinenberg's book has no sustained policy section and the question of how to renew the decaying US social infrastructure is dealt with briefly in his conclusion. The Bennett Institute report has a more substantial seven pages on policy. The recommendations here are general and focus on, for example, new institutions, including introduce a social infrastructure fund, start to collect data on the topic, establish social infrastructure as a category of investment for the new National Infrastructure Bank and support local authorities in developing a social infrastructure strategy. If we are to get any further than this from a foundational liveability point of view, we must think more analytically about the diverse forms of social infrastructure provision, the historical development of that provision and its business models and how it has culminated in the current UK crisis in tax-funded provision of public goods.

The starting point has to be that many different actors – community groups, social and private entrepreneurs, not-for-profits, faith organisations and local authorities – are involved in the daily production and reproduction of social infrastructure for households. And, in making sense of all this, two points stand out.

- On the supply side, free or cheaply accessible provision is associated with public or civic provision because private providers will usually need to recover their capital costs with a margin on turnover from customers. Contrast a theme park whose private owner charges via entry tickets and a public park maintained at public expense from local authority tax revenue. Or again, contrast a gym or swimming pool in a public leisure centre with a private gym that charges a subscription.
- On the demand side, high income districts can to some extent sustain private social infrastructure because residents can pay for it. An affluent district will always have an infrastructure of gyms, music venues, attractive cafes and restaurants and bookshops. With respect to some categories of social infrastructure then, higher income households can realise the market citizenship ideal through private consumption. Depending on time and place, there may also be publicly provided parks and libraries because high income districts generate more tax revenue. By way of contrast, in low income districts in Europe and North America, community self-provision, publicly funded provision and charity provision are much more common and relevant in supplying or maintaining community centres, youth centres, playgrounds, working men's clubs and suchlike.

The privatisation of the material infrastructure of pipe and cable utilities after 1979 was a damaging project because the whole society suffers from under-investment in the reliance systems that provide utility services like water or electricity distribution. The privatisation of social infrastructure by the closure and run down of public facilities in our own time is a divisive project because high income districts can to some extent switch to private provision (including people driving themselves to places) while low income districts must rely on community self-provision and local government funding. The problem in the UK by the 2020s is that local authority capital and revenue funding for social infrastructure is increasingly hard to find and community self-provision depends on activists with organisational capacity including for fundraising. So, closure or decay are the norms.

It is important not to exaggerate the achievements of municipal provision through 'gas and water socialism' in the late nineteenth century. The few available historical studies suggest[38] that the initial development of social infrastructure in Europe and North America owes much to community self-organisation because nineteenth-century municipalities understandably prioritised what makes people survive ahead of what makes people thrive. Many English towns and cities by the late nineteenth century ran portfolios of trading companies variably including public services like water, town gas, electricity and tramways.[39] In some cases, the profits from town gas were applied to finance prestige new-build projects like Manchester Town Hall. But generally, the policy was to break even with the ratepayers' dividend coming in the form of locally available services at a reasonable price.[40] By implication, around 1900, a local tax surplus from rates on property was more important than cross-subsidy from trading services in funding social infrastructure.

Equally, it is important to be realistic about the potential and capacity of 'new municipalism(s)' to fund social infrastructure in the UK. Here new municipal experiments may represent a 'newly politicised and radical reformist orientation towards the local state'[41] but external constraint and limited internal capability effectively exclude UK municipalities from cash generative trading businesses which could supplement local tax income and central grants. Profitable utilities like water and broadband are in the hands of private monopolists and out of reach of enterprising local authorities. As we note in Chapter 6, outsourced services can be taken back into control as Liverpool has done with Streetscene Services, but services like refuse collection and street cleaning are at best only marginally profitable and also come with pension liabilities.[42] The losses of more than £65 million incurred on energy intermediation by Bristol and Nottingham[43] suggest risk investment is best avoided because councils lack the necessary judgement and governance.

The business model reality is that the capital and revenue funding for social infrastructure in the UK has to come from local taxes and central grants in aid, and that requires a discretionary surplus after local authorities have met their statutory duties for adults and children. Since the post-2010 austerity cuts in central funding, the available surplus has been grossly inadequate, especially in low income local authorities. Hence the closed youth clubs and libraries and neglected public parks. According to CIPFA, library spend was cut by 30 per cent over the austerity decade of the 2010s and nearly one-fifth of library branches were closed.[44] The sense of neglect, underfunding and falling apart is pervasive and the latest manifestation is the threat of swimming pool closure as many of the municipal pools constructed in the 1960s and 1970s reach the end of their useful life, and the rest struggle to afford their energy bills.[45]

The immediate priority in the UK is reversing the austerity cuts of the 2010s in central government grants to local authorities. These cuts dramatically reduced the municipal surpluses available for support of hard and soft infrastructure and (as we noted in Section 3.3 of Chapter 3) did so in an unequal way so that low GVA urban areas of greatest need suffered the greatest cuts. The UK needs an explicit return to central government needs-based grants which especially recognised the extra needs of low income municipalities including for social infrastructure funding. Extra funds could also result from reform of local taxation because the property rates system does not tap local income or wealth; while recognising that inequalities in the availability of local tax revenue need to be addressed through central government allocations. Reforms of taxation and funding mechanisms need to be connected to positive and ambitious politics and policies that directly improve foundational liveability through the three pillars. The political case for prioritising social infrastructure is that it is highly visible, locally valued and already to some extent connects with community organisations. And prioritising social infrastructure is less of a large step if we connect it with central government starter, stealth and switch policies as recommended in Chapter 6. This would take us towards policies like a national public parks fund and a solidly funded, nationwide social prescribing system in NHS primary care.

PART IV

What to do

Introduction to Part IV

The crisis of foundational liveability is acute, but it is not new. We are in the later stages of a chronic and worsening 20-year situation, the direct result of the failure of the market citizenship project over 40 years. The UK political classes have generally refused to recognise all this, and the result is a policy quagmire centred on ends like 'levelling up' and means like 'devolution', where policy makers can neither achieve their aims nor admit defeat. The cost-of-living crisis simply exposes the inadequacy of mainstream thinking. At the same time, the necessary reset is very difficult because rebuilding the pillars of foundational liveability and rebalancing private and collective consumption is a generational project that does not easily fit into an electoral cycle of four years. Equally, the project does not fit the model of electoral competition because the project of rebuilding and rebalancing is one which Labour would have to share with other parties, especially the Greens and Scottish and Welsh nationalists, who are all in different ways the residuary legatees of social democracy. So what is to be done politically?

Chapter 6

What to do? Politics and policy

Introduction

This book has criticised the policy aims of faster growth and higher wages as economically unattainable and/or irrelevant to the current crisis of deteriorating liveability for low and middle income groups in a society which is aggravating nature and climate emergency. The irony is that we do not have enough of the right goods and services for our households in a society whose consumption and production systems are wasting the planet. The problems are serious and embedded because the acute foundational liveability crisis overlays chronic problems which successive governments have exacerbated with inept economic policies.

The foundational liveability aim is that households on low and middling incomes should not suffer constraining disadvantage in present day society. More positively, the aim is that many more diverse households from across the income range should have what Amartya Sen and others have described as the freedom to pursue the lives they have reason to value. This policy agenda is different from one-dimensional mandating of universal minima providing basic income or basic services or social infrastructure. It is about reversing decline and putting our society back onto an upward trajectory of foundational liveability by better provision of essential services *and* social infrastructure *and* residual income.

The challenge then is what is to be done politically, by whom and how to deliver improved foundational liveability by rebuilding all three pillars of liveability. We can begin by discounting the romantic hope that central government can or will deliver heroic resolution in one or two terms. Heroic resolution requires an incoming UK government, with an intellectual vision and a clear popular mandate that captures and holds the central state while delivering a new settlement; or at least changing the Overton window around what is politically thinkable and doable. Romantics can point to the Attlee and Thatcher Governments in the UK who did achieve some of this shift in vision, mandate and possibility. But both were special cases: in 1945, an organised working class could not be cheated of reward for its war effort, as it was after 1918; in 1979, the task was breaking up a settlement with benefit of the windfall fiscal gain of North Sea oil.

Successive economic crises in high income countries since 2008 have manifestly led not to system-wide change but to deepening mess without central government addressing the sector specific problems exposed by these crises. After the Great Financial Crisis, uncontrolled credit creation continued, and the low interest rate regime averted recession and mass unemployment by boosting asset prices and feeding the 'everything bubble'. After the Covid-19 pandemic, under-resourcing of disorganised public health continues and, in the UK, unmanageable treatment backlogs have built up in the acute hospital system. Responses to the overlapping food and energy emergencies in 2022–23 are probably taking us further away from any kind of balance between security of supply and environmental responsibility.

This political experience of ineffectuality in all high income countries feeds electoral division and scepticism about centrist politicians who effectively promise, 'vote for us and we will fix the economy for you'. The challenge in this chapter is to shift from economic to political analysis and address two key issues. First, how do political processes frustrate the political classes so that mainstream policy promises end in disappointment? Second, how could an alternative politics deliver the policies that can improve foundational liveability?

From a foundational point of view, politics has some key characteristics of a service activity with a front office and a back office. As in other service activities, back office processes both limit what can be delivered and are an opportunity for innovators. In national systems of multi-level government and dispersed governance, the central state's ability to exert control and clean up messes is limited by many breaks and resistances. Mainstream policies are front office promises which deliver little because they ignore these back office constraints. Government and opposition are united in the pretence that they have agency when they have a delivery problem.

But how to do better politically and deliver improved foundational liveability? Our recommendation is for adaptive reuse which delivers slow, steady progress starting from what is/where we are at, recognising constraints and developing workarounds. The descriptive term adaptive reuse is borrowed from the French architects Lacaton and Vassal who specialise in the refurbishment of failed modernist developments as a first best, responsible, creative and effective way of working with what exists. Demolition and new build is rejected because this disrupts social communities, has a high embodied carbon cost and the next grand design is likely to create new problems not anticipated at the design stage.

If the aim is increased foundational liveability, the central state cannot be bypassed politically because so much local delivery of essentials is centrally formatted. Of course, the central state cannot in one or two terms fix the current mess which is the result of 40 years of misguided efforts. But there are creative opportunities to address the foundational liveability crisis and make a meaningful difference to households by working around back office constraints at and below the central state level. Practically, this means central state starter and stealth policies to address service provision and income deficiencies. Equally necessary are switch policies which pass the initiative from central state to other actors and encourage distributed social innovation so that bottom-up initiative can meet top-down support.

Thus, the foundational approach is to shift attention from policy and front office promises (which generally cannot be delivered) and add focus on politics as back office processes with the opportunity for workarounds that increase the deliverable. Policy and politics are understood through the lens of the front office/back office distinction in service activities and in the belief that adaptive reuse has potential in rebuilding the three pillars of foundational liveability. From this point of view, the political domain has a dual character as a set of both constraints and opportunities. Those constraints that frustrate mainstream central state policies for economic growth and public service reform can also be opportunities for a central state that presses its own adaptive reuse policies and empowers other actors to deliver foundational liveability. This argument is developed in three sections of this chapter: Section 6.1 introduces our grey skies thinking about back office constraints on mainstream policies; Section 6.2 proposes central state policies of adaptive reuse; and Section 6.3 considers how distributed social innovation depends on alliances for change.

6.1 Back office constraints on central state policies

Politics is many things, but from an organisational perspective, it can be seen as a service activity which, like other service activities, from restaurants to banks, has a front office and back office. The front office is about the customer facing part of the operation which the customer sees and directly experiences. The back office has the out-of-sight processes and operations that determine what can be delivered, which can be both a constraint on delivering front office promises and an opportunity for innovation. The back office will typically include internal service operations and external links to independent providers, with many back office functions outsourced. The problem of present-day politics is its preoccupation with devising front office promises to get elected, while being insufficiently focused on analysing the back office processes. These determine what can be delivered and therefore also act as a driver of credibility in terms of re-election prospects.

The front office/back office distinction is most obvious in a restaurant. The menu constitutes the front office offer, and behind that there is the kitchen, the cellar and a supply chain which determine what can be delivered front of house on the plate when the chef calls service at the pass. It is relatively easy to construct an attractive offer on a menu but much more difficult to organise a kitchen and supply chain so that fastidious design can be consistently delivered to a price point. That is why Michelin stars are hard to get and so many high-end restaurants lose money. The interactions are different in something like internet banking, but the basic principle of back office constraint applies, especially to the business systems of large, complex organisations like UK high street banks whose legacy software prevents delivery of new services.

This front office/back office distinction is obviously important in politics. It is not difficult to come up with attractive public facing policies that promise much but it is much more difficult to organise the political processes for implementation and delivery at scale for intended results. This is because delivery is dominated by actors, financial and power relations and pre-existing organisational capabilities that constrain or limit as well as open possibilities. This is especially so if we want to change the complex reliance systems behind foundational service provision, such as health and care. Here there would typically be incomplete system knowledge, limited understanding of what will work and how, and in many cases actors and processes that can be difficult to change. Moreover, much that matters is outside the one system when healthcare is connected to food, housing and much more. If we had a choice, we would not start from here.

None of this is a major problem for the radical right political actors and forces whose successes threaten to displace or transform the centre right and centre left parties which have been the established parties of central governments in Europe since 1945. This kind of new right politics – from Trump to Brexit in the Anglosphere – is always front office dominated. Whatever animates the electorate will flavour electoral campaigns which aim to capture the central state with an opportunist electoral pitch. When in power the new right will not deliver for the majority and increasingly nothing works. But that is no insuperable obstacle to winning the next election because their economic transformations are about meaningless slogans – *Make America Great Again* or *Take Back Control* – with identity and culture war issues used to distract the electorate.

If the centre left and centre right are not to be displaced or move onto this dismal terrain, they need to address politics as process and figure out how to deliver something meaningful on foundational liveability within back office constraints. We cannot in policy terms avoid the central state in countries like the UK which are highly centralised. While wage income, foundational services and social infrastructure are all locally delivered to households, the earning of income and the provision of foundational services and social infrastructure all take place within a central state framework which structures local delivery. But it is easy then to jump from this observation to overestimating central state power to deliver and failing to think through what is deliverable.

The first point here has to be that it is a mistake to suppose that central state politicians are engaged in conversation with an informed and engaged electorate. Central state elections are won and lost according to how national moods are tapped by party narratives encapsulated in cheap slogans and embodied in party leaders who must project an aura of competence while contending with disruptive events. Hence the endless demands by sympathetic political commentators for some kind of 'compelling narrative' to underpin the policy offer of opposition leaders.[1] Polling and focus groups track how electors relate not just to policies but to personalities, because in every UK election since 1979, the party leader with the highest approval ratings has won the election.[2]

In consequence well-thought-through economic and social radicalism will often be misunderstood and undervalued by the electorate and reactionary policies can be endorsed or ignored. And there is nothing new about this. In the 1959 UK general election voters rejected Labour which offered a National Superannuation Scheme with retirement on half pay for all except the low paid who would get two-thirds.[3] Instead, they returned the Tories whose offer was in effect low, flat-rate state benefits and private pensions for only half the workforce. The same electorate neither knew nor cared when in its next term the Tory government stopped the public purchase of land at unimproved value and incidentally completely undermined the business model of the new town development corporations.

The novelty since 2010 or thereabouts is that the electorate's superficiality is increasingly reflected in volatile voting behaviour in high income countries. The collapse of private sector unionism and the end of the stolid mass membership party have everywhere created electorates which are increasingly untethered from settled party loyalties. In consequence, politicians are increasingly preoccupied with polls and focus groups which allow alignment of policy promises with electoral sentiment and values. Hence the audience for Claire Ainsley's argument[4] that Labour can win electorally if it adopts policies that fit with widely shared elector values of family, fairness, decency and hard work. The problem is that other parties are playing this game using the same poll and focus group techniques, and values like family and hard work are not the property of one party.

If parties are searching for promises the electorate will buy, the mainstream preoccupation with promises of higher economic growth is peculiar because more than half their electorate does not understand their technocratic national income language. In a 2015 UK survey by YouGov, only 39 per cent chose the correct definition of GDP from a short list and 25 per cent ticked 'don't know'.[5] This result was broadly confirmed in a subsequent 2020 survey which added that in focus groups 'the vast majority of ... participants demonstrated little or no understanding of GDP'.[6] As ethnographers like Anna Killick and Jack Mosse[7] have demonstrated, the dominant popular understanding of the economy is as a pot of money. This is exactly the opposite of modern monetary theory or classic Keynesianism and plays in favour of austerity and sound finance in every crisis.

These problems of communication and the fading prospect of achieving higher growth in the 2020s are not so far reflected in the promises of the political classes. Capturing and holding the central state is now a remote possibility for the centre left in mainland European countries like France and Italy where social democracy has been marginalised. But it remains a real possibility for the centre left through coalition in Germany and through first-past-the-post in the UK. As we noted in Chapter 1, under its present leadership, a newly elected Labour government would come into office promising and planning to deliver higher growth. The mainstream constraint argument can be pulled into focus by considering what an incoming

Labour government could and could not deliver in one term after a 2024 or 2025 general election. Our argument is that constraints will not only frustrate higher economic growth promises but also limit central state sponsored pro-liveability reform in other policy areas.

In economic policy, any large-scale fiscal move to stimulus through unfunded borrowing (for capital or revenue purposes) or any radical change in the tax regime would be limited by adverse financial market reaction. The UK has a trade deficit and a pile of government debt, with the interest rate on 25 per cent of that debt index linked to inflation. In the first quarter of 2022, the UK current account deficit reached £51.7 billion or 8.3 per cent of GDP[8] and the ratio of debt to GDP rose above 100 per cent after the Covid pandemic and before the costs of energy price subvention kicked in. The trade deficit has increased sharply with the rising price of energy and food. The financial market's reaction to Kwasi Kwarteng's September 2022 mini-budget shows the markets have a limited tolerance for reactionary fiscal experiments and they may be equally averse to progressive experiments.

Furthermore, the government does not control monetary policy which is the responsibility of an independent Bank of England formally charged with curbing inflation and informally responsible for preventing a sustained, substantial fall in the pound. With inflation embedded or the pound falling, the Bank would have no choice but to raise interest rates regardless of disruptive domestic consequences for households, firms and government. In 2016 Mark Carney, as Governor of the Bank of England, observed that the UK depended on 'the kindness of strangers' to finance the current account deficit of a consumption-led economy. These constraints are now very real, and the risk is that any Labour fiscal experiment would end in something like the French austerity watershed and François Mitterrand's 'tournant de la rigueur' in 1983, when progressive social policies were abandoned.[9] Expansionary fiscal policy could not deliver for the French Socialists because the French government did not control the Banque de France's monetary policy when the position of the franc in the European Monetary System was under external pressure.

Practically, the financial market and institutional constraints are such that they will most likely prevent (rather than cut short) any radical fiscal experiment. An incoming Labour government would internalise expectations of fiscal responsibility, make no abrupt change and adopt continuity policies on tax and spend in an economy scarred by recession, inflation and austerity. If an incoming Labour government cannot and does not fund costly, bold fiscal policies, then the issue is what can be done to address the foundational liveability crisis without immediately spending large amounts of money. The problem here is that at every turn there are central state capability limits and opposition from vested interests.

Implementation of a foundational liveability programme that improves essential services, social infrastructure and residual income, while paying attention to the nature and climate emergency, requires a central state machine that can set and enforce standards, plan material infrastructure programmes and organise activities. But the organisational capacity to deal with complex problems is lacking in the UK where we have limited expertise in central ministries, design and appraisal by consultants, execution by hierarchies of contractors and subcontractors and behaviour change resting on often short-lived and uncoordinated financial incentives for magic bullet solutions.

For example, better insulated and more airtight homes are an urgent priority for limiting emissions, improving health and improving residual income: UK homes account for 15 per cent of greenhouse gas emissions and, on a frosty winter day, UK homes lose heat up to three times faster than German homes.[10] The limits of the English system of owner decisions incentiv-ised by grants are demonstrated by grant-funded insulation of cavity walls which has produced all kinds of problems with damp and mould. Moreover, 20 per cent of English dwell-ings are pre-1918 construction with solid walls requiring more expensive insulation methods.[11] And the limits of insulation as a standalone solution are demonstrated by research which shows a rebound effect in energy usage so that gas consumption is sometimes only reduced for the first year or two after the instal-lation of loft or cavity wall insulation.[12]

Control of privatised utilities is another priority for the foundational liveability agenda. But large-scale renational-isation of utilities is likely to be prohibitively expensive if current owners are to be compensated. The alternative of regulation is not straightforward. The problem here is that completely ineffectual UK regulators have operated with an economics-based understanding of markets without any accounting understanding of how extractive capitalist own-ers behave. And these owners will defend their sheltered positions against the threat of public interest reform that threatens the extraction of cash and/or loading of balance sheets with debt.

For example, the energy regulator encouraged competition through new entrant intermediary firms without regard to balance sheet resource or any requirement to hedge against price movements. Consumers had to pick up the tab when the companies fell over and the cost of bailing out one large supplier, Bulb, had risen to £6.5 billion by November 2022 (more than £200 per household), the largest bailout since that of the Royal Bank of Scotland in 2008.[13] In the English water industry, the regulator failed to restrain the financial engineering of extractive investors who by 2020 had distributed £50 billion in profits and financed investment by loading the firms with £47 billion of debt,[14] so that an estimated 20 per cent of the average household bill for water and sewerage now covers interest and dividend payments.[15] Environmental improvements, like limiting fertiliser or slurry run-off into water courses[16] add cost and will be obstructed by another set of vested interests complaining about the regulatory burdens.

Under pressure from investors, funds and large corporates work their business models for shareholder value. The market citizenship project produced not low prices for consumers but low risk, monopoly positions in privatised utilities and outsourced services with a lien on household income or taxpayer revenue. Such sheltered positions are hugely valuable compared with high risk positions in competitive and fast changing markets. They will be defended resolutely by the lobbying and PR which is an adjunct of sheltered business. The number employed in UK public relations increased from 38,000 in 2010 to 71,000 in 2022[17] and much media reporting relies heavily on corporate press releases.

It is difficult to control extractive investors who resist change and can outsmart regulators[18] when politicians, media and the public are not engaged until things go spectacularly wrong. But the behaviour of under-regulated corporations can become a public issue, as it has in the case of private water companies in England. Here civil society, some media and politicians understand that large profits have been made and distributed while regulators have failed to sustain let alone improve water quality and the companies have underinvested in renewing ageing infrastructure so as to limit sewerage discharges and anticipate water shortage.[19] One important issue is what to do in such cases when regulatory failure and corporate breach of public interest have become public issues.

We have previously advocated social licensing[20] whereby government would impose explicit social obligations on for-profit and not-for-profit providers of foundational goods and services. But, realistically, the central state, national and regional governments currently do not have the capability to negotiate and enforce social licences. Hence, we now propose an adaptive reuse reform of regulation to shift the focus from regulated returns and competition in two ways. First, lead with physical requirements for service provision and environmental clean-up, recognising these will reduce financial returns and lead to restructuring and corporate retreat by those who cannot meet return expectations and deliver public interest service. Second, on the financial side, hire accountants who can police extraction and balance sheet manipulation by fund investors and corporate investors. The public interest in the utilities requires a more active version of the forensic financial analysis that is providing 'leverage' for successful trade union negotiations in the private sector.[21]

The problem for the Labour Party in the UK (and by extension the international dilemma of the centre left) is that, if and when a right-wing government loses a central state election, the centre left may inherit office, but it will struggle to use and hold power in a world of multiple constraints on its mainstream policy options for economic growth and foundational liveability. But, if these constraints are recognised, that is no reason to despair. As in the case of water supply, there are opportunities for workarounds in some policy areas. The next two sections of this chapter broaden the argument to sketch a central state strategy of adaptive reuse where the central state could work with a revitalised trade union movement and local providers of essential services to ensure that top-down connects with bottom-up distributed social innovation.

This overlaps with a long-term project of rebuilding lost capabilities. In the heroic first period of foundational provision between 1870 and 1950, central government learnt how to organise utility networks, operate unemployment insurance, distribute old age pensions, organise hospital and school provision, plan new towns and suchlike. This capability was built up over more than eight decades just as it has been slowly destroyed over the last five decades. What we need now is to rebuild this back office capability in new forms which are appropriate to the mid-twenty-first-century world in that they are less bureaucratically state centred and deal with new challenges like adaptation to climate change. How, for example, can local authorities and housing associations work together to organise housing retrofit around expert survey and impartial advice? This is the foundational equivalent of mainstream supply side policies but geared in the foundational case to rebuilding our collective capability for action (not trying to make the market work better). But shifting constraints by improving back office processes won't deliver meaningful foundational liveability improvements in a five-year term. Therefore, in the next section, we turn to the opportunity of workarounds.

6.2 Adaptive reuse opportunities: starter, stealth and switch policies

Back office processes are paradoxically both a constraint and an opportunity. As a constraint, they frustrate what a central state government with mainstream policies can achieve in one term, making it difficult to secure a second term. But the same processes can be an opportunity for a central state government with an adaptive reuse strategy which uses starter and stealth policies to open closed issues, plus switch policies which empower and enable other actors to take the initiative and effectively deliver what the central state cannot. Before turning to establish the nature and potential of such policies, it is helpful to explain adaptive reuse and how it fits into the foundational approach which starts from the basis that the solutions of the last generation often become the problems of the next.

The many socio-technic systems delivering foundational goods and services including health, utilities and public

transport were a huge modernist achievement of the 1870–
1950 period,[22] which came with all kinds of limits and unintended consequences. The foundational liveability machine of
the 1950s and 1960s was patriarchal and on a growth trajectory
that was in every way unsustainable because more than half
our emissions now come from foundational provision, especially food, transport and energy. Instead of intelligent adaptation, the UK after 1979 pursued market citizenship. Under
Thatcher and Blair, as factories were demolished, new build
created edge-of-town retail and off-roundabout owner occupier
estates while the neglected urban fabric became increasingly
unfit for purpose. Rather like the social housing tenants of a
neglected 1970s tower block, UK households are now living in
a failed modernist experiment.

Hence the relevance of *adaptive reuse* rather than a grand
design for demolition and rebuilding.[23] The term adaptive
reuse is borrowed from the French architects Anne Lacaton
and Jean-Philippe Vassal[24] who resisted French government
programmes of the 2000s for demolishing post-war social
housing developments.[25] Their response was 'never demolish,
never remove or replace, always add, transform, and reuse'.
Rebuilding to a new design has a high embodied carbon cost[26]
and will design in unintended new problems. But adaptive
reuse can fix issues for existing users and modify structures to
sustain new uses and accommodate new users. This can be not
simply as a response to existing conditions but in anticipation
of future changes like nature and climate crisis, which require
new kinds of resilience.

In adaptive reuse, progress involves multiple small transi-
tions which move us beyond the limited vision of our earlier

constructions. In foundational systems like health or care, the constructions are less physical structures and more the organisation of people, things and money flows. The principle is that what already exists provides the basis from which we must start and what we should adapt, extend and improve. Stopping doing things that are damaging and dysfunctional is often a very good first step. The adaptive reuse process is a kind of Lévi-Straussian bricolage which uses what is to hand rather than goal driven science and engineering which has the freedom to construct tools and instruments. Or again, the outcome of adaptive reuse is the socio-political equivalent of Kaizen in the classic Japanese factory, that is, continuous small improvement. The Kaizen metaphor is apt because in politics as in the factory much of the initiative for improvement should come from lower-level operators and supervisors.

We are not of course opposed to all large-scale central redesign of systems. In the British system of representative democracy, for example, no sensible person could be against reform of the House of Lords. But the benefits of system redesign are usually limited in large-scale, complex, interacting systems of multi-level government and governance. Here system redesign is disruptive at the operating level, consumes a great deal of management time, comes with unintended consequences and often leads to KPI-chasing which does little for service quality. At worst, as in the NHS after the early 1990s, system redesign turns into hyper-innovation where the failure of one structural reform justifies the next in an exhausting process of churn that achieves very little. The accumulating evidence of quagmire suggests that reach exceeds grasp in the case of technological centrism in economic policy and 'public service reform' in social policy. Both rest on an overestimate of the intelligence, benevolence and capacity of central state political and technical elites and their ability to directly influence key outcomes by changing structures and objectives.

If adaptive reuse involves a major change of emphasis, what does this approach imply in practical terms and how could it be applied by the central state to improve foundational liveability through essential services, social infrastructure and residual income in a country like the UK? That question has a threefold answer in central state starter, stealth and switch policies which together can begin to take economic and social policy out of the quagmire.

- Starter policies push emotional buttons and establish connections to constructively harness affect and performance, just like the radical right's destructive wedge policies. Examples would include free school meals and extended social insurance.
- Stealth policies are technical adjustments on issues which are politically uncontroversial because an inattentive electorate neither knows nor cares much about them. The big UK opportunity here is to move in steps to a much less aggressive Universal Credit taper.
- Switch policies support a division of labour and empower other state and non-state actors to do effectively what central state policies and reform initiatives cannot do. So, trade unions should be empowered to pursue higher wages and many local and regional actors can be empowered to drive a process of distributed social innovation in public service delivery.

Starter policies can push emotional buttons because inattentive electorates are also well meaning and emotionally engaged by some foundational economy objectives which are then put above and beyond party politics. Thus, decent basics for all our children is a trope that plays in a 'who could be against it?' way to justify all kinds of reform and wrongfoot opponents. It worked for Archbishop Temple in 1942–43[27] and almost 80 years later it worked for Marcus Rashford when campaigning that 'no child should go hungry in this country'.[28] It is easy, though no more than a start, to make the case against the English denial of free school meals to those on Universal Credit whose net household income after tax and before cash benefit is above £7,400.[29] Other Westminster campaigns should be fronted with compassion and solidarity policies not only for children but also for the carers, sick and disabled. Raising sickness benefit is an obvious first step in the UK, as is the real living wage for English care workers, bringing them to parity with Scottish and Welsh care workers.

Starter policies can also be used in a performative way not just to change outcomes but to establish connections which have been broken in the minds of the electorate. The most important broken connection is the link between paying taxes and getting some kind of benefit in return. As we noted in Chapter 3, all the lower household deciles are heavily dependent on health, education, care and welfare benefits in-kind. But households do not understand the cash equivalent value of these services, and many suspect the state spends wastefully – hence, the importance of rescuing UK social insurance from its present status as a convenient source of general state revenue which serves the

Treasury practically as an adjunct to income tax. Pay-as-you-go social insurance should be established as a completely separate hypothecated system with its own set of accounts at the same time as the system is extended to cover the costs of care in old age. This should be combined with an aggressive public information campaign to explain the difference between private and social insurance and how the latter can re-establish a sustainable revenue base for welfare service provision.

More ambitiously, starter policies could also be used more generally to begin to address the existing tax system's limited capacity to raise general revenue which is a fundamental constraint on central state capacity to support disposable and residual household income or fund foundational services like local buses and social infrastructure like public parks. The immediate big issue here is how to start taxing the wealth of upper decile households when such reforms would produce vocal losers whose sense of grievance would be fanned by the right-wing press.

The ratio of household net wealth to GDP has more or less doubled since the 1970s and 1980s so that it is now some seven times GDP,[30] largely as a result of unearned capital gains on house property and pension assets. From 2008–18, more than three-quarters of the household gains in wealth were the result of windfall asset price increases rather than savings[31] and it is therefore completely anomalous that taxes on wealth raise less than 10 per cent of UK total tax revenue. This is both problem and opportunity. A starter policy would involve taxing unearned gains on house property at the point of sale or inheritance and bringing back issues that have not been publicly discussed since the abolition of Schedule A for owner occupiers in 1960.[32]

The highly technical nature of the tax system also creates opportunities for what we can call 'stealth' policies which adjust technicalities. Stealth policies have been used by successive UK chancellors to raise revenue by freezing income tax thresholds not raising income tax rates. But they could be used with progressive intent in a 'stealth for good' approach which should first be applied to lowering the Universal Credit taper rate in steps in successive budgets. This would address 40 years of dismal policy failure. When Family Credit was introduced in 1986, a claimant who paid income tax would retain less than 20p of any extra £1 of pay.[33] Under current Universal Credit rules, the retention (after paying tax and losing benefits) is still no more than about 30p out of any £1 of extra pay. This problem of high marginal rates of income loss now applies to those earning up to £40,000 or more if they are private renters and live in the south of England or other places with high rents.

The effective marginal tax rate for low income households earning between £25,000 and £30,000 is around 70 per cent. This is consistently higher than for a well-paid manager or professional earning between £100,000 and £120,000 a year who faces a 60 per cent marginal tax rate because the individual's tax-free personal allowance goes down by £1 for every £2 of adjusted net income above £100,000. It would be possible to spend a lot of moralising rhetoric on denouncing this anomaly. But it might be more effective to just include three successive 5 per cent cuts in the Universal Credit taper rate in budget announcements. This could open the way to detaching Universal Credit from its monomania about disciplining the work-shy so that uplifts in weekly benefits for the sick, disabled and carers got onto the agenda. The starter here could be lifting the two-child limit on benefits, which affects one in twelve of all children. This would bring direct gains for many low income families who cannot afford essentials and which at the same time begin to re-establish the basic social security principle that family support should be related to need.[34]

The starter and stealth policies described above could be disparaged as tinkering, but sustained, purposive, broad front, radical tinkering is what adaptive reuse is all about. In justification, we would reiterate that, when it has taken 40 years of misguided efforts to create the present mess, any government can in one term only begin to inflect the curve of damage to foundational liveability and establish the basis for doing much more in a second term. It would be sensible to resist general notions of 'transformation' and 'transition' which, as with sustainability, might actually result in little actual change in practice rather than empowering progressive reforms. But, at the same time, there has to be meaningful change in foundational liveability for ordinary citizens in their everyday lives because the status quo is onerous and dysfunctional.

If the central state wishes to accelerate the pace of change, it must also adopt switch policies which eschew central direction and sponsor actors who have the capacity to do what the centre cannot. The first great UK opportunity is to empower unions politically to pursue higher wages and better conditions. This opportunity should be pursued instead of persisting with the techno centrist pro-productivity policies which in one form or another date back to the Anglo-American Council on Productivity in the 1940s and have achieved almost nothing. The second opportunity is to empower state and non-state actors at local and regional levels to pursue social innovation through improving public services. This should be pursued instead of returning to centrally sponsored public service reform as with successive reorganisations of the NHS after the early 1990s or schools reform under Michael Gove in the 2010s.

What central state policy can do for higher wages is to empower unions, including by repealing anti-union legislation, encouraging bargaining and facilitating union organisation in the many activities where employment is dispersed. This would of course need to be combined with reform of the tax and benefits system so that the benefits of negotiated pay increases come through as disposable income. This is a precondition for households' ability to manage the cost of essentials like housing or energy so that low and medium income households have some residual income. In parallel, the central state should regulate employment conditions to address the problem of zero hours and fluctuating weekly incomes which undermine domestic budgeting. More enforcement is also urgent in the UK given problems like the continued exploitation of vulnerable workers, as in the Leicester garment industry.[35] Within that governmental frame, the rest is up to the unions.

What is required for higher private sector wages (regardless of the trend rate of GDP growth and productivity) is a change in the balance of forces between labour and capital so that labour can begin to claw back some of the share of output that it has lost and capital has gained over the past 50 years. This requires employer-by-employer, sector-by-sector labour market organisation which increases union density and power. This has to be backed by approaches like that of Sharon Graham's

Unite, with hard bargaining based on forensic accounting anal-ysis of what specific employers can afford to pay. The central state should recognise that investment in skills and public trans-port is not going to deliver higher productivity and wages but remains a priority because it promotes access to employment and reduces cultural and material exclusion.

Any rebalancing of power towards labour is of course prob-lematic for the central state when it is a major employer and public sector industrial action is necessary to obtain higher settlements than those delivered through existing mechanisms such as public sector pay review boards staffed by members of the non-executive director class. But here, there is a greater public good argument. The results of present arrangements in health and education have sustained real pay cuts pressed to the point where recruitment and retention problems are under-mining service delivery. This much is clear from the Institute for Government's annual performance tracker verdict on nine public services in autumn 2022.[36] In GP services, hospitals, adult care, children's care, courts and prisons, it is 'unlikely' that sufficient staff can be recruited or retained to return service performance to 2019–20 levels; in schools, children's care and neighbourhood services, this outcome is 'uncertain'.

There may be some role for new machinery in setting sec-toral wages where employment is dispersed amongst multiple small, private employers as in social care. But tripartism and social dialogue have to be backed by the threat of strike by organised workers who are empowered to claim higher wages from employers. Strikes which inconvenience consumers are a necessary part of the rebalancing process, especially in the case of low paid workers playing catch-up after they have been left behind. Where employers (public or private) cannot pay, some costs will have to be passed to customers or taxpayers. This can be a virtuous process where the private service is cheap because the workforce is being exploited as in the case of private parcel delivery. Similarly, it can be virtuous when public service delivery is failing as in health and care, where low wages limit recruitment and retention and thereby undermine service delivery.

The other area for switch policies is public service improvement, where any incoming progressive government needs to recognise the limits of top-down reform from the centre and the opportunity of supporting distributed bottom-up social innovation. The limits of reform from the centre can be illustrated by considering the case of the English NHS where the Westminster Secretary of State for health is rather like a staff general who makes plans but then has very little control over operations in the field. The Department of Health and Social Care controls funding and the organisation of service delivery units. But it has weakened the NHS with too much reorganisation and not enough funding and then added confusion through inept management by key performance indicators.

In the 20 years up to and including the Lansley reforms of 2012, hyper-innovation and churning NHS reorganisation was a major distraction. Between 1990 and 2009, less than 40 per cent of constituent NHS organisations survived for ten years[37] and the enduring legacy of reorganisation was service fragmentation through the creation of quasi-autonomous service providers. When reorganisation paused in the 2010s, aggressive under-funding was then combined with attempts at control of operations for efficiency by key performance indicators like productivity. But there is no consistently high productivity group of hospitals over time, much of the variation in productivity between hospitals is unexplained and many units under pressure offered productivity gains which were one-off cost cuts not improvements in process efficiency.[38]

Even if the English NHS had more funding, less reorganisation and more scepticism about productivity, effective change depends on addressing a whole series of problems that are outside the organisational boundaries of the NHS and require coordinated sustained commitment.

- First, none of the health system's long-term problems is soluble without some form of demand management to control chronic illness arising from environment and lifestyle. But public health has been partly devolved to local authorities and broader responsibilities for diet, air quality, housing and active lifestyles are divided between many government departments and have never been prioritised.
- Second, the short-term problems of the hospital system with nearly 7 million on the waiting list in England alone are only soluble if adult care is improved so that hospital patients can be safely discharged home or into appropriate community settings. But care is commissioned by local authorities from multiple outsourced providers, and central government, even if it put more money into care, can directly control very little.

Hence, the importance of distributed social innovation if we want reform in activities like health and care.

6.3 Distributed social innovation and alliances for change

The foundational starting point here is simple. If we want greater foundational liveability in complex systems of multi-level government and governance, the central state should mostly empower rather than attempt to control and direct. Because the central state has limited capacity to initiate and manage intelligent top-down reform and control for foundational liveability, James C. Scott's[39] argument about 'seeing like a state' does recognise a real problem. Insofar as the central state relies on the 'thin simplifications' of knowledge at a distance, it is extraordinarily difficult to provide strategic direction which exploits local opportunities and responds to changing circumstances to engage local specifics in a way that allows operational control with feedback loops. But Scott does at the same time place too much emphasis on the role of local knowledge and practice. If the aim is reform for increased foundational liveability, the dynamic is not just local knowledge but knowledge *empowered* by local alliances for change.

Our pro-liveability argument does not start from a fixed position on the central state's role but focuses on enabling and empowerment as functions that should be developed in different ways, according to context. Key to this, the central state needs to move towards supporting social innovation that draws on distributed sources of initiative and mobilises alliances of state and non-state actors to deliver something meaningful at regional and local level. Pragmatically, this is in the interest of both a reforming Westminster government and the many over-stretched local authorities and other public bodies and organisations on the front line of public service delivery.

• The central state has much to gain from empowering and enabling lower-level success in improving foundational liveability. An incoming government which implements starter, stealth and switch policies in a messed-up economy cannot assume that it will secure a second term because meaningful improvement from a low base of liveability will take time. This suggests that Labour in the UK should also be looking towards what it can do at city region and devolved levels, where it has reliable majorities in the large English cities and in Wales. This is important in itself and could have feedback effects at the Westminster level when many electors are sceptical of all promises by politicians. Performative success at the lower levels would in a 'show and tell' way make Westminster promises much more credible.

• Networking local authorities with other actors could also deal with the problem of limited capacity and the dangers of overreach in local authorities which have been hollowed out by outsourcing and austerity cuts. Re-municipalisation of mundane activities like street services and waste does take back control from outsourcing firms and can allow better employment conditions and service improvements. But such activities are never going to be a cash genera-tor that can help support other services. More ambitious local authority attempts to meet social objectives and/ or generate cash by moving into trading and investment have had disastrous outcomes in the UK as with unhedged municipal energy intermediation at Nottingham,[40] Bristol[41] and Warrington.[42] Without enhanced internal capabilities and more supportive regulation and governance, English municipalities should not operate in trading or investment activities which involve risk because local councillors and officers do not understand business models and the governance controls on local risk taking are wholly inadequate. But there is much else that they can do for foundational liveability in alliance with other local actors.

The immediate challenge with rebuilding foundational liveability in the UK is a controlling central state which cannot let go of doing. Hence, 'decentralisation' (as with Michael Gove's educational reforms) is a façade which covers the reassertion of control by different means, while 'devolution' (under City Deals or the Brown Commission proposals) transfers resources and powers within a framework of priorities and objectives defined by the central state. As we outline in Chapter 1, one underlying cause of this control freakery is the techno centrist preoccupation with the unachievable quagmire objectives of growth and higher wages through productivity increase. Local, regional and national actors can never be allowed to resile from the next phase of this quixotic struggle.

Decentralisation can be a façade, as with the Gove/Gibbs English educational reforms of 2010–14 which pressed further with Labour policies of direct funding of academy schools removed from local authority control. This is sometimes represented as decentralisation which freed up headmasters to become school leaders. More accurately, the reforms removed schools from local government control and enmeshed them in a new curriculum system with prescriptive assessment requirements and key performance indicators that reflected the agenda of Westminster education ministers. Curriculums were narrowed in English and in history, where this was done against the advice of historians.[43] Baseline assessment in reception classes was backed up by compulsory multiplication and phonics checks. Secondary teachers understood that they needed to deliver GCSE and A-level grades in unseen examinations which were the prescribed modes of assessment.[44]

Devolution as we know it in the UK operates in much the same way to enforce the agenda of the central state. In 2014, George Osborne offered Greater Manchester an elected Mayor and a City Deal which was represented as a devolution of powers and resources to a combined authority bringing together ten boroughs. But the central government concept of devolution, in this and subsequent deals, was that the Treasury at the centre would control the framework and the regions should implement and deliver. The Brown Commission in 2022 sketches a new devolution plan for an incoming Labour government after the next election in 2024 or 2025 and appears novel insofar as it argues that over-centralised political power is the cause of geographically concentrated prosperity in the UK. But, on closer inspection, it shows how the UK political classes cannot move on from quagmire tropes and central control.

In the original Greater Manchester City Deal, the city region gained some funds and extra powers on the Treasury's condition that Manchester targeted GVA growth and promised to build a local economy to generate tax revenues that covered government expenditure in Greater Manchester. In subsequent deals, it is very clear that the centre has a mainstream economics agenda about jobs and growth through skills, physical infrastructure and job-creating projects. As the Coalition Government explained when it launched the first wave of city region deals, 'City Deals give local areas specific powers and freedoms to help the region support economic growth, create jobs, or invest in local projects'.[45] The supported projects vary from one deal to the next[46] but the overwhelming focus is on training and skills and transport infrastructure with cities making pledges about apprenticeships and jobs created.[47]

The Brown Commission's report starts from a classic quagmire definition of the problem as regional GVA gaps which can be cured by a 'new pro-growth strategy' to 'provide the high paying jobs we need'.[48] It then prescribes the productivity fix of a devolved high tech industrial strategy where the role of the local authorities is to deliver on Brown's central agenda. Local authorities, businesses and universities should come together 'to deliver locally led economic strategies' whose role will be to create 'a supportive environment for the dynamic new clusters in the digital, medical, environmental and creative industries'.[49] This fix is complemented in the area of social policy by the recommendation that more services should be delivered 'at a neighbourhood level' with 'greater use of deliberative and participative processes'.[50] But it is not clear what this means when these social policy arguments are not developed in the report.

If we leave the quagmire behind, how then should we rethink the foundational liveability issues here from an adaptive reuse point of view? The first point has to be that the main challenge is not economic innovation but social innovation. Economic innovation is spread semi-automatically by financial incentives and industrial policy specialists have spent too much time worrying about early-stage research and development where the financial incentives are weakest. There have also been too many financial resources channelled to corporates and fund investors doing early-stage innovation. The larger challenge is social innovation which covers the many changes in product and process that require (re)organisation beyond a market frame. The general problem is that in systems of multi-level government and governance, there are many resistances to innovative change amongst state, civil society and for-profit actors. These obstacles can only be overcome by alliances for change with shared pro-liveability ambitions that can mobilise distributed intelligence, knowledges and motivating values.

The initial primary sphere for social innovation must be the providential services of health, education and care because of their scale and partly off-market position. Health, education and adult care are the big-ticket items of state expenditure at local level,[51] accounting for nearly 20 per cent of GDP and a larger percentage of the workforce in many localities. Productivity thinking, fixed on the input/output efficiency of a single service, is a seriously limited way of thinking about our delivery problems in these activities. Because, as Hilary Cottam argues, 'we have reached the limits of our post-war services and institutions'[52] and their ways of responding to dependent needs rather than supporting individuals and households to grow their capabilities.

The problem Cottam diagnoses is not the inefficiency of a single service but the ineffectuality of multiple systems which will always be overwhelmed by demand that they have failed to manage. All the various providential systems need adaptive reworking so that prevention and early intervention have value. Effective social innovation is possible where siloed agencies in services like health or housing recognise that they are dealing with aspects of larger household problems that present different aspects to various agencies. It is then possible for services to respond flexibly and adaptively to the needs of the individual person. Services can move beyond the gatekeeping and bureaucracy that produces adult care assessment as a preliminary to time and task support in 15 or 30 minute care worker visits for a narrow range of tasks around bathing, dressing and feeding. The fact that social innovation of this kind already exists in some localities should set the agenda for supporting more households in more places.

The good news here is also that social innovation thinking can be applied to problems of economic development, including the development of the tradeable and competitive sectors. In this case, we shift from thinking of individual worker skills as the limit and instead focus on the stock of capable firms or, more exactly, those capable firms grounded in the region by ownership and/or some form of human or physical resource. This is particularly relevant in the deindustrialised regions of North and West Britain which have a problem about the 'missing middle' of small and medium-sized enterprises (SMEs) and ever more micro firms of limited ambition and capability. In Wales in 2019 micro firms had a growing 35 per cent share of employment and just 13 per cent of turnover whereas SMEs had a 28 per cent share of employment and 25 per cent of turnover with neither share increasing.[53] Our Welsh study of food processing – the largest UK manufacturing sector – revealed problems about capable SME firms with narrow margins unable to expand from their retained earnings or secured bank borrowing.

Innovative alternatives do exist if we want more effectual providential services or a larger number of grounded SMEs. Domiciliary care reform for older people usually involves replacing a fixed time and task round system with a local patch system where care is varied according to the changing social and physical needs of clients without the assumption of continued and increasing dependence, and care workers can then take more responsibility for continuous effective support. On building capable SMEs, the shift has to be away from skills and cheap funding to developing all the different kinds of soft and hard infrastructure which could sustain SMEs in unglamorous sectors. Hence, in food processing, our recommendation of continued funding of the three Welsh food innovation centres, which support new product and process development, and an extension of the food park system offering rented units that reduce the capital costs of expansion.[54]

When all this has been said, there is then the distributed innovation puzzle about 'why we do not do more of the right stuff?'. If we know or half know what to do, why do we have many isolated experiments (such as those described by Hilary Cottam) but so little replication and scaling up into large-scale social innovation? This failure is remarkable when 'how to do it' consultancies like Vanguard already offer 'systems thinking' toolkits for worthwhile single service reform. These build on important insights about change as a normative process where doubters are convinced not by arguments but by seeing a future that works.[55] We can understand more of the possibilities and limits of distributed social innovation by considering the case of Wales.

Wales is a Celtic nation with a devolved government and a social democratic consensus which is in fitful recovery from a period of front office excess without sufficient back office focus. The 2008 Brundtland Commission definition of sustainability was enacted in the Welsh Government's 2015 Well-Being of Future Generations Act. This was about improving the social, economic, environmental and cultural well-being of Welsh people by requiring all public bodies to consider the long-term impact of their decisions. The ambition was commendable and a precondition of change, but the Act was built on naïveté which made delivery unlikely. The Act never confronted the issue of trade-offs between goals like 'prosperity' and 'global responsibility'. Delivery was the responsibility of Public Service Boards as newly formed local committees and a small Commissioner's office which has not taken an evidence-based approach to sector or place specifics. The Commissioner's recent Section 20 review of public procurement contained vignettes but no numbers at all except for one exaggerated estimate of the total value of Welsh public procurement expenditure.[56]

In Wales, policy reach often exceeds political grasp. But here at least problems are being recognised and Welsh Government has commissioned a template for review of foundational policies. As noted in Section 2.3 of Chapter 2, the working group of Welsh foundational economy practitioners and researchers who constructed that template proposed not just aims but also three ways of working which would act as adaptive reuse guardrails for a discovery process of social innovation. The first of these is to engage system and place specifics; the second is to use relevant evidence to guide action; and the third is to mobilise alliances for change. What works and how will depend partly on the way those alliances for change are built at local level, just as scalability at sectoral level will come from communities of practice which spread learning with variation to accommodate local specifics.

The greatest difficulty which stands in the way of achieving greater foundational liveability in Wales is the need for new ways of working and learning to act in alliance to support innovation inside and outside government. Alliances for change are the necessary but difficult precondition for initiating social innovation and for replication with variation for local circumstance. And they are practically very difficult to put together when Wales is a country of splintered political agency. Here Westminster Government often cuts across Welsh Government, which has limited powers of home rule and has to manage relations with 22 local authorities, seven Health Boards and many not-for-profit organisations like housing associations and further education colleges. This is a polity where many leave their organisations to listen politely in committee without giving too much ground before going back to their own corridor realities and business models.

Against this background, the incubation of an emerging Welsh liveability agenda is both encouraging and unsettling because it suggests Wales must begin to rethink politics as much as policy. Inside government, Welsh Government is beginning to rethink its role as an enabler of change rather than an ineffectual strategic controller. In the newly created Welsh Climate

Change Ministry, the language is explicitly about 'alliances for change' to press sectoral progress, with the Ministry organising 'deep dives' on issues like afforestation, town centres and renewable energy. These bring together stakeholders and experts in a round of intensive meetings to hammer out objectives and policies. Outside government, the Foundational Alliance Wales is putting together sectoral 'round tables' for reform in activities like care and housing.

Underneath these first attempts to put together Welsh national alliances, there is a ferment of local social innovation for liveability with much of the initiative for change coming from driver institutions outside the electoral system and party politics. Thus, the Hywel Dda and Aneurin Bevan Health Boards have policies of 'grow your own' workforce development and have reworked training pathways so that healthcare support workers with attitude and ambition but few academic qualifications can become registered nurses.[57] The housing association Clwyd Alyn has a business plan about 'addressing the causes and impacts of poverty' which is backed up by a joint venture which distributes meal packs from mobile shops in food deserts and much else.[58] Local authorities are both joining in and initiating social innovation. Flintshire Council works in partnership on food with Clwyd Alyn while Gwynedd Council is initiating reform of home care for older adults.

At this point, it is unclear whether the Welsh can put together the necessary alliances for change to turn imaginative experiments into reformed national practice. But at least the need to search for new pathways to social innovation has been recognised and taken on board in some policy. The Welsh work in progress reinforces the message of this book about how we must find a new foundational starting point on what is deliverable and how. The starting point must be a break with mainstream economic thinking to install the aim of foundational liveability, and this needs to be supported by a gradualist political practice of adaptive reuse. The central state political classes must recognise the limits of resetting central policy levers and go for starter, stealth and switch policies. At the lower levels, distributed social innovation has huge potential but requires new ways of working and alliances for change which require active effort but can realise opportunities to learn and share.

Notes

Introduction: behind the great anxiety

1 Josh Glancy, 11 June 2022, 'Why is nothing working in broken Britain?', *The Times*. https://www.thetimes.co.uk/article/why-nothing-working-broken-britain-brexit-covid-t22pjbrsp

2 *The Economist*, 9 August 2022, 'Almost nothing seems to be working in Britain. It could get worse'. https://www.economist.com/britain/2022/08/09/almost-nothing-seems-to-be-working-in-britain-it-could-get-worse

3 Andrew Neil, 26 November 2022, 'Britain is paralysed by a toxic brew of political incompetence and impotence. No wonder millions are now asking … why can't this Government get ANYTHING done?', *Daily Mail*. https://www.dailymail.co.uk/debate/article-11470995/ANDREW-NEIL-Britain-paralysed-Government-done.html

4 Hannah Rose Woods, 29 December 2022, 'Why does nothing work in the UK anymore?', *New Statesman*. https://www.newstatesman.com/quickfire/2022/12/nothing-work-uk-anymore-inflation-strikes-nhs

5 Madeline Grant, 23 August 2022, 'Britain is broken – and nobody can be bothered to do anything about it', *The Telegraph*. https://www.telegraph.co.uk/news/2022/08/23/britain-broken-nobody-can-bothered-do-anything/

6 Zoe Williams, 22 September 2022, '"Everything is broken because of 12 years of Tory government" – why can't Starmer just say it?', *The Guardian*. https://www.theguardian.com/commentisfree/2022/sep/22/uk-broken-12-years-starmer-tory-government-labour

Notes

7 https://peoplepolling.org/2022/gb-voting-intention-week-51
-2022/

8 George Parker, Jim Pickard and Sarah Neville, 12 December 2022, 'Attempt to avert nurses' strike fails after Barclay refuses to discuss pay', *Financial Times*. https://www.ft.com/content/1184930f-8b5d -4c29-80bc-756123846df0

9 Sebastian Payne, 1 December 2022, 'To woo voters, Rishi Sunak must fix the UK's "palpable economy"', *Financial Times*. https:// www.ft.com/content/09dc03f4-e280-4089-a3ad-7b5d55f9b850

10 John McDonnell, 24 June 2019, 'Speech on the economy and Labour's plans for sustainable investment'. https://labour.org.uk/ press/john-mcdonnell-speech-economy-labours-plans-sustainable -investment/

11 The list of essentials could be extended, for example, to include childcare, or mobile phone and broadband expenses. But we draw the line at the four essentials because spending on them can be easily tracked for households ranked by income deciles. The exclusion of important services like these means that residual income needs to be positive and sufficient to cover their cost.

12 Pat McFadden, 19 November 2022, 'Labour is committed to main-taining financial stability', *Financial Times*. https://www.ft.com/con-tent/8e665812-0dfd-47c1-8ba7-f6181f9ee855

13 David Huber, 26 January 2016, 'Lacaton & Vassal have pioneered a strategy for saving France's social housing', *Metropolis*. https://metropolismag.com/profiles/lacaton-vassal-pio neered-strategy-saving-france-social-housing/

1 Economic policy as quagmire

1 For more details see: Joe Earle, Cahal Moran and Zach Ward-Perkins (2016) *The Econocracy: The Perils of Leaving Economics to the Experts*, Manchester University Press.

2 Lawrence Freedman (1991) 'Escalators and quagmires: expectations and the use of force', *International Affairs*, 67(1), pp. 15–31.

Notes

3 'Escalators and quagmires', p. 26.

4 HM Treasury, 23 September 2022, 'The Growth Plan 2022: investment zones factsheet'. https://www.gov.uk/government/publications/the-growth-plan-2022-factsheet-on-investment-zones/the-growth-plan-2022-investment-zones-factsheet

5 Department for Work and Pensions, 27 January 2022, Press release. https://www.gov.uk/government/news/new-jobs-mission-to-get-500-000-into-work

6 *Financial Times* editorial, 30 November 2022, 'The mystery of Britain's missing workers'. https://www.ft.com/content/dee332d0-0c1d-4590-bad5-2c37006d9b90

7 CEIC database, UK Private Consumption: % of GDP. https://www.ceicdata.com/en/indicator/united-kingdom/private-consumption--of-nominal-gdp#:~:text=United%20Kingdom%20Private%20Consumption%20accounted,63.7%20%25%20in%20the%20previous%20quarter. Note that the other components of GDP are government expenditures, investment and net exports. Internationally, the share of private consumption in the UK is significantly higher than in several other European economies, including Germany and France.

8 Gordon Brown (2022) *A New Britain: Renewing Our Democracy and Rebuilding Our Economy*, Report of the Commission on the UK's Future, p. 22. https://labour.org.uk/wp-content/uploads/2022/12/Commission-on-the-UKs-Future.pdf

9 Keir Starmer speech, 25 July 2022. https://labour.org.uk/press/keir-starmer-speech-on-labours-mission-for-economic-growth/

10 Rachel Reeves speech, 13 July 2022. https://labour.org.uk/press/rachel-reeves-speech-at-stagnation-nation-the-economy-2030-inquiry-conference/

11 Resolution Foundation and Centre for Economic Performance (2022) *Stagnation Nation: Navigating a Route to a Fairer and More Prosperous Britain*, Resolution Foundation, pp. 110, 9. https://economy2030.resolutionfoundation.org/wp-content/uploads/2022/07/Stagnation_nation_interim_report.pdf

12 Secretary of State for Levelling Up, Housing and Communities (2022) *Levelling Up the United Kingdom*, HM Government, London.

Notes

Executive summary p. 5 and main report p. 192. https://assets.
publishing.service.gov.uk/government/uploads/system/uploads/
attachment_data/file/1052708/Levelling_up_the_UK_white
_paper.pdf

13 Keir Starmer speech, 7 October 2022. https://labour.org.uk/press
/keir-starmer-speaks-ahead-of-visit-to-british-food-manufacturing
-site/

14 Martin Wolf, 6 February 2022, 'The levelling-up white paper is a
necessary call to arms', *Financial Times*. https://www.ft.com/content
/19c28c15-cd88-40b6-bd7a-15115b624ef5

15 Alix Culbertson, 20 September 2022, 'Truss admits that tax cuts will
disproportionately benefit the rich', *Sky News*. https://news.sky.com
/story/liz-truss-prepared-to-be-unpopular-with-tax-policy-to-boost
-economic-growth-12702039

16 Kwasi Kwarteng, 23 September 2022, 'The Growth Plan 2022
speech' (transcript of House of Commons speech), HM Treasury.
https://www.gov.uk/government/speeches/the-growth-plan-2022
-speech

17 Kate Devlin, 24 September 2022, 'Tax cuts will not suddenly unlock
growth, CBI boss warns Chancellor', *Independent*. https://www
.independent.co.uk/news/uk/politics/tax-cut-growth-tony-danker
-b2174405.html

18 Jeremy Hunt, 17 October 2022, Chancellor's Statement. https://
www.gov.uk/government/speeches/chancellor-statement-17
-october

19 Jeremy Hunt, 16 October 2022, interview with Laura Kuenssberg,
Sunday with Laura Kuenssberg. https://www.bbc.co.uk/programmes/
m001d7z4

20 Iain Duncan Smith, 25 October 2022, interview, *Today Programme*.
https://www.bbc.co.uk/programmes/m001ddmf

21 Liz Truss, 18 October 2022, 'I'll lead Tories into the next election',
BBC interview. https://www.bbc.co.uk/news/uk-politics-63293891

22 Colin Crouch (2009) 'Privatised Keynesianism: an unacknowledged
policy regime', *British Journal of Politics and International Relations*, 11(3),
pp. 382–99.

Notes

23 LSE Growth Commission (2012) *Investing for Prosperity*, LSE Centre for Economic Performance. https://cep.lse.ac.uk/LSE-Growth -Commission/files/LSEGC-2012-report.pdf

24 *Stagnation Nation.*

25 Mariana Mazzucato and George Dibb (2019) *Missions: A Beginner's Guide*. UCL Institute for Innovation and Public Purpose, IIPP Policy Brief 09. https://www.ucl.ac.uk/bartlett/public-purpose/publica-tions/2019/dec/missions-beginners-guide. See also https://assets .publishing.service.gov.uk/government/uploads/system/uploads/ attachment_data/file/664563/industrial-strategy-white-paper-web -ready-version.pdf

26 HM Treasury (March 2021) *Build Back Better: Our Plan for Growth*, HM Treasury. https://www.gov.uk/government/publications/build -back-better-our-plan-for-growth/build-back-better-our-plan-for -growth-html

27 Roger Tym and Partners (1984) *Monitoring Enterprise Zones, Third Year Report*, HMSO.

28 See, for example, Rosemary Bromley and Richard Morgan (1985) 'The effects of enterprise zones: evidence from Swansea', *Regional Studies*, 19(5), pp. 403–14.

29 European Environmental Agency, 11 January 2021, 'Growth with-out economic growth', Briefing. https://www.eea.europa.eu/publi-cations/growth-without-economic-growth

30 Matthew Taylor and Helena Horton, 8 February 2022, 'Tories fight-ing net zero plans are dragging climate into new culture war, experts say', *The Guardian*. https://www.theguardian.com/politics/2022 /feb/08/tories-fighting-net-zero-plans-are-dragging-climate-into -new-culture-war-experts-say

31 Keir Starmer, 25 July 2022.

32 Jason Hickel and Georgos Kallis (2020) 'Is green growth possible?', *New Political Economy*, 25(4), pp. 469–86.

33 Timothée Parrique *et al.*, July 2019, *Decoupling Debunked: Evidence and Arguments Against Green Growth as a Sole Strategy for Sustainability*, European Environmental Bureau. https://eeb.org/wp-content/ uploads/2019/07/Decoupling-Debunked.pdf

34 ONS (2019) 'The decoupling of economic growth from carbon emissions: UK evidence'. https://www.ons.gov.uk/economy/ nationalaccounts/uksectoraccounts/compendium/economicreview /october2019/thedecouplingofeconomicgrowthfromcarbonemis sionsukevidence#:~:text=The%20UK%20has%20shown%20evi- dence,CO2%20emissions%20fell%20by%2034.2%25.

35 ONS, 'Decoupling of economic growth'.

36 Simon Cran-McGreehin (2019) 'UK energy and emissions: where does the country get its energy from? And what's producing its car- bon emissions?', Energy and Climate Intelligence Unit. https://eciu .net/analysis/briefings/uk-energy-policies-and-prices/uk-energy -and-emissions

37 Climate Change Committee (CCC), 29 June 2022, 'Current pro- grammes will not deliver Net Zero'. https://www.theccc.org.uk /2022/06/29/current-programmes-will-not-deliver-net-zero/

38 Oxfam. https://oxfamilibrary.openrepository.com/bitstream/han- dle/10546/621052/mb-confronting-carbon-inequality-210920-en .pdf

39 World Wide Fund For Nature (WWF). https://wwf.panda.org/dis- cover/knowledge_hub/teacher_resources/webfieldtrips/ecological _balance/eco_footprint/

40 Daniel W. O'Neill, Andrew L. Fanning, Williams F. Lamb and Julia K. Steinberger (2018) 'A good life for all within planetary bounda- ries', *Nature Sustainability*, 1(2), pp. 900–12.

41 See Tim Jackson (2016) *Prosperity Without Growth: Foundations for the Economy of Tomorrow*, Second edition, Taylor & Francis; Kate Raworth (2017) *Doughnut Economics: Seven Ways to Think Like a 21st Century Economist*, Chelsea Green Publishing.

42 Nye Cominetti, Charlie McCurdy and Hannah Slaughter (2021) 'Low Pay Britain: 2021', Resolution Foundation, p. 5. https://www .resolutionfoundation.org/app/uploads/2021/06/Low-Pay-Britain -2021.pdf

43 'Real' refers to the total after accounting for inflation.

44 ONS (2022) 'X09: real average weekly earnings using consumer price inflation (seasonally adjusted) dataset XO9', Office for National Statistics. https://www.ons.gov.uk/employmentandlabour

market/peopleinwork/earningsandworkinghours/datasets/x09real
averageweeklyearningsusingconsumerpriceinflationseasonallyad
justed

45 ONS (2021) 'Productivity economic commentary, UK: October to
December 2020', Office for National Statistics. https://www.ons
.gov.uk/employmentandlabourmarket/peopleinwork/labourpro-
ductivity/articles/ukproductivityintroduction/octobertodecemb
er2020#:~:text=During%20the%20downturn%20(2008%20
to,known%20as%20the%20productivity%20puzzle

46 The Centre for Macroeconomics (2022) 'The latest thinking of
European macroeconomists: levelling up productivity gaps in the
UK'. https://cfmsurvey.org/

47 Matthew Whittaker (2020) *Dead-End Relationship? Exploring the
Link Between Productivity and Workers' Living Standards*, Resolution
Foundation. https://www.resolutionfoundation.org/publications/
dead-end-relationship/

48 Tony Cutler, John Williams and Karel Williams (1986) *Keynes,
Beveridge and Beyond*, Routledge & Kegan Paul, Table 3.9, p. 81.

49 Julie Froud, Sukhdev Johal, John Law, Adam Leaver and Karel
Williams (2011) 'Rebalancing the economy (or buyer's remorse)',
CRESC Working Paper No. 87, Centre for Research on Socio-
Cultural Change, p. 30. https://foundationaleconomycom.files
.wordpress.com/2017/01/wp87.pdf

50 Eurostat, 'Glossary: high-tech'. https://ec.europa.eu/eurostat/sta-
tistics-explained/index.php?title=Glossary:High-tech

51 Eurostat, 'Archive: high-tech statistics – employment'. https://ec
.europa.eu/eurostat/statistics-explained/index.php?oldid=409153

52 Enrico Moretti (2013) *The New Geography of Jobs*, Harcourt.

53 John Buchanan, Julie Froud, Sukhdev Johal, Adam Leaver and
Karel Williams (2009) 'Undisclosed and unsustainable: problems of
the UK National Business Model', *CRESC Working Paper No. 75*, p.
19. https://hummedia.manchester.ac.uk/institutes/cresc/working-
papers/wp75.pdf

54 Luke Sibieta, 11 March 2022, 'The even longer squeeze on teacher
pay', Institute for Fiscal Studies. https://ifs.org.uk/articles/even
-longer-squeeze-teacher-pay

55 Julie Froud, Colin Haslam, Sukhdev Johal, John Law and Karel Williams (2020) 'When systems fail: UK acute hospitals and public health after Covid-19', Research Report, Foundational Economy Collective, pp. 16–28. https://foundationaleconomycom.files.word-press.com/2020/08/when-systems-fail-uk-acute-hospitals-and-public-health-after-covid-19.pdf

56 See, for example: Karel Williams, Colin Haslam, John Williams, Tony Cutler, Andy Adcroft and Sukhdev Johal (1992) 'Against lean production', *Economy and Society*, 21(3), pp. 321–54.

57 For a broad ranging discussion of productivity in the foundational economy see Julie Froud, Colin Haslam, Sukhdev Johal and Karel Williams (2020) '(How) does productivity matter in the foundational economy?', *Local Economy*, 35(4), pp. 316–36.

2 Households and foundational liveability

1 Tim Jackson (2009) *Prosperity without Growth*, Earthscan, pp. 194–202.

2 Jason Hickel (2020) *Less Is More: How Degrowth Will Save the World*, Penguin.

3 Julian M. Allwood *et al.* (2019) *Absolute Zero*, UK FIRES. https://www.ukfires.org/wp-content/uploads/2019/11/Absolute-Zero-online.pdf

4 Benjamin Seebohm Rowntree (1901) *Poverty: A Study of Town Life*, Macmillan, pp. 3, 16–25.

5 William Temple (1942) *Christianity and Social Order* (1987 reprint), Penguin Books, pp. 87, 96–7.

6 Lizzie Edmonds, 21 May 2021, 'Marcus Rashford: I would force myself to sleep so I didn't feel hungry as a child', *Evening Standard*. https://www.standard.co.uk/news/uk/marcus-rashford-child-poverty-hungry-sleep-manchester-united-b936306.html

7 Billy Perrigo, 23 October 2020, 'The UK is facing a child hunger crisis: a sports star won't wait for the Government to act', *Time*. https://time.com/5903453/marcus-rashford-child-food-poverty/

8 Tim Adams, 17 January 2021, 'Marcus Rashford: the making of a food superhero', *The Guardian*. https://www.theguardian.com/football/2021/jan/17/marcus-rashford-the-making-of-a-food-superhero-child-hunger-free-school-meals

9 OECD, 'Glossary of statistical terms: household'. https://stats.oecd.org/glossary/detail.asp?ID=1255

10 OECD, 'Glossary'.

11 The Howard League for Penal Reform, 'Prison Watch'. https://howardleague.org/prison-watch/

12 Statista, 'Number of personnel in the armed forces of the United Kingdom from 1900 to 2022'. https://www.statista.com/statistics/579773/number-of-personnel-in-uk-armed-forces/

13 Wendy Wilson and Hannah Cromarty (2019) 'Houses in multiple occupation (HMOs) England and Wales', Briefing Paper Number 0708, House of Commons Library. https://researchbriefings.files.parliament.uk/documents/SN00708/SN00708.pdf

14 Statista, 'Numbers of beds in registered nursing and residential homes in England from April 2015 to November 2020'. https://www.statista.com/statistics/827861/number-of-beds-in-nursing-and-residential-homes-england/

15 ONS, 'Families and households 2021', Dataset. https://www.ons.gov.uk/peoplepopulationandcommunity/birthsdeathsandmarriages/families/bulletins/familiesandhouseholds/2021

16 ONS, 'Families and households 2021'.

17 ONS, 'Living alone in the UK, Reference tables 2019'. https://www.ons.gov.uk/peoplepopulationandcommunity/birthsdeathsandmarriages/families/datasets/livingaloneintheuk

18 ONS, 'Births in England and Wales: 2020'. https://www.ons.gov.uk/releases/birthsinenglandandwales2020

19 IPPR, 5 April 2012, 'Modern women marrying men of the same or lower social class'. https://www.ippr.org/news-and-media/press-releases/modern-women-marrying-men-of-the-same-or-lower-social-class

20 Foundational Economy Research Limited (FERL) is a research-based consultancy whose principals are four of the authors of this book. See https://foundationaleconomyresearch.com/. Foundational

Economy Alliance Wales is a membership organisation which brings together many different stakeholders to promote and improve the foundational economy. The Foundational Economy Collective is a European research network with several active groups, including in Italy, Austria, Belgium and the UK. Their publications and activities can be found at: https://foundationaleconomy.com/

21 Justin Bentham *et al.* (2013) 'Manifesto for the foundational economy', CRESC Working Paper 131, Centre for Research on Socio-Cultural Change (CRESC). https://foundationaleconomycom.files.wordpress.com/2017/01/wp131.pdf

22 Luca Calafati, Jill Ebrey, Julie Froud, Colin Haslam, Sukhdev Johal and Karel Williams (2019) *How an Ordinary Place Works: Understanding Morriston.* https://foundationaleconomycom.files.wordpress.com/2019/05/morriston-report-v6-13-may-2019.pdf

23 Lowri Cunnington Wynn, Julie Froud and Karel Williams (2022) *A Way Ahead: Empowering Restanza in a Slate Valley*, Foundational Economy Research Ltd and Cwmni Bro Ffestiniog. https://foundationaleconomycom.files.wordpress.com/2022/04/restanza-english-version-as-of-7-feb-2022.pdf

24 Julie Froud, Colin Haslam, Sukhdev Johal and Karel Williams (2020) '(How) does productivity matter in the foundational economy?', *Local Economy*, 35(4), pp. 316–36.

25 Luca Calafati, Julie Froud, Colin Haslam, Sukhdev Johal and Karel Williams (2021) 'Diversity in leading and laggard regions: living standards, residual income and regional policy', *Cambridge Journal of Regions, Economy and Society*, 13(1), pp. 117–39. In this original paper, residual income was calculated after housing, transport and utilities.

26 Luca Calafati, Julie Froud, Colin Haslam, Steve Jeffels, Sukhdev Johal and Karel Williams (2022) *Jobs and Liveability*, A report by Foundational Economy Research Ltd for Karbon Homes.

27 Local Trust (2020) 'Left behind areas missing out on community facilities and places to meet'. https://localtrust.org.uk/news-and-stories/news/left-behind-areas-missing-out-on-community-facilities-and-places-to-meet/

28 Tenure groups include social and private renters, mortgage payers and owner occupiers.

29 Ruth Green, Harriet Agerholm and Libby Rogers, 8 August 2022, 'Full extent of NHS dentistry shortage revealed by far-reaching BBC research', *BBC News*. https://www.bbc.co.uk/news/health-62253893

30 EIU (2022) *The Global Liveability Index 2022*. https://pages.eiu.com/rs/753-RIQ-438/images/Liveability-free-report-V13-revised.pdf

31 Demos-PwC (2022) 'Good growth for cities: taking action on levelling up'. https://www.pwc.co.uk/industries/government-public-sector/good-growth.html

32 EIU, *Global Liveability Index*, p. 1.

33 Demos-PwC, 'Good growth for cities', p. 11.

34 EIU, *Global Liveability Index*, p. 8.

35 Demos-PwC, 'Good growth for cities', p. 8.

36 EIU, *Global Liveability Index*, p. 2.

37 Demos-PwC, 'Good growth for cities', pp. 6–7.

38 Quoted in Tyce Herrman and Rebecca Lewis (undated) 'What is livability?', Sustainable Cities Initiative, University of Oregon. https://sci.uoregon.edu/sites/default/files/sub_1_-_what_is_livability_lit_review.pdf

39 For the concept of reliance system, see Alex Schafran, Matthew Noah Smith and Stephen Hall (2020) *The Spatial Contract: A New Politics of Provision for an Urbanized Planet*, Manchester University Press.

40 Diane Burns, Luke Cowie, Joe Earle, Peter Folkman, Julie Froud, Paula Hyde, Sukhdev Johal, Ian Rees Jones, Anne Killett and Karel Williams (2016) 'Where does the money go? Financialised chains and the crisis in residential care', CRESC Public Interest Report, Centre for Research on Socio-Cultural Change (CRESC). https://foundationaleconomycom.files.wordpress.com/2017/01/where-doesthemoneygo.pdf

41 Luca Calafati, Julie Froud, Colin Haslam, Sukhdev Johal and Karel Williams (2021) *Small Towns Big Issues*, FERL. https://foundationaleconomycom.files.wordpress.com/2021/08/small-towns-big-issues-report-june-2021.pdf

42 Luca Calafati, Julie Froud, Colin Haslam, Sukhdev Johal and Karel Williams (2021) *Meeting Social Needs on a Damaged Planet*, FE Collective

Working Paper 8. https://foundationaleconomycom.files.wordpress
.com/2021/01/fe-wp8-meeting-social-needs-on-a-damaged-planet
.pdf

43 Stockholm Environment Institute and GHD (2015) 'Ecological
and carbon footprints of Wales: Update to 2011', Stockholm
Environment Institute and GHD. https://gov.wales/sites/default/
files/publications/2019-04/ecological-and-carbon-footprint-of-w
ales-report.pdf

44 Luca Calafati, Julie Froud, Colin Haslam, Sukhdev Johal and Karel
Williams (2020) 'Serious about green? Building a Welsh wood
economy through co-ordination', Report by Foundational Economy
Research Ltd for WoodKnowledge Wales. https://woodknowledge
.wales/wp-content/uploads/Serious-about-Green-WKW-FERL
-report-Oct-2020-vB-002.pdf

3 Inequalities between households and places

1 Matt Prior, 24 April 2020, 'The Volvo XC90 is a real drag', *Autocar*.
https://www.autocar.co.uk/opinion/tester%27s-notes/matt-prior
-volvo-xc90-real-drag

2 M. Gurdon, 16 February 2022, 'The death of old bangers', *Spectator*.
https://www.spectator.co.uk/article/the-death-of-the-old-banger/

3 For information about Quooker, see https://www.quooker.co.uk/
about-quooker

4 https://www.bathroomandkitchenupdate.com/quookers-dealer
-first-business-strategy-why-it-pays-to-invest-in-supplier-retailer
-relationships/

5 Office for National Statistics (2022) 'Family Resources Survey:
financial year 2020 to 2021'. https://www.gov.uk/government/
statistics/family-resources-survey-financial-year-2020-to-2021/fam-
ily-resources-survey-financial-year-2020-to-2021#using-the-frs-for
-analysis

6 The Food Foundation, 30 September 2022, 'As energy prices rise
again, a quarter of parents have cut back on the quantity of food

to afford essentials'. https://foodfoundation.org.uk/press-release/
energy-prices-rise-again-quarter-parents-have-cut-back-quantity-
food-afford

7   Patrick Jenkins, 3 October 2022, 'Failure to learn lessons of 2008
    caused LDI pension blow up', *Financial Times*. https://www.ft.com/
    content/6ca2ff89-e59b-4529-8448-4c09b27af480

8   ONS (2022) 'Household total wealth in Great Britain: April 2018 to
    March 2020'. https://www.ons.gov.uk/peoplepopulationandcom-
    munity/personalandhouseholdfinances/incomeandwealth/bulle-
    tins/totalwealthingreatbritain/april2018tomarch2020

9   George Bangham (2019) *Game of Homes. The Rise of Multiple Property
    Ownership in Great Britain*, Resolution Foundation. https://www.res
    olutionfoundation.org/app/uploads/2019/06/Game-of-Homes
    .pdf

10 George Bangham and Jack Leslie (2020) *Rainy Days: An Audit of
    Household Wealth and the Initial Effects of the Coronavirus Crisis on Saving
    and Spending in Great Britain*, Resolution Foundation, p. 5. https://
    www.resolutionfoundation.org/publications/rainy-days/

11 Rowena Crawford, Dave Innes and Cormac O'Dea (2016)
    'Household wealth in Great Britain: distribution, composition and
    changes 2006–12', *Fiscal Studies*, 37(1), pp. 35–54.

12 Adam Corlett, Felicia Odamtten and Lalitha Try (2022) 'The Living
    Standards Audit 2022', Resolution Foundation, pp. 14–18. https://
    www.resolutionfoundation.org/app/uploads/2022/07/Living
    -Standards-Audit-2022.pdf

13 Government Office for Science (2021) 'Trend Deck 2021:
    Urbanisation'. https://www.gov.uk/government/publications/
    trend-deck-2021-urbanisation/trend-deck-2021-urbanisation

14 The estimates are made at the MSOA (middle super output area)
    level, which is a district defined by the ONS as having a minimum
    population of 5,000 and a mean population of 7,200. ONS (2020)
    'Income estimates for small areas, England and Wales'. https://www
    .ons.gov.uk/peoplepopulationandcommunity/personalandhousehol
    dfinances/incomeandwealth/bulletins/smallareamodelbasedinco
    meestimates/financialyearending2018/relateddata. Notes: Total
    annual household income is the sum of the gross income of every

member of the household plus any income from benefits such as Working Families Tax Credit. The number of households is based on the 2011 Census data.

15 Bespoke data from the ONS, 2020.

16 Paul Swinney (2021) *So You Want to Level Up?*, Centre for Cities, p. 3. https://www.centreforcities.org/wp-content/uploads/2021/06/So-you-want-to-level-up-Centre-for-Cities.pdf

17 See, for example, research by Ron Martin (2015) 'Rebalancing the spatial economy: the challenge for regional theory', *Territory, Politics, Governance*, 3(3), pp. 235–72; Ron Martin (1999) 'The new "geographical turn" in economics: some critical reflections', *Cambridge Journal of Economics*, 23, pp. 65–91.

18 Resolution Foundation and Centre for Economic Performance, LSE (2022) *Stagnation Nation: Navigating a Route to a Fairer and More Prosperous Britain*, p. 15. https://economy2030.resolutionfoundation.org/wp-content/uploads/2022/07/Stagnation_nation_interim_report.pdf

19 *Stagnation Nation*, p. 18.

20 *Stagnation Nation*, p. 20.

21 Paul Swinney, 21 September 2022, 'How to make investment zones work for levelling up?', Centre for Cities, blog post. https://www.centreforcities.org/blog/how-to-make-investment-zones-work-for-levelling-up/

22 Department for Levelling Up, Housing and Communities, 1 August 2022, 'UK Shared Prosperity Fund: prospectus', GOV.UK (www.gov.uk). Department for Digital, Culture, Media and Sport, 10 November 2020, 'Headline Findings from the 2020 Community Life Recontact Survey', HM Government. https://www.gov.uk/government/statistics/headline-findings-from-the-2020-community-life-recontact-survey

23 Secretary of State for Levelling Up, Housing and Communities (2022) *Levelling Up the United Kingdom*, CP604, HM Government, London. Executive summary p. 5 and main report p. xviii. https://assets.publishing.service.gov.uk/government/uploads/system/uploads/attachment_data/file/1052708/Levelling_up_the_UK_white_paper.pdf

Notes

24 Department for Digital, Culture, Media and Sport, 29 July 2021, 'Neighbourhood and Community – Community Life Survey 2020/21', HM Government. https://www.gov.uk/government/statistics/community-life-survey-202021-neighbourhood-and-community/neighbourhood-and-community-community-life-survey-202021

25 Department for Digital, Culture, Media and Sport, 31 August 2018, 'DCMS Community Life Survey: Ad-hoc statistical releases', HM Government. https://www.gov.uk/government/statistical-data-sets/dcms-community-life-survey-ad-hoc-statistical-releases

26 Courtney Stephenson and Kate Harrison (2022) *Movers and Stayers: Localising Power to Level Up Towns*, Demos, p. 35. https://demos.co.uk/wp-content/uploads/2022/07/FT-final-final.pdf

27 *Movers and Stayers*, p. 7.

28 Wikipedia, 'Multiple deprivation index'. https://en.wikipedia.org/wiki/Multiple_deprivation_index

29 These districts are MSOAs, as described previously.

30 Calafati *et al.* (2022) *Jobs and Liveability*.

31 Department for Work and Pensions (2022) 'Universal Credit statistics, 29 April 2013 to 13 January 2022', Official Statistics, HM Government. https://www.gov.uk/government/statistics/universal-credit-statistics-29-april-2013-to-13-january-2022/universal-credit-statistics-29-april-2013-to-13-january-2022

32 See for example: Graham Atkins and Stuart Hoddinott (2022) *Neighbourhood Services Under Strain*, Institute for Government. https://www.instituteforgovernment.org.uk/sites/default/files/publications/neighbourhood-services-under-strain.pdf; and Annette Hastings, Nick Bailey, Glen Bramley, Maria Gannon and David Watkins (2015) *The Cost of the Cuts: The Impact on Local Government and Poorer Communities*, Joseph Rowntree Foundation. https://www.jrf.org.uk/sites/default/files/jrf/migrated/files/Summary-Final.pdf

33 *Neighbourhood Services Under Strain*, p. 5.

34 Chris Thomas, 5 November 2019, 'Hitting the poorest worst? How public health cuts have been experienced in England's most deprived communities', blog post, IPPR. https://www.ippr.org/blog/public-health-cuts

35 https://www.gov.uk/government/publications/uk-shared-prosper-ity-fund-prospectus/uk-shared-prosperity-fund-prospectus

36 Vito Teti (2022) *La Restanza* (Italian Edition), Einaudi.

37 Vito Teti (2018) *Bread into Stones*, Guernica, p. 18.

38 Desirè Gaudioso, 2 February 2021, 'Shrinking areas as dynamic spaces of care and resilience', blog post, *Welcoming Spaces*. https://www.welcomingspaces.eu/tag/restanza/

39 Building Communities Trust (undated) 'Our Local Communities: Case study – Social Enterprise in Bro Ffestiniog'. http://cwmni-bro.cymru/pdf/BCT%20Cwmni%20Bro%20Ffestiniog%20Case%20Study(e5).pdf

40 Grace Blakeley (2022) 'Radical Ffestiniog', *Tribune*. https://trib-unemag.co.uk/2022/08/radical-ffestiniog

41 Lowri Cunnington Wynn, Julie Froud and Karel Williams (2022) *A Way Ahead: Empowering Restanza in a Slate Valley*, Foundational Economy Research. https://foundationaleconomyresearch.com/wp-content/uploads/2022/04/Restanza-English-version-as-of-7-feb-2022.pdf

4 Nothing works

1 Andrew Neill, 26 November 2022, 'Britain is paralysed by a toxic brew of political incompetence and impotence. No wonder millions are now asking … why can't this Government get ANYTHING done?', *Daily Mail*. https://www.dailymail.co.uk/debate/article-11470995/ANDREW-NEIL-Britain-paralysed-Government-done.html

2 Nuffield Trust, 31 October 2022, 'Ambulance response times'. https://www.nuffieldtrust.org.uk/resource/ambulance-response-times#background

3 Heritage Fund (2016) *State of UK Public Parks 2016*. https://www.her-itagefund.org.uk/about/insight/research/state-uk-public-parks-2016

4 APSE (2021) *State of Public Parks 2021*. https://www.apse.org.uk/apse/?LinkServID=6F6C3880-FBA4-259F-18889D4F13AC7765

5 Andrew Gimson (2013) 'How Macmillan built 300,000 houses a year'. https://conservativehome.com/2013/10/17/how-macmillan-built-300000-houses-a-year/

6 John Kenneth Galbraith (1998) *The Affluent Society*, Houghton Mifflin Company, p. 100.

7 The Overton window refers to the range of ideas the public is willing to consider and accept.

8 Paul Addison (1996) *British Historians and the Debate over the 'Post-War Consensus'*, College of Liberal Arts, University of Texas.

9 HM Treasury (1954) *Report of the Committee on the Economic and Financial Problems of the Provision for Old Age* (Cmd 93333), The Stationery Office.

10 Karel Williams, John Williams and Dennis Thomas (1983) *Why Are the British Bad at Manufacturing?*, Routledge.

11 Karel Williams, Colin Haslam, Sukhdev Johal and John Williams (1994) *Cars: Analysis, History, Cases*, Berghahn Books.

12 Department for Communities and Local Government (2015) *English Housing Survey: Annual Report on England's Households, 2013–14*, HM Government, pp. 17–18. https://assets.publishing.service.gov.uk/government/uploads/system/uploads/attachment_data/file/461439/EHS_Households_2013-14.pdf

13 Richard Blundell, David Green and Wenchao Jin (2018) 'The UK education expansion and technological change', Working Paper, UCL, p. 1. https://www.ucl.ac.uk/~uctp39a/BGJ_Jan_22_2018.pdf

14 Kirstine Hansen, Heather Joshi and Georgia Verropoulou (2005) 'Childcare and mothers' employment: approaching the millennium', Working Paper, Institute of Education, University of London, p. 9. https://discovery.ucl.ac.uk/id/eprint/1528547/1/Hansen2006Childcare84.pdf

15 Fred Hirsch (1977) *The Social Limits to Growth*, Routledge & Kegan Paul, pp. 8–10.

16 Horst Rittel and Melvin Webber (1973) 'Dilemmas in a general theory of planning', *Policy Sciences*, 4(2), pp. 155–69.

17 ONS, 'Consumer price inflation time series (MM23)'. https://www.ons.gov.uk/economy/inflationandpriceindices/datasets/consumerpriceindices

18 ONS, 'Consumer price inflation time series (MM23)'.

19 ONS, 'Consumer price inflation time series (MM23)'.

20 Paul Bolton and Iona Stewart, 9 November 2022, 'Domestic energy prices', Research Briefing, House of Commons Library. https://researchbriefings.files.parliament.uk/documents/CBP-9491/CBP-9491.pdf

21 ONS, 'Consumer price inflation, UK: September 2022'. https://www.ons.gov.uk/economy/inflationandpriceindices/bulletins/consumerpriceinflation/september2022

22 The Trussell Trust, 'Mid-year stats'. https://www.trusselltrust.org/news-and-blog/latest-stats/mid-year-stats/

23 Lindsay Judge, Jack Leslie and Krishnan Shah (2022) *Interesting Times: Assessing the Impact of Rising Interest Rates on Mortgagors' Living Standards*, Resolution Foundation. https://www.resolutionfoundation.org/publications/interesting-times/

24 ONS, 5 August 2022, 'What actions are people taking because of the rising cost of living?'. https://www.ons.gov.uk/peoplepopulationandcommunity/personalandhouseholdfinances/expenditure/articles/whatactionsarepeopletakingbecauseoftherisingcostofliving/2022-08-05

25 Molly Broome and Jack Leslie (2022) *Arrears Fears: The Distribution of UK Household Wealth and the Impact on Families*. Resolution Foundation. https://www.resolutionfoundation.org/app/uploads/2022/07/Arrears-fears.pdf; Morgan Wild, 28 July 2022, 'Our new cost of living dashboard: the crisis we're seeing unfolding', Citizens Advice. https://wearecitizensadvice.org.uk/our-new-cost-of-living-dashboard-the-crisis-were-seeing-unfold-aac74fb98713

26 Source: Statista, 'Percentage of population covered by public or private health insurance in the United Kingdom from 2000 to 2019'. https://www.statista.com/statistics/683451/population-covered-by-public-or-private-health-insurance-in-united-kingdom/

27 John Burn-Murdoch, 28 April 2022, 'UK healthcare is already being privatised, but not in the way you think', *Financial Times*, https://www.ft.com/content/dbf166ce-1ebb-4a67-980e-9860fd170ba2. Note that out of pocket private expenditure excludes private health plans which account for a much larger proportion of private medical costs in the US.

28 BMA, 'NHS backlog data analysis'. https://www.bma.org.uk/ advice-and-support/nhs-delivery-and-workforce/pressures/nhs -backlog-data-analysis

29 Nuffield Trust, 31 October 2022, 'A and E waiting times'. https:// www.nuffieldtrust.org.uk/resource/a-e-waiting-times#background

30 BMA, 'NHS backlog data analysis'.

31 Julie Froud, Colin Haslam, Sukhdev Johal, John Law and Karel Williams (2020) *When Systems Fail: UK Acute Hospitals and Public Health After Covid-19*, Foundational Economy Collective, pp. 42–6. https:// foundationaleconomycom.files.wordpress.com/2020/08/when-sys- tems-fail-uk-acute-hospitals-and-public-health-after-covid-19.pdf

32 *When Systems Fail*, pp. 39–40.

33 British Medical Association (undated) 'Demanding fair pay for NHS consultants'. https://www.bma.org.uk/pay-and-contracts/pay/ consultants-pay-scales/demanding-fair-pay-for-nhs-consultants

34 NHS Pay Review Body (2022) 'Thirty-Fifth Report 2022', HMSO, p. 77. https://assets.publishing.service.gov.uk/government/uploads /system/uploads/attachment_data/file/1092270/NHSPRB_2022 _Accessible.pdf#page=88

35 NHS Confederation, 25 November 2021, 'Still no clear plan on NHS staffing to meet the needs of the population'. https://www.nhsconfed .org/news/still-no-clear-plan-nhs-staffing-meet-needs-population

36 Nursing and Midwifery Council (2022) 'The NMC register: 1 April 2021–31 March 2022', p. 3. https://www.nmc.org.uk/globalassets /sitedocuments/data-reports/march-2022/nmc-register-march -2022.pdf

37 World Health Organization (June 2022) 'Health workforce', WHO. https://www.who.int/health-topics/health-workforce#tab=tab_1

38 *When Systems Fail.*

39 Office for National Statistics (2022) 'Deaths involving COVID-19 in the care sector, England and Wales: deaths registered between week ending 20 March 2020 and week ending 21 January 2022'. https://www.ons.gov.uk/peoplepopulationandcommunity/birthsd eathsandmarriages/deaths/articles/deathsinvolvingcovid19inthe caresectorenglandandwales/deathsregisteredbetweenweekending20 march2020andweekending21january2022

40 Leo Ewbank, James Thompson, Helen McKenna, Siva Anandaciva and Deborah Ward, 5 November 2021, 'NHS hospital bed numbers: past, present, future', The Kings Fund.

41 *When Systems Fail*, pp. 17–19.

42 *When Systems Fail*, pp. 19–20.

43 *When Systems Fail*, pp. 22–3.

44 *When Systems Fail*, p. 21.

45 National Health Service (2022) 'Delivery plan for tackling the COVID-19 backlog of elective care', p. 5. https://www.england.nhs .uk/coronavirus/wp-content/uploads/sites/52/2022/02/C1466 -delivery-plan-for-tackling-the-covid-19-backlog-of-elective-care.pdf

46 Natasha Curry and Elizabeth Fisher, 2 February 2022, 'Chart of the week: what's happening to hospital discharges?', Nuffield Trust. https://www.nuffieldtrust.org.uk/resource/chart-of-the-week -what-s-happening-to-hospital-discharges?gclid=CjwKCAjwsMG YBhAEEiwAGUXJaTmKSr-VUI1SRnbJSxK9oOW-ZGheUoG5 -ZPHSQ9_OxW8fP343yOJ5RoCnzgQAvD_BwE

47 John Burn-Murdoch, 11 August 2022, 'The NHS is being squeezed in a vice', *Financial Times*. https://www.ft.com/content/f36c5daa -9c14-4a92-9136-19b26508b9d2

48 Care Quality Commission (2022) *The State of Health Care and Adult Social Care in England 2021–2* HC724 https://www.cqc.org.uk/sites/ default/files/2022-10/20221024_stateofcare2122_print.pdf

5 Why the low paid need more than a pay rise

1 Sky News, 2 October 2022, 'Cut consumption or get a new higher paid job'. https://news.sky.com/video/cut-consumption-or-get-a -new-higher-paid-job-says-conservative-party-chair-12710016

2 Sarah O'Connor, 16 November 2017, 'Left behind: can anyone save the towns the UK economy forgot', *Financial Times*. https://www.ft .com/blackpool

3 Hélène Mulholland, 8 October 2012, 'George Osborne: austerity may last until 2018', *The Guardian*. https://www.theguardian.com/ politics/2012/oct/08/george-osborne-austerity-2018

Notes

4 Alan Clark (1991) *The Donkeys*, Pimlico.

5 Luca Calafati, Julie Froud, Colin Haslam, Steve Jeffels, Sukhdev Johal and Karel Williams (2022) *Jobs and Liveability*, A report by Foundational Economy Research Ltd for Karbon Homes. https://foundationaleconomyresearch.com/wp-content/uploads/2022/12/FERL-Report-Jobs-Liveability-for-Karbon-Homes-Sept-2022.pdf

6 See, for example, House of Lords Economic Affairs Committee (2020) *Universal Credit Isn't Working: Proposals for Reform*, 2nd report of Session 2019–21, House of Lords. https://committees.parliament.uk/publications/2224/documents/20325/default/

7 For example, the New Economics Foundation shows that benefits levels for those claimants who are out of work have fallen significantly since 2010: Sarah Arnold, Dominic Caddick and Lukasz Krebel (2021) *How Our Benefits System Was Hollowed Out Over 10 Years*. https://neweconomics.org/2021/02/social-security-2010-comparison; see also the Resolution Foundation's review of a decade of changes to the social security system: Laura Gardiner (2019) *The Shifting Shape of Social Security*. https://www.resolutionfoundation.org/publications/the-shifting-shape-of-social-security/

8 Department of Work and Pension, Stat-Xplore database.

9 In this illustration we include a 4 per cent deduction for pension contributions. Workplace pensions require a minimum contribution of 8 per cent, at least 3 per cent of which should be paid by the employer. Our example assumes that the 8 per cent is evenly split between employer and employee. https://www.gov.uk/workplace-pensions/what-you-your-employer-and-the-government-pay

10 OECD (2020) *Is Childcare Affordable?*, Policy brief on employment, labour and social affairs. https://www.oecd.org/els/family/OECD-Is-Childcare-Affordable.pdf

11 For useful reviews of the concept of transport poverty and a range of empirical studies see: Graham Currie and Alexa Delbosc (2011) 'Transport disadvantage: a review' in G. Currie (ed.), *New Perspectives and Methods in Transport and Social Exclusion Research*, Emerald Group Publishing. https://www.emerald.com/insight/content/doi/10.1108/9781780522012-002/full/html

12 See: Kelly Clifton and Karen Lucas (2004) 'Examining the empirical evidence of transport inequality in the US and UK', in K. Lucas
(ed.), *Running on Empty: Transport, Social Exclusion and Environmental
Justice*, Policy Press. Also Richard Crisp, Ed Ferrari, Tony Gore,
Steve Green, Lindsey McCarthy, Alasdair Rae, Kesia Reeve and
Mark Stevens (2018) *Tackling Transport-Related Barriers to Employment
in Low Income Neighbourhoods*, Joseph Rowntree Foundation. https://
shura.shu.ac.uk/24128/1/tackling_transport-related_barriers_low
-income_neighbourhoods.pdf

13 Shivonne Gates, Fiona Gogescu, Chris Grollman, Emily Cooper
and Priya Khambhaita (2019) *Transport and Inequality: An Evidence
Review for the Department for Transport*, NatCen, pp. 4, 10. https://nat-
cen.ac.uk/our-research/research/transport-and-inequality/

14 *Jobs and Liveability*, p. 39.

15 Office for National Statistics (2020) 'Driving licences'. https://
www.ethnicity-facts-figures.service.gov.uk/culture-and-commu-
nity/transport/driving-licences/latest#:~:text=between%202015
%20and%202019%2C%20an,had%20a%20full%20driving
%20licence

16 Office for National Statistics (2022) 'Effects of taxes and benefits on
household income'. https://www.ons.gov.uk/peoplepopulationand
community/personalandhouseholdfinances/incomeandwealth/
datasets/theeffectsoftaxesandbenefitsonhouseholdincomefinancialy
earending2014

17 Leasing (i.e., renting for a fixed period) is in principle cheaper than
hire purchase (buying by instalments). However, used car leases are
generally available only on cars which are under four years and
50,000 miles. The low income household would be considering
cheaper, older cars where HP (hire purchase) is the only available
form of credit. In this instance the poor pay more.

18 RAC, 'Petrol and diesel prices in the UK: Latest fuel price data from
the RAC'. https://www.rac.co.uk/drive/advice/fuel-watch/

19 Census 2011, Nomis. https://www.nomisweb.co.uk/query/select/
getdatasetbytheme.asp?theme=75

20 See, for example, the work of Curl *et al.* on Glasgow: Angela Curl,
Julie Clark and Ade Kearns (2017) 'Household car adoption and

financial distress in deprived urban communities over time: a case of "forced car ownership"?', *Transport Policy*, 65, pp. 61–71. See also see Graham Currie and Alexa Delbosc (2011) 'Transport disadvantage: a review' in G. Currie (ed.) *New Perspectives and Methods in Transport and Social Exclusion Research*, Emerald Group Publishing.

21 Tom Kelsey and Michael Kenny (2021) *The Value of Social Infrastructure*, Townscapes Policy Report, Bennett Institute for Public Policy. https://www.bennettinstitute.cam.ac.uk/wp-content/uploads/2020/12/Townscapes_The_value_of_infrastructure.pdf

22 Eric Klinenberg (2018) *Palaces for the People: How Social Infrastructure Can Help Fight Inequality, Polarization, and the Decline of Civic Life*, Crown Publishing Group, p. 5.

23 For a more detailed explanation of the categories of the foundational economy such as 'material', 'providential' and 'overlooked' see the Foundational Economy Collective (2022) *Foundational Economy: The Infrastructure of Everyday Life*, 2nd edition, Manchester University Press.

24 Amartya Sen (1999) *Development as Freedom*, Oxford University Press, p. 293.

25 Iris Marion Young (1999) *Justice and the Politics of Difference*, Princeton University Press.

26 *Palaces for the People*, p. 33.

27 Public Health England (2020) 'Prescribed medicines review: summary', PHE. https://www.gov.uk/government/publications/prescribed-medicines-review-report/prescribed-medicines-review-summary#:~:text=antidepressants%207.3%20million%20people%20(17%25%20of%20the%20adult%20population)

28 NHS Digital (2020) 'Statistics on obesity, physical activity and diet, England, 2020 (Part 3: Adult overweight and obesity)', NHS. https://digital.nhs.uk/data-and-information/publications/statistical/statistics-on-obesity-physical-activity-and-diet/england-2020/part-3-adult-obesity-copy

29 Debra Umberson and Jennifer Karas Montez (2010) 'Social relationships and health: a flashpoint for health policy', *Journal of Health and Social Behavior*, 51(Suppl), S54–S66.

30 Scott B. Kaufman, 14 June 2016, 'Both introverts and extra-verts get exhausted from too much socializing' (blog), *Scientific American*. https://blogs.scientificamerican.com/beautiful-minds/both-introverts-and-extraverts-get-exhausted-from-too-much-socializing/

31 Debora Rizzuto, Nicola Orsini, Chenxuan Qiu, Hui-Xin Wang and Luara Fratiglioni (2012) 'Lifestyle, social factors, and survival after age 75: population based study', *BMJ*, 345, e5568.

32 Robert Newton and Daniel Galvão (2008) 'Exercise in prevention and management of cancer', *Current Treatment Options in Oncology*, 9, pp. 135–46.

33 Antonino Patti, Daniele Zangla, Fatma Nese Sahin, Stefanis Cataldi, Gioacchino Lavanco, Antonio Palma and Francesco Fischietti (2021) 'Physical exercise and prevention of falls: effects of a Pilates train-ing method compared with a general physical activity program', *Medicine (Baltimore)*, 100(13), e25289.

34 Health and Safety Executive (undated), 'Working days lost in Great Britain'. https://www.hse.gov.uk/statistics/dayslost.htm; Maria Minor, 20 January 2021, 'Mental health in the workplace: the high cost of depression', *Forbes*. https://www.forbes.com/sites/mariaminor/2021/01/20/mental-health-in-the-workplace-the-high-cost-of-depression/?sh=5f3dbeb86666

35 Abraham H. Maslow (1962) 'Creativity in self-actualizing people' in Maslow (ed.), *Toward a Psychology of Being*, D. Van Nostrand, pp. 127–37; and Frank Barron (1963) *Creativity and Psychological Health*, D. Van Nostrand.

36 Tamlin S. Conner, Colin G. DeYoung and Paul J. Silvia (2016) 'Everyday creative activity as a path to flourishing', *The Journal of Positive Psychology*, 13(2), pp. 181–9.

37 Michael R. Irwin (2008) 'Human psychoneuroimmunology: 20 years of discovery', *Brain, Behavior, and Immunity*, 22(2), pp. 129–39.

38 The history of community centres as social infrastructure in the UK, Europe or US is not rich. But on the UK see: Mark K. Smith (2002) 'Community centres (centers) and associations', *The Encyclopedia of Pedagogy and Informal Education*, Infed. https://infed.org/mobi/community-centers-and-associations/

39　John Maud and S. E. Finer (1960) *Local Government in England and Wales*, Oxford University Press; Malcolm E. Falkus (1987) *Britain Transformed: An Economic and Social History, 1700–1914*, Causeway Press; Leslie Hannah (1979) *Electricity Before Nationalisation*, Palgrave Macmillan.

40　Hugh Coombs and John R. Edwards (2008) 'Capital accounting in municipal corporations 1884–1914: theory and practice', *Financial Accountability & Management*, 8(3), p. 200.

41　Matthew Thompson (2021) 'What's so new about New Municipalism?', *Progress in Human Geography*, 45(2), pp. 317–42.

42　Liverpool Streetscene Services (undated), 'Business Plan 2018–2023', Liverpool Streetscene Services Limited, p. 29. lssl-business-plan-final-version-2018-2023.pdf (liverpool.gov.uk)

43　Kit Sandeman, 7 September 2020, 'How Robin Hood Energy went from political dream to financial nightmare in five years', *Nottinghamshire Live*. https://www.nottinghampost.com/news/local-news/how-robin-hood-energy-went-4491806; and Adam Postans, 2 December 2021, 'City council auditor defends Bristol Energy report after deputy mayor comments', *Bristol Live*. https://www.bristolpost.co.uk/news/bristol-news/city-council-auditor-defends-bristol-6293486

44　Alison Flood, 6 December 2019, 'Britain has closed almost 800 libraries since 2010, figures show', *The Guardian*. https://www.theguardian.com/books/2019/dec/06/britain-has-closed-almost-800-libraries-since-2010-figures-show

45　Alice Hancock, 27 May 2022, 'Swimming pools under threat as operators fear industry collapse', *Financial Times*. https://www.ft.com/content/7760087e-d4fd-43e5-a07d-c4afbc42e16f

6 What to do? Politics and policy

1　Sebastian Payne, 29 September 2022, 'Complacency is Keir Starmer's biggest adversary', *Financial Times*. https://www.ft.com/content/b17a7655-63b8-4bc7-b305-8ab50a656472

Notes

2 Deborah Mattison (2020) *Beyond the Red Wall*, Biteback Publishing, p. 147.

3 Labour Party, *1959 Election Manifesto*. http://labourmanifesto.com /1959/1959-labour-manifesto.shtml

4 Claire Ainsley (2018) *The New Working Class: How to Win Hearts, Minds and Votes*, Policy Press.

5 Joe Earle, Cahal Moran and Zach Ward-Perkins (2016) *The Econocracy: The Perils of Leaving Economics to the Experts*, Manchester University Press, p. 19.

6 Johnny Runge and Nathan Hudson-Sharp (2020) 'Public under- standing of economic statistics', NIESR, p. 9. https://www.niesr .ac.uk/projects/public-understanding-economics-and-economic -statistics

7 See for example, Anna Killick (2020) *Rigged: Understanding 'the Economy' in Brexit Britain*, Manchester University Press; Jack Mosse (2021) *The Pound and the Fury: Why Anger and Confusion Reign in an Economy Paralysed by Myth*, Manchester University Press.

8 ONS, 'UK posts widest current account gap on balance of pay- ments, UK: January to March 2022'. https://www.ons.gov.uk/ economy/nationalaccounts/balanceofpayments/bulletins/balan- ceofpayments/januarytomarch2022#:~:text=The%20underlying %20UK%20current%20account,billion%20from%20the%20pre- vious%20quarter

9 Jeffrey Sachs and Charles Wyplosz (1986) 'The economic conse- quences of President Mitterrand', *Economic Policy*, 1(2), pp. 261–306.

10 Tado, 20 February 2020, 'UK homes losing heat up to three times faster than European neighbours', Press release. https://www.tado .com/gb-en/press/uk-homes-losing-heat-up-to-three-times-faster -than-european-neighbours

11 Department for Communities and Local Government (October 2010) *English Housing Survey: Housing Stock Report 2008*. https://assets .publishing.service.gov.uk/government/uploads/system/uploads/ attachment_data/file/6703/1750754.pdf

12 Cristina Penasco and Laura Diaz Andon (2023) 'Assessing the effec- tiveness of energy efficiency measures on the residential sector gas consumption', *Energy Economics*, January 2023, 106435. https://www .sciencedirect.com/science/article/pii/S0140988322005643

13 Gill Plimmer and David Sheppard, 17 November 2022, 'Bulb Energy bailout to cost UK taxpayers £6.5bn', *Financial Times*. https://www.ft.com/content/2d19da21-b79f-4ee3-8c74-5c61abca7a13

14 University of Greenwich, 16 June 2020, 'Privatised water: a system in need of repair?', Press release. https://www.gre.ac.uk/news/articles/public-relations/2018/privatised-water-failure

15 CMA, 9 April 2021, 'CMA issues final decision on water price controls'. https://www.gov.uk/cma-cases/ofwat-price-determinations. The companies referred to are Anglian Water Services Limited, Bristol Water plc, Northumbrian Water Limited and Yorkshire Water Services, p. 46.

16 Sandra Laville, 31 March 2022, 'Raw sewage discharged into English rivers 375,000 times by water firms', *The Guardian*. https://www.theguardian.com/environment/2022/mar/31/sewage-released-into-english-rivers-for-27m-hours-last-year-by-water-firms

17 Statista (2022) 'Estimated number of public relations professionals in the UK from 2010 to 2022' (based on NOMIS standard occupational classification, 2493). https://www.statista.com/statistics/319801/number-of-public-relations-professionals-in-the-uk/#:~:text=Number%20of%20public%20relations%20professionals%20in%20the%20UK,37%2C500%20in%202010%2C%20a%20decrease%20of%20around%2033%2C600.

18 Kate Bayliss, Elisa Van Waeyenberge and Benjamin Bowles (2022) 'Private equity and the regulation of financialised infrastructure: the case of Macquarie in Britain's water and energy networks', *New Political Economy* (online June 2022), DOI: 10.1080/13563467.2022.2084521

19 See for example: Gill Plimmer and Jonathan Ford, 12 October 2018, 'Investors benefit from water group's borrowing at expense of customers', *Financial Times*. https://www.ft.com/content/b60e062e-9712-11e8-b67b-b8205561c3fe

20 Julie Froud and Karel Williams in Rachel Reeves (ed.) (2019) *Everyday Socialism: How to Rebuild Britain*, Fabian Society, pp. 23–32. https://fabians.org.uk/wp-content/uploads/2019/09/FABJ7429-Socialism-Pamphlet-0819-WEB-002.pdf

21 Randeep Ramesh, 2 December 2021, 'Unite will use "brains as well as brawn" to fight bad employers, says boss', *The Guardian*. https://

Notes

www.theguardian.com/politics/2021/dec/02/unite-will-use-brains
-as-well-as-brawn-to-fight-bad-employers-says-boss

22 Foundational Economy Collective (2018) *Foundational Economy*, Manchester University Press.

23 On adaptive reuse, see the introduction to the new edition of Foundational Economy Collective (2022) *Foundational Economy* (2nd edition), Manchester University Press.

24 Anne Lacaton and Jean-Philippe Vassal (2015) *Freedom of Use*, Sternberg Press.

25 Ana Tostoes and Jaime Silva (2020) 'Rescuing the "machine à habiter"', *Revista de Arquitectura*, 22, pp. 170–87.

26 UCL Engineering (no date) 'Embodied carbon: factsheet'. https://www.ucl.ac.uk/engineering-exchange/sites/engineering-exchange/files/fact-sheet-embodied-carbon-social-housing.pdf

27 William Temple (1943) *Christianity and Social Order*, Penguin.

28 End Child Food Poverty. https://endchildfoodpoverty.org/

29 Apply for free school meals. https://www.gov.uk/apply-free-school-meals

30 Anthony Atkinson (2018) 'Wealth and inheritance in Britain from 1896 to the present', *The Journal of Economic Inequality*, 16(2), pp. 137–69.

31 Arun Advani, George Bangham and Jack Leslie (2020) *The UK's Wealth Distribution*, Resolution Foundation, p. 16. https://www.resolutionfoundation.org/publications/the-uks-wealth-distribution-and-characteristics-of-high-wealth-households/

32 Hansard (1960) 'New clause (relief from Schedule A for owner-occupiers)', HC Deb, 21 June 1960, vol. 625 cc233–87. https://api.parliament.uk/historic-hansard/commons/1960/jun/21/new-clause-relief-from-schedule-a-for

33 Anthony I. Ogus and E. M. Barendt (1988) *The Law of Social Security*, Butterworths, p. 472.

34 Patrick Butler, 14 July 2022, 'One in 12 UK children now in families hit by two-child benefit limit', *The Guardian*. https://www.theguardian.com/society/2022/jul/14/one-in-12-uk-children-now-in-families-hit-by-two-child-benefit-limit; and Kate Anderson, Ruth Patrick and Aaron Reeves (2022) *Needs Matter: How the Two-Child Limit and the*

Benefit Cap Harm Children, Nuffield Foundation. https://largerfamilies
.study/publications/needs-matter/

35 See Rights Lab, University of Nottingham and School of Law, De
    Montfort University, Leicester (April 2022) 'Fashioning a beautiful
    future? Supporting workers and addressing labour exploitation in
    Leicester's textile and garment industry'. https://www.nottingham
    .ac.uk/Research/Beacons-of-Excellence/Rights-Lab/resources/
    reports-and-briefings/2022/June/Fashioning-a-beautiful-future
    .pdf; and Low Pay Commission (July 2022) 'Compliance and enforce-
    ment of the National Minimum Wage: the case of the Leicester
    textiles sector'. https://assets.publishing.service.gov.uk/government
    /uploads/system/uploads/attachment_data/file/1093191/2022
    _LPC_enforcement_report_FINAL.pdf

36 Institute for Government (2022) *Performance Tracker 2022: Public
    Services.* https://www.instituteforgovernment.org.uk/publication/
    performance-tracker-2022/cross-service

37 Julie Froud, Colin Haslam, Sukhdev Johal, John Law and Karel
    Williams (2020) *When Systems Fail: UK Acute Hospitals and Public Health
    after Covid-19*, Foundational Economy Collective, p. 51. https://fou
    ndationaleconomycom.files.wordpress.com/2020/08/when-sys-
    tems-fail-uk-acute-hospitals-and-public-health-after-covid-19.pdf

38 *When Systems Fail*, pp. 24–8.

39 John Scott (1998) *Seeing Like a State: How Certain Schemes to Improve the
    Human Condition Have Failed*, Yale University Press.

40 Kit Sandeman, 7 September 2020, 'How Robin Hood Energy went
    from political dream to financial nightmare in five years', *Nottingham
    Post.* https://www.nottinghampost.com/news/local-news/how
    -robin-hood-energy-went-4491806

41 Andrew Arthur, 18 January 2022, 'Bristol Energy and parent com-
    pany collapse', *Business Live*. https://www.business-live.co.uk/retail
    -consumer/energy-crisis-bristol-energy-parent-22793906

42 Aran Dhillon, 29 July 2022, 'Warrington Council faces possible £18
    million loss', *Cheshire Live*. https://www.cheshire-live.co.uk/news
    /chester-cheshire-news/warrington-council-faces-possible-18m
    -24612516

43 https://www.theguardian.com/theobserver/2013/feb/16/history-curriculum-letters

44 Sean Coughlan, 11 June 2013, 'GCSEs: Gove pledges "challenging" exam changes', BBC News. https://www.bbc.co.uk/news/education-22841266

45 Cabinet Office and Deputy Prime Minister's Office, 5 July 2013, 'City deals'. https://www.gov.uk/government/collections/city-deals

46 Matthew Ward (2020) 'City deals', House of Commons Briefing paper, Number 7158. https://researchbriefings.files.parliament.uk/documents/SN07158/SN07158.pdf

47 Centre for Cities, 'City assets: how can cities use public sector assets to support economic growth?'. https://www.centreforcities.org/event/city-assets-how-can-cities-use-public-sector-assets-to-support-economic-growth/

48 Brown Commission (Commission on the UK's Future) (2022) *A New Britain: Renewing Our Democracy and Rebuilding Our Economy*, pp. 5, 9, 12. https://labour.org.uk/wp-content/uploads/2022/12/Commission-on-the-UKs-Future.pdf

49 Brown Commission, p. 9.

50 Brown Commission, p. 98.

51 In 2020, UK healthcare spend was £257.6 billion of which the government funded £213 billion. In 2020–21 the UK government, mainly through local government, spent £22 billion on adult social care and the spend on education was £99 billion in 2020–21. In total this equates to over 19 per cent of UK GDP in 2020. https://www.ons.gov.uk/peoplepopulationandcommunity/healthandsocialcare/healthcaresystem/bulletins/ukhealthaccounts/2020; https://view.officeapps.live.com/op/view.aspx?src=https%3A%2F%2Ffiles.digital.nhs.uk%2FDE%2F22E3C9%2FAdult%2520Social%2520Care%2520Statistics%2520in%2520England%2520An%2520Overview%2520-%2520Data%2520Tables.xlsx&wdOrigin=BROWSELINK; https://ifs.org.uk/publications/2021-annual-report-education-spending-england

52 Hilary Cottam (2019) *Radical Help: How We Can Remake the Relationships Between Us and Revolutionise the Welfare State*, Virago, p. 14.

Notes

53 Andrew Bowman, Luca Calafati, Julie Froud, Colin Haslam, Sukhdev Johal, Kevin Morgan and Karel Willians (2021) *What Can Welsh Government Do to Increase the Number of Grounded SME Firms in Food Processing and Distribution?*, pp. 11–12. https://www.gov.wales/what-can-welsh-government-do-increase-number-grounded-sme-firms-food-processing-and-distribution

54 *What Can Welsh Government Do.*

55 Vanguard Method. https://whatisthevanguardmethod.net/about-vanguard-method/#:~:text=The%20Vanguard%20method%20employs%20the,respond%20effectively%20to%20customer%20demands

56 Future Generations Commission (2021) *Procuring Well-Being in Wales.* https://www.futuregenerations.wales/resources_posts/procuring-well-being-in-wales/

57 Luca Calafati, Julie Froud, Colin Haslam, Sukhdev Johal, Ian McGrady and Karel Williams (2022) *NHS Wales as a Driver of Economic Value*, report for Welsh Government.

58 Well Fed. https://www.cancook.co.uk/about-well-fed/

Index

adaptive reuse 4–5, 20–2, 24,
    220–1, 231–6, 240, 249,
    253–6
Ainsley, Claire 225
alliances for change 24, 100,
    245–6, 250, 254–6
Archbishop William Temple 69
assortative mating 17, 79
austerity 39, 41, 132, 134, 174–5,
    212–13, 228, 246

back office 4, 20–1, 219–24,
    232–3, 253
benefits 12–13, 18–20, 77–9, 85,
    89–94, 114–16, 144, 150,
    154–8, 183–94, 239–41
    see also Universal Credit (UC)
benefits in-kind 18–19, 89–94,
    156–7
Bennett Institute 205–6, 209
Blaenau Ffestiniog 82, 136–8
Blakeley, Grace 136
Brexit 126, 223–4
Brown Commission 10, 34, 247–9
Bulb 230
Byker 15, 121–2, 130–1, 188–9,
    192–3, 198

car ownership and use 147–9,
    197–207

central state 20–1, 23–4, 61–2,
    180, 218–24, 226–9, 231–3,
    236–42, 245–9
childcare 72–3, 85, 153–5, 182–4,
    196
CO_2 emissions 8, 47–52, 229
    see also decoupling
Community Life Survey 127, 134
Conservative Party 27–8, 37–9,
    183
cost of essentials 18, 85, 158–71,
    241
cost-of-living crisis 1, 13, 18, 68,
    77, 80, 82, 85, 107, 144,
    158–62
    energy costs 37–8, 40, 158–60,
    171
    food costs 85, 88, 107, 159–60,
    163–5
    motoring costs 195–201
Cottam, Hilary 250, 252
Covid-19 43, 50, 107, 142, 173,
    177–9

decoupling 47–52, 54
Demos 95, 97, 128
devolution 217, 247–9
disposable income 12, 14–15, 40,
    85, 87–91, 114–15, 164–5,
    182–4, 186–93, 199, 241

Index

early-stage innovation 35, 45, 250
earnings retention 18, 130, 191–3, 239–40
see also tax and benefits system
ecological footprint 8, 47, 52–4, 101–2, 201
economically active 57, 70, 77–80, 111, 141, 156–7
Economy 2030 Inquiry 45
equity release 8, 42
essential services 10, 61, 70–1, 81–6, 89, 96–8, 132, 134, 136–7, 142, 145, 171, 184, 204, 218, 228, 232, 236
European Research Group 35
everyday economy 36

financialisation 111, 151
Foundational Alliance Wales 255
foundational balance 86
foundational economy 22, 71, 82, 98, 101–2, 122, 237, 253
    FE 1.0 101
    FE 2.0 101–2
    Manifesto for the Foundational Economy 82
foundational liveability 3–5, 10, 12–16, 20–1, 23–5, 81–7, 94–9, 102–3, 121, 129, 132, 134, 136–8, 142–4, 146, 171, 204–5, 209, 217–21, 228–9, 232–4, 236, 240
    three pillars of 4, 12–14, 20, 81–6, 97–8, 132, 139, 142, 221
foundational politics 20–1, 99–102, 219–21, 228–31, 233–44
Freedman, Lawrence 29
front office 21, 219–23, 253
frontier sectors 36, 59–60

Gove, Michael 36, 241, 247
Graham, Sharon 241–2
Great Financial Crisis 28, 43, 55, 157, 219
Green New Deal 44
Gross Domestic Product (GDP) 9–10, 22, 33, 42–3, 48–51, 53–4, 57, 109–12, 144, 155, 226–7, 238
    GDP per capita 33, 51, 54, 68, 146
    see also growth
gross income 12, 78–9, 87–8, 111–12, 121–2, 163–4, 191–3
    see also disposable income; residual income
gross value added (GVA) 6, 10, 42, 46, 68, 97, 108–9, 120–1, 123–7, 129–30, 132, 213, 248–9
    per capita 10, 14–15, 33, 36, 68, 82, 123
    see also value added
growth 3, 5–10, 24, 31–48, 50–2, 54–7, 61, 67–8, 110, 113–15, 126, 144–5, 151, 153, 217, 226–7, 234, 247–9
    green growth 8, 36, 47–53
    low growth 6–7, 36, 45–7

household 68–70, 72–6, 80–1, 83–5, 95–6, 98–9
    size and composition 11, 40, 72–3, 75–8, 81, 87–9
housing costs 13–15, 67, 81, 85–8, 123–4, 162–3, 165–9, 188–9, 192–3
Hutton, Will 32, 37

improvement 4, 11, 16, 20, 22–3, 235, 243–4, 246–7

Index

Kaizen 22, 235
inequalities 30, 36, 77–9, 111,
    114, 116–20, 125, 129–33,
    213
    of income 77, 114–16, 121–3
    of wealth 116–20, 123
inflation 1, 18, 41, 44, 134, 144–5,
    159–60, 163–4, 168–71,
    182–3, 195, 227–8
investment 35–6, 45–6, 56, 100,
    113, 125–7, 209–10, 212–13,
    230, 242, 246–7
    zone 30, 45–7

Jackson, Tim 54
job creation 44, 60–1, 151–3
Johnson, Boris 30, 32, 36, 45

Killick, Anna 226
Klinenberg, Eric 205–6,
    209–10
knowledge-intensive sectors 56–7,
    59–60
Kwarteng, Kwasi 38, 44, 227

Labour Party 7, 21, 27, 35–6,
    150–1, 226–8, 232
labour share of GDP 57–8, 105,
    109–14
Lacaton, Anne 22, 220, 234
Lawson, Nigel 44, 157
left-behind places 36, 84, 103,
    125, 127–9
levelling up 10, 30, 36–7, 39, 80,
    126–7, 134, 217
liveability 3–5, 10–16, 19–21,
    23–4, 65, 70–1, 81–7, 94–9,
    102–4, 128–9, 132, 134,
    136–8, 142, 144, 146, 182,
    194, 204–5, 209, 217–21,
    227–9, 234–6, 240, 245–7,
    249–50, 254–6

London School of Economics
    (LSE) Growth Commission
    45
low wages 11, 19–20, 36, 41,
    55–7, 69, 130, 132, 144,
    146, 151, 153–7, 185–7,
    194

Macmillan, Harold 146
market citizenship 19, 33–4, 86,
    91, 94, 141, 144–7, 153–6,
    210, 230, 234
May, Theresa 45, 174
Morriston 82
municipal experiments 211–13,
    246–7

National Health Service (NHS)
    23, 92, 142–3, 155, 171–81,
    235, 241, 243–4
    funding 38, 145, 172–5
    hospitals 62–3, 173, 177–81
    workforce 24, 176, 255
National Superannuation Scheme
    225
nature and climate emergency 6,
    47, 99–101, 217, 228
Newcastle-upon-Tyne 14–15,
    82, 121–2, 130–1, 187–91,
    195–6, 198–9, 202–4
North East England 87–9, 130,
    152–3, 203
nothing works 1–2, 13, 141–3,
    151–81, 223

Oakeshott, Michael 23
outsourcing 22, 60, 111, 113, 172,
    246

para-state 59–62
planetary limits 48–53, 98,
    101–2

Index

privatisation 22, 60, 111, 113, 172, 210, 229–31
privatised Keynesianism 8, 42
productivity 7, 9–10, 31, 33, 35–6, 39–42, 55–9, 71, 82, 110, 121, 126, 150–2, 240–2, 249
and place 123–6
and public services 62–3, 174–5, 244, 250
public goods 155, 209–10

quagmire 3, 5–6, 9, 24, 27–37, 39–47, 105, 134, 215, 235–6, 247–9

Rashford, Marcus 69, 237
Raworth, Kate 54
Reeves, Rachel 32, 36
residual income 4, 10–13, 18–19, 81–5, 87–9, 123, 142, 144–5, 158–70, 182, 186–96, 241
resilience 12, 63, 176, 207, 234
Resolution Foundation 36, 40, 116, 120, 125, 168
restanza 128–9, 135–8

Sen, Amartya 206, 218
Shared Prosperity Fund 30, 126–7, 134
social infrastructure 10–14, 16, 20, 70–1, 81–4, 86–7, 132, 134, 142–3, 158, 184–5, 204–13, 224, 238
social innovation 23–4, 221, 232, 236, 241, 243–7, 249–56
starter policies 23, 236–8
stealth policies 23, 221, 236, 239–40
Sunak, Rishi 7, 32, 37–8
supply side policy 35, 38, 41, 45–7, 98, 233
switch policies 23, 221, 233, 236, 240–4, 246

tax and benefits system 23, 25, 77, 82, 114, 184, 186–94, 241
techno centrists 7, 9–10, 34–5, 37–9, 41, 45, 47, 55–6, 108–9, 226, 240, 247
trade unions 23, 58, 111–12, 232, 236, 241–2
transformation 4, 21, 103, 224, 240
transition 4, 21, 44, 47, 240
transport disadvantage 197, 202–4
Truss, Liz 7, 30, 32, 37–9

UK Climate Change Committee 52
Ukraine War 20, 43, 159
Universal Credit (UC) 18–19, 23, 90, 93, 130–1, 133, 153–4, 158, 182–6, 190–1, 193–4, 236–7, 239

value added 33, 57–9, 62, 68, 105, 110–12
see also gross value added (GVA)
Vassal, Jean-Philippe 22, 220

Wales 24, 73, 101–3, 121, 135–7, 246, 251–5
Welsh Government 98–9, 136, 253–5
see also Foundational Alliance Wales
water industry 100, 211–12, 230–1, 238
wealth 17, 79, 116–20, 123–4
Well-Being of Future Generations Act 253
Wolf, Martin 32, 37
workforce development 24, 255
see also National Health Service (NHS), workforce

Young, Iris Marion 206